1001
LEGAL
WORDS
You Need to Know

Other titles in the series:

1001 Finance Words You Need to Know

1001 Computer Words You Need to Know

1001 LEGAL WORDS

You Need to Know

JAY M. FEINMAN
Editor

ERIN McKEAN
Series Editor

With Topical Essays by **JAMES E. CLAPP**

OXFORD
UNIVERSITY PRESS

OXFORD
UNIVERSITY PRESS

Oxford University Press, Inc., publishes works that further
Oxford University's objective of excellence
in research, scholarship, and education.

Oxford   New York
Auckland   Cape Town   Dar es Salaam   Hong Kong   Karachi
Kuala Lumpur   Madrid   Melbourne   Mexico City   Nairobi
New Delhi   Shanghai   Taipei   Toronto

With offices in
Argentina   Austria   Brazil   Chile   Czech Republic   France   Greece
Guatemala   Hungary   Italy   Japan   Poland   Portugal   Singapore
South Korea   Switzerland   Thailand   Turkey   Ukraine   Vietnam

First published by Oxford University Press, Inc.
198 Madison Avenue, New York, New York 10016
www.oup.com

First issued as an Oxford University Press paperback, 2005
ISBN-13: 978-0-19-518133-3
ISBN-10: 0-19-518133-6

Oxford is a registered trademark of Oxford University Press

The Library of Congress has cataloged the cloth edition as follows:
1001 Legal words you need to know / Jay M. Feinman, James E. Clapp,
Erin McKean, editors.—1st. ed.
p. cm.
Includes bibliographical references.
ISBN-13: 978-0-19-516503-6
ISBN-10: 0-19-516503-9
1. Law—United States—Dictionaries. I. Title: One thousand and one
legal words you need to know. II. Feinman, Jay M. III. Clapp, James E.
(James Edward), 1943– IV. McKean, Erin
KF156 .A113 2003   349.73′03—dc21   2003009869

EDITORIAL STAFF

Erin McKean, *Series Editor*
Constance Baboukis, *Managing Editor*
Christine Lindberg, Orin Hargraves, *Editors*
Katherine Sietsema, Marina Padakis, *Proofreaders*
Ryan Sullivan, *Editorial Assistant*

3 5 7 9 8 6 4
Printed in the United States of America

PREFACE

This book, *1001 Legal Words You Need to Know*, is part of a new Oxford University Press series of concise, helpful guides to the vocabularies of significant fields. We have distilled and enhanced the general dictionary entries (taken from our groundbreaking *New Oxford American Dictionary*) to make useful, browsable books that present the most important words needed to understand a particular topic, selected and updated by recognized experts. By stripping away the words you don't immediately need, we bring these complicated topics into sharper focus.

In addition to these essential 1001 words, we've included explanatory essays about important (and often confusing) related concepts and a list of essential resources for further reading, making this more than just a dictionary—a truly practical all-around guide and reference book.

Erin McKean
Senior Editor, U.S. Dictionaries,
Oxford University Press

CONTENTS

INTRODUCTION

Law is everywhere in American life. The daily newspaper and the evening news report about the latest sensational criminal trial, massive lawsuit, or constitutional claim. Dramas about crime and lawyers are staples of prime-time television, and real-life courtroom shows rival soap operas in popularity. Credit card agreements and other contracts, landlord-tenant disputes, personal injury litigation, and other legal matters are common features of everyday life.

Because law is everywhere, the language of the law is everywhere, too. News stories, televison shows, and legal transactions are filled with special words and phrases. Instead of simply asking a court to get out of jail, a prisoner seeks a "writ of *habeas corpus*." The standard-form contract for the sale of a computer typically will disclaim "consequential damages." When police make an arrest, they advise a suspect of the right to remain silent and have an attorney by giving a "Miranda warning." A homeowner owns a house in "fee simple absolute," which is much better than having a "life estate" or a "defeasible fee."

The language of the law can seem mysterious, as if lawyers are priests muttering incantations in a secret tongue kept hidden from the laity. Sometimes it even seems as if lawyers deliberately obfuscate, using magic words and awkward constructions to make the simple complex and the obvious obscure. In drafting a will, is it really necessary to "give, bequeath, and devise" property, or in a deed to "grant, bargain, sell, and convey" all of one's "right, title, and interest" to "lands, tenements, and hereditaments"?

Actually, legal language has been getting more accessible in recent years. Statutes such as the federal Truth in Lending Act specify disclosures and how they have to be made in documents such as loan agreements and solicitations for credit cards. The plain language movement has caused insurance policies and other forms to be written, organized, and presented more simply. Increasingly, lawyers have recognized that legal transactions and the law in general work better when they are understandable. All of these developments have combined to reduce legalese, retire antiquated terms, and make ordinary legal documents and discourse simpler and clearer.

But reform can go only so far. Law is a specialized subject, and it needs a specialized language. Every discipline, profession, or trade, from anthropology and medicine to computer engineering and auto mechanics, uses technical terms that are familiar to its practitioners and foreign to the rest of us. A technical vocabulary is the only way to be precise and to describe concepts that are not in common use outside the field.

Like any other language, legal language expands and contracts to fit the changing needs of its users. As legal rules and principles develop, old terms are redefined or discarded and new terms are added. The specialized language of the law in the United States is an amalgam of ancient terms and more recent additions.

The United States has a "common law" legal system, which means it is derived from English law. Our legal vocabulary has its origins in medieval English law, and it contains many terms in Latin and French. Some of the Latin terms come from Roman law, but most of them arose because Latin was the technical language of the educated classes in medieval times and later. *Habeas corpus,* for example, often referred to as "the Great Writ" because it provides a powerful remedy for wrongful imprisonment, has been in use since the 14th century and was later enshrined in the U.S. Constitution. Its name is old, but no English language substitute has replaced it and its meaning is well understood. After their conquest of England in 1066, the Normans' French language made its way into the law as well. Even today, lawyers engage in *voir dire*—Norman French for 'to speak the truth'—qualifying a jury by making sure potential jurors are being truthful about their ability to decide fairly. Other legal words, such as "arrest" and "mortgage," have become so familiar that their French origin is generally unrecognized.

Most of the language of the law is English, of course, but not necessarily everyday English. Some words are unique to the law, having no meaning in ordinary discourse. To die "intestate," for example, means 'to die without a will', and the term has no significance in any other context. Other English words have legal meanings that are more technical and precise than their ordinary usage. In common parlance, "consideration" means 'careful thought', or sometimes 'a payment or reward'. To lawyers, however, "consideration" has a specialized meaning for the element of bargain and exchange that makes a contract enforceable, with a complex body of law defining what can and cannot constitute consideration.

Law must contain technical terms, but "technical" does not have to equate to 'incomprehensible'. In a democratic society, law belongs not to the lawyers but to the people, and ordinary people need to be able to understand the law. That is the purpose of this book: to make the language of the law accessible to the layperson and the beginning student of the law.

The typical law dictionary is a massive tome, weighty in size, scope, and style. (One law dictionary on my bookshelf is four inches thick and weighs seven pounds.) This book is different. It defines and explains the usage of the basic legal terms that non-lawyers are likely to encounter in news stories, fictional legal dramas, and their personal lives. This book excludes archaic legal terms or words that only lawyers need to know. Its definitions are drawn from the *New Oxford American Dictionary*, but they have been edited and revised to meet the particular purpose of this volume, focusing on the special legal meanings of words. It includes many examples and usage notes to make the meaning of the language of law clear and lively.

Because this volume is designed as a basic resource for the non-lawyer, it includes two special features. First, ten short articles answer questions people commonly ask about the law, from "What is a power of attorney?" and "How do I choose a lawyer?" to "What should I watch for in lawyer shows on television?" and "Is law school for me?" (For a complete list of these articles, see page vii.) Second, for readers who want to find out more about the law, a bibliography of useful books on law is included at the end of the volume.

Legal issues, cases, and problems are important in our society. They also can be interesting and even entertaining. This dictionary is designed to enrich your understanding of the law so that you can participate more fully in observing, thinking about, debating, and shaping the law.

Jay M. Feinman
Rutgers University
School of Law, Camden

USING THIS DICTIONARY

The "entry map" below explains the different parts of an entry.

Syllabification

Pronunciation set off with slashes / /

Grammar information in square brackets [ ]

dis•miss /dis'mis/ ▶ v. [trans.] refuse further hearing to (a case): *the judge dismissed the case for lack of evidence.*
■ revoke an order of a court: *the writ of certiorari is dismissed as improvidently granted.*
DERIVATIVES **dis•miss•al** /dis'misəl/ **n.**; **dis•miss•i•ble** /dis'misəbəl/ **adj.**
ORIGIN late Middle English: from medieval Latin *dismiss-*, variant of Latin *dimiss-* 'sent away,' from the verb *dimittere.*

Derivative section, derivatives in **bold face**

Etymology section

Subsenses signalled by ■

con•sor•ti•um /kən'sôrsH(ē)əm; -'sôrṯēəm/ ▶ **n.** (pl. **con•sor•ti•a** /kən'sôrsH(ē)ə; -'sôrṯēə/ or **con•sor•ti•ums**) the right of association and companionship with one's husband or wife.
PHRASES **loss of consortium** damage to a spouse for loss of companionship (often including sexual relations) due to injury to their spouse: *the extent to which a spouse may apply for loss of consortium damages in a wrongful death claim.*

Phrases section, phrases in **bold face**

Examples in *italic*

pub•lic law /'pəblik 'lô/ ▶ **n. 1** the law of relationships between individuals and the government, such as constitutional, criminal, and administrative law.
2 another term for PUBLIC ACT.

Cross references in BOLD SMALL CAPITALS

Main entries and other boldface forms

Main entries appear in boldface type, as do inflected forms, idioms and phrases, and derivatives. The words PHRASES and DERIVATIVES introduce those elements. Main entries and derivatives of two or more syllables show syllabification with centered dots.

Parts of speech

Each new part of speech is introduced by a small right-facing arrow.

Senses and subsenses

The main sense of each word follows the part of speech and any grammatical information (e.g., [trans.] before a verb definition). If there are two or more main senses for a word, these are numbered in boldface. Closely related subsenses of each main sense are introduced by a solid black box. In the entry for **dismiss** above, the main sense of "refuse further hearing to" is followed by a related sense, "revoke an order of a court."

Example sentences

Example sentences are shown in italic typeface; certain common expressions appear in bold italic typeface within examples.

Cross references

Cross references to main entries appear in small capitals. For example, in the entry **public law** seen previously, a cross reference is given in bold small capitals to the entry for PUBLIC ACT.

PRONUNCIATION KEY

This dictionary uses a simple respelling system to show how entries are pronounced, using the following symbols:

æ   *as in* **hat** /hæt/, **fashion** /'fæsHən/, **carry** /'kærē/

ā   *as in* **day** /dā/, **rate** /rāt/, **maid** /mād/, **prey** /prā/

ä   *as in* **lot** /lät/, **father** /'fäTHər/, **barnyard** /'bärn‚yärd/

b   *as in* **big** /big/

CH   *as in* **church** /CHərCH/, **picture** /'pikCHər/

d   *as in* **dog** /dôg/, **bed** /bed/

e   *as in* **men** /men/, **bet** /bet/, **ferry** /'ferē/

ē   *as in* **feet** /fēt/, **receive** /ri'sēv/

er   *as in* **air** /er/, **care** /ker/

ə   *as in* **about** /ə'bowt/, **soda** /'sōdə/, **mother** /'məTHər/, **person** /'pərsən/

f   *as in* **free** /frē/, **graph** /græf/, **tough** /təf/

g   *as in* **get** /get/, **exist** /ig'zist/, **egg** /eg/

h   *as in* **her** /hər/, **behave** /bi'hāv/

i   *as in* **guild** /gild/, **women** /'wimin/

ī   *as in* **time** /tīm/, **fight** /fīt/, **guide** /gīd/, **hire** /hīr/

ir   *as in* **ear** /ir/, **beer** /bir/, **pierce** /pirs/

j   *as in* **judge** /jəj/, **carriage** /'kærij/

k   *as in* **kettle** /'ketl/, **cut** /kət/

l   *as in* **lap** /læp/, **cellar** /'selər/, **cradle** /'krādl/

m   *as in* **main** /mān/, **dam** /dæm/

n   *as in* **honor** /'änər/, **maiden** /'mādn/

NG   *as in* **sing** /siNG/, **anger** /'æNGgər/

ō   *as in* **go** /gō/, **promote** /prə'mōt/

ô   *as in* **law** /lô/, **thought** /THôt/, **lore** / lôr/

oi   *as in* **boy** /boi/, **noisy** /'noizē/

o͝o   *as in* **wood** /wo͝od/, **football** /'fo͝ot‚bôl/, **sure** /SHo͝or/

o͞o   *as in* **food** /fo͞od/, **music** /'myo͞ozik/

ow   *as in* **mouse** /mows/, **coward** /'kowərd/

p   *as in* **put** /po͝ot/, **cap** /kæp/
r   *as in* **run** /rən/, **fur** /fər/, **spirit** /'spirit/
s   *as in* **sit** /sit/, **lesson** /'lesən/
SH   *as in* **shut** /SHət/, **social** /'sōSHəl/, **action** /'ækSHən/
t   *as in* **top** /täp/, **seat** /sēt/
t̩   *as in* **butter** /'bət̩ər/, **forty** /'fôrt̩ē/, **bottle** /'bät̩l/
TH   *as in* **thin** /THin/, **truth** /tro͞oTH/
T̲H̲   *as in* **then** /T̲H̲en/, **father** /'fäT̲H̲ər/
v   *as in* **never** /'nevər/, **very** /'verē/
w   *as in* **wait** /wāt/, **quick** /kwik/
(h)w *as in* **when** /(h)wen/, **which** /(h)wicH/
y   *as in* **yet** /yet/, **accuse** /ə'kyo͞oz/
z   *as in* **zipper** /'zipər/, **musician** /myo͞o'zisHən/
ZH   *as in* **measure** /'mezHər/, **vision** /'vizHən/

Foreign Sounds
KH   *as in* **Bach** /bäKH/
N   *as in* **en route** /äN 'ro͞ot/, **Rodin** /rō'dæN/
œ   *as in* **hors d'oeuvre** /ôr 'dœvrə/, **Goethe** /'gœtə/
Y   *as in* **Lully** /lY'lē/, **Utrecht** /'Y‚treKHt/

Stress marks

Stress marks are placed before the affected syllable. The primary stress mark is a short vertical line above the letters ['] and signifies greater pronunciation emphasis should be placed on that syllable. The secondary stress mark is a short vertical line below the letters [‚] and signifies a weaker pronunciation emphasis.

A

a•bate /ə'bāt/ ▶ v. [trans.] lessen, reduce, or remove (esp. a nuisance): *this action would not have been sufficient to abate the odor nuisance.*
ORIGIN Middle English (in the legal sense 'put a stop to (a nuisance)'): from Old French *abatre* 'to fell,' from *a-* (from Latin *ad* 'to, at') + *batre* 'to beat' (from Latin *battere, battuere* 'to beat').

a•bate•ment /ə'bātmənt/ ▶ n. the ending, reduction, or lessening of something: *noise abatement | an abatement in the purchase price.*
ORIGIN Middle English: from Anglo-Norman French, from Old French *abatre* 'fell, put an end to' (see **ABATE**).

ab•duc•tion /æb'dəksHən/ ▶ n. the action or an instance of forcibly taking a person or persons away against their will: *they organized the abduction of Mr. Cordes on his way to the airport | abductions by armed men in plain clothes.*
■ the illegal removal from parents or guardians of a child.

a•bet /ə'bet/ ▶ v. (**abetted, abetting**) [trans.] encourage or assist (someone) to do something wrong, in particular, to commit a crime or other offense: *he was not guilty of murder but was guilty of **aiding and abetting** others.*
■ encourage or assist someone to commit (a crime): *we are **aiding and abetting** this illegal traffic.*
DERIVATIVES **a•bet•ment** n.; **a•bet•tor** /ə'betər/ (also **a•bet•ter**) n.
ORIGIN late Middle English (in the sense 'urge to do something good or bad'): from Old French *abeter*, from *a-* (from Latin *ad* 'to, at') + *beter* 'hound, urge on.'

ab•jure /æb'jŏŏr/ ▶ v. [trans.] formal solemnly renounce (a belief, cause, or claim): *the state has abjured the authority to execute custodial arrests for such minor offenses.*
DERIVATIVES **ab•ju•ra•tion** /ˌæbjə'rāsHən/ n.
ORIGIN late Middle English: from Latin *abjurare*, from *ab-* 'away' + *jurare* 'swear.'

a•bridge /ə'brij/ ▶ v. [trans.] (usu. **be abridged**) curtail (rights or privileges): *even the right to free speech can be abridged.*
ORIGIN Middle English (in the sense 'deprive of'): from Old French *abregier*, from late Latin *abbreviare* 'cut short'.

ab•ro•gate /'æbrəˌgāt/ ▶ v. [trans.] formal repeal or do away with (a law,

right, or formal agreement): *a proposal to abrogate temporarily the right to strike.*
DERIVATIVES **ab•ro•ga•tion** /ˌæbrə'gāsHən/ **n.**
ORIGIN early 16th cent.: from Latin *abrogat-* 'repealed,' from the verb *abrogare*, from *ab-* 'away, from' + *rogare* 'propose a law.'

ab•scond /æb'skänd/ ▶ **v.** [intrans.] leave hurriedly and secretly, typically to avoid detection of or arrest for an unlawful action such as theft: *she absconded with the remaining thousand dollars.*
■ (of someone on bail) fail to surrender oneself for custody at the appointed time. ■ (of a person kept in detention or under supervision) escape: *176 detainees absconded.*
DERIVATIVES **ab•scond•er n.**
ORIGIN mid 16th cent. (in the sense 'hide, conceal (oneself)'): from Latin *abscondere* 'hide,' from *ab-* 'away, from' + *condere* 'stow.'

ab•so•lute ti•tle /'æbsə,lo͞ot 'tīt̲l/ ▶ **n.** guaranteed title to the ownership of a property or lease.

ab•stract of ti•tle /'æbstrækt əv 'tīt̲l/ ▶ **n.** a summary giving details of the title deeds and documents that prove an owner's right to dispose of land, together with any encumbrances that relate to the property.

ac•ces•sion /æk'seSHən/ ▶ **n. 1** the attainment or acquisition of a position of rank or power, typically that of monarch or president: *the queen's accession to the throne* | *lost the vote on the Fortas accession to the chief justiceship.*
■ the action or process of formally joining or being accepted by an association, institution, or group: *the accession of Spain and Portugal into the European Community.*
2 a new item added to an existing collection of books, paintings, or artifacts.
■ an amount added to an existing quantity of something: *did not anticipate any further accession of wealth from the man's estate.*
3 the formal acceptance of a treaty or agreement: *accession to the Treaty of Paris.*
▶ **v.** [trans.] (usu. **be accessioned**) record the addition of (a new item) to a library, museum, or other collection.
ORIGIN late 16th cent. (in the general sense 'something added'): from Latin *accession-*, from the verb *accedere* 'approach, come to' (see **ACCEDE**).

ac•ces•so•ry /æk'ses(ə)rē/ (also **ac•ces•sa•ry**) ▶ **n.** (pl. **ac•ces•so•ries**) someone who gives assistance to the perpetrator of a crime, without directly committing it, sometimes without being present: *she was charged as an accessory to murder.* Compare with **PRINCIPAL**.
PHRASES **accessory before** (or **after**) **the fact** dated a person who incites or assists someone to commit a crime (or knowingly aids someone who has committed a crime).
ORIGIN late Middle English: from medieval Latin *accessorius* 'additional thing,' from Latin *access-* 'increased,' from the verb *accedere*.

ac•com•plice /ə'kämplis/ ▶ n. a person who helps another commit a crime.
ORIGIN mid 16th cent.: alteration (probably by association with *accompany*) of Middle English *complice* 'an associate,' via Old French from late Latin *complex, complic-* 'allied,' from *com-* 'together' + the root of *plicare* 'to fold.'

ac•cu•sa•to•ri•al /ə,kyo͞ozə'tôrēəl/ ▶ adj. [attrib.] (esp. of a trial or legal procedure) involving accusation by a prosecutor and a verdict reached by an impartial judge or jury. Often contrasted with INQUISITORIAL.

ac•quaint•ance rape /ə'kwäntəns ,rāp/ ▶ n. rape by a person who is known to the victim.

ac•quit /ə'kwit/ ▶ v. (**acquitted, acquitting**) [trans.] (usu. **be acquitted**) free (someone) from a criminal charge by a verdict of not guilty: *she was acquitted on all counts* | *the jury* **acquitted** *him of murder.*
ORIGIN Middle English (originally in the sense 'pay a debt, discharge a liability'): from Old French *acquiter,* from medieval Latin *acquitare* 'pay a debt,' from *ad-* 'to' + *quitare* 'set free.'

ac•quit•tal /ə'kwitl/ ▶ n. a judgment that a person is not guilty of the crime with which the person has been charged: *the trial resulted in an acquittal* | *the women felt their chances of acquittal were poor.*

act /ækt/ ▶ v. [intrans.] (**act for/on behalf of**) represent (someone) on a contractual, legal, or paid basis: *he chose an attorney to act for him.*
▶ n. **1** (often as **criminal act**) a constituent element of a crime or tort: *they argued over whether the burning of the flag is a criminal act.*
2 a written ordinance of Congress, or another legislative body; a statute: *the act to abolish slavery.*
■ a document attesting a legal transaction. ■ (often **acts**) dated the recorded decisions or proceedings of a committee or an academic body.
PHRASES **act of God** an instance of uncontrollable natural forces in operation (often used in insurance claims). **read the Riot Act** see RIOT ACT.
ORIGIN late Middle English: from Latin *actus* 'event, thing done,' *act-* 'done,' from the verb *agere,* reinforced by the French noun *acte.*

ac•tion /'ækSHən/ ▶ n. a legal process; a lawsuit: *an action for damages.*
ORIGIN late Middle English: via Old French from Latin *actio(n-),* from *agere* 'do, act.'

ac•tion•a•ble /'ækSHənəbəl/ ▶ adj. giving sufficient reason to take legal action: *slanderous remarks are actionable.*

ac•tus re•us /,æktəs 'rēəs; 'rāəs/ ▶ n. action or conduct that is a constituent element of a crime, as opposed to the mental state of the accused: [as modifier] *the statutes do not characterize hate and bias as actus reus conditions.* Compare with MENS REA.
ORIGIN early 20th cent.: Latin, literally 'guilty act.'

ad li•tem /æd 'lītəm/ ▶ adj. (esp. of a guardian) appointed to act in a lawsuit on behalf of a child or other person who is not considered capable of representing themselves: *you'll have to discuss that with the girls' guardian ad litem.*
ORIGIN mid 18th cent.: Latin, literally 'for the lawsuit.'

ad•min•is•tra•tion /ədˌminəˈstrāsHən/ (abbr.: **admin.**) ▶ **n.** the management and disposal of the property of an intestate, deceased person, debtor, or other individual, or of an insolvent company, by a legally appointed administrator: *the company* ***went into administration*** | [as adj.] *an administration order.*
ORIGIN Middle English: from Latin *administratio(n-)*, from the verb *administrare.*

ad•min•is•tra•tor /ədˈminəˌstrātər/ ▶ **n.** a person legally appointed to manage and dispose of the estate of an intestate, deceased person, debtor, or other individual, or of an insolvent company.

ad•min•is•tra•trix /ədˈminəˌstrātriks/ ▶ **n.** a female administrator of an estate.

ad•mi•ral•ty /ˈædmərəltē/ ▶ **n.** (pl. **ad•mi•ral•ties**) the jurisdiction of courts of law over cases concerning ships or the sea and other navigable waters (maritime law).
ORIGIN late Middle English: from Old French *admiralte*, from *admirail* 'emir, leader.'

ADR ▶ **abbr.** alternative dispute resolution.

a•dult /əˈdəlt; ˈædˌəlt/ ▶ **n.** a person who has reached the age of majority.
ORIGIN mid 16th cent.: from Latin *adultus*, past participle of *adolescere* 'grow to maturity.'

a•dul•ter•y /əˈdəlt(ə)rē/ ▶ **n.** voluntary sexual intercourse between a married person and a person who is not his or her spouse: *she was* ***committing adultery with*** *a much younger man.*
ORIGIN late 15th cent.: from the obsolete noun *adulter*, from Latin *adulter* 'adulterer,' replacing an earlier form *avoutrie*, from Old French *avouterie*, likewise based on Latin *adulter.*

ad va•lo•rem /ˌæd vəˈlôrəm/ ▶ **adv. & adj.** (of the levying of tax or customs duties) in proportion to the estimated value of the goods or transaction concerned: [as adj.] *the property owner may be eligible for a reduction in ad valorem taxes.*
ORIGIN late 17th cent.: Latin, literally 'according to the value.'

ad•vance di•rec•tive /ədˈvæns dəˌrektiv/ ▶ **n.** a written statement of a person's wishes regarding medical treatment, often including a living will, made to ensure those wishes are carried out should they be unable to communicate them to a doctor.

ad•ver•sar•i•al /ˌædvərˈserēəl/ ▶ **adj.** (of a trial or legal procedure) in which the parties in a dispute have the responsibility for finding and presenting evidence: *equality between prosecution and defense is essential in an adversarial system of justice.* Compare with INQUISITORIAL.

ad•verse pos•ses•sion /ˈædvərs pəˈzesHən/ ▶ **n.** the acquisition of property by a trespasser whose occupation of the property is exclusive, open, and continuous for a statutory period.

ad•vo•ca•cy /ˈædvəkəsē/ ▶ **n.** the profession or work of a legal advocate.
ORIGIN late Middle English: via Old French from medieval Latin *advocatia*, from *advocare* 'summon, call to one's aid' (see ADVOCATE).

ad•vo•cate ▸ n. /'ædvəkit/ a pleader in a court of law; a lawyer: *Marshall was a skilled advocate but a mediocre judge.*

ORIGIN Middle English: from Old French *avocat*, from Latin *advocatus*, past participle (used as a noun) of *advocare* 'call (to one's aid),' from *ad-* 'to' + *vocare* 'to call.'

af•fi•ant /ə'fīənt/ ▸ n. a person who swears to an affidavit: *your affiant, Special Agent Perez, has been a sworn police officer for 22 years.*

ORIGIN early 19th cent.: from French, present participle of *afier*, from medieval Latin *affidare* 'declare on oath.'

af•fi•da•vit /ˌæfi'dāvit/ ▸ n. a written statement confirmed by oath or affirmation, for use as evidence in court.

ORIGIN mid 16th cent.: from medieval Latin, literally 'he has stated on oath,' from *affidare*.

af•firm /ə'fərm/ ▸ v. [trans.] declare, support, or defend as fact, specifically: ■ accept or confirm the validity of (a judgment or agreement); ratify: *we affirm the judgment of the trial court.* ■ (of a court) uphold (a decision) on appeal: *the committee shall have the power to affirm, modify, or reject the decision.* ■ [intrans.] make a formal declaration rather than taking an oath (e.g., to testify truthfully): *I solemnly affirm.*

ORIGIN Middle English (in the sense 'make firm'): via Old French from Latin *affirmare*, from *ad-* 'to' + *firmus* 'strong.'

af•firm•a•tion /ˌæfər'mᴀsʜən/ ▸ n. a formal declaration by a person who declines to take an oath for reasons of conscience.

ORIGIN late Middle English: from Latin *affirmation-*, from the verb *affirmare* (see **AFFIRM**).

af•fray /ə'frā/ ▸ n. dated an instance of group fighting in a public place that disturbs the peace: *Lowe was charged with **causing an affray** | a person guilty of affray.*

ORIGIN Middle English (in the general sense 'disturbance, fray'): from Anglo-Norman French *afrayer* 'disturb, startle,' based on an element of Germanic origin related to Old English *frithu*'peace, safety' (compare with German *Friede* 'peace').

a•fore•thought /ə'fôrˌᴛʜôt/ ▸ adj. see **MALICE AFORETHOUGHT**.

AG ▸ abbr. attorney general.

age of con•sent /'āj əv kən'sent/ ▸ n. the age at which a person's, typically a girl's, consent to sexual intercourse is valid in law.

ag•gra•vat•ed /'ægrəˌvātid/ ▸ adj. [attrib.] (of an offense) made more serious by attendant circumstances (such as frame of mind): *aggravated burglary.*

■ (of a penalty) made more severe in recognition of the seriousness of an offense: *aggravated damages.*

DERIVATIVES **ag•gra•vat•ing** adj.: *aggravating factors in a death penalty case.*

a•gree•ment /ə'grēmənt/ ▸ n. a typically legally binding arrangement between parties as to a course of action: *a trade agreement | a verbal agreement to sell.*

ORIGIN late Middle English: from Old French, from *agreer* 'make agreeable to.'

al•ien•a•ble /'ālēənəbəl; 'ālyən-/ ▸ **adj**. able to be transferred to new ownership: *alienable common stock.*

DERIVATIVES **a•lien•a•bil•i•ty** /ˌālēənə'bilitē; ˌālyən-/ n.

al•ien•ate /'ālēəˌnāt; 'ālyə-/ ▸ **v**. [trans.] transfer ownership of (property rights) to another person or group: *he had the right to alienate the property.*

PHRASES **alienate someone's affections** induce someone to transfer their affection from a person (such as a spouse) with legal rights or claims on them: *the plaintiff sued a colleague for alienating the affections of plaintiff's wife.*

ORIGIN early 16th cent.: from Latin *alienat-* 'estranged,' from the verb *alienare*, from *alienus* 'of another.'

al•ien•a•tion /ˌālēə'nāSHən; ˌālyə-/ ▸ **n**. the transfer of the ownership of property rights.

ORIGIN late Middle English: from Latin *alienatio(n-)*, from the verb *alienare* 'estrange,' from *alienus*.

al•i•mo•ny /'æləˌmōnē/ ▸ **n**. a husband's or wife's court-ordered provision for a spouse after separation or divorce.

ORIGIN early 17th cent. (in the sense 'nourishment, means of subsistence'): from Latin *alimonia* 'nutriment,' from *alere* 'nourish.'

al•lo•cu•tion /ˌælə'kyo͞oSHən/ ▸ **n**. the right of a convicted defendant to speak on their own behalf before sentencing is pronounced: *the trial court determined Goodwin was not granted allocution at his original sentencing.*

■ an unsworn statement delivered (to the sentencing court) by a convicted defendant in which the defendant attempts to win a lesser sentence by such persuasion as requesting mercy, expressing regret, or giving a reasonable explanation for the criminal conduct: *the sentencing court indicated on the record that the defendant's allocution did not affect its sentencing decision.*

DERIVATIVES **al•lo•cute** /ˌælə'kyo͞ot/ v.; **al•loc•u•tor•y** /ˌælə'kyo͞otərē/ adj.

ORIGIN early 17th cent.: from Latin *allocutio(n-)*, from *alloqui* 'speak to,' from *ad-* 'to' + *loqui* 'speak.'

al•ter•na•tive dis•pute res•o•lu•tion /ôl'tərnətiv dis'pyo͞ot rezəˌlo͞oSHən/ (abbr.: **ADR**) ▸ **n**. the use of methods such as mediation or arbitration to resolve a dispute instead of litigation.

a•me•na•ble /ə'mēnəbəl; ə'men-/ ▸ **adj**. (**amenable to**) (of a thing) capable of being acted upon in a particular way; susceptible: *the defendant was amenable to suit in the jurisdiction.*

DERIVATIVES **a•me•na•bil•i•ty** /əˌmēnə'bilitē; əˌmen-/ n.; **a•me•na•bly** /ə'mēnəblē; ə'men-/ adv.

ORIGIN late 16th cent. (in the sense 'liable to answer (to a law or tribunal)'): an Anglo-Norman French legal term, from Old French *amener* 'bring to,' from *a-* (from Latin *ad*) 'to' + *mener* 'bring' (from late Latin *minare* 'drive (animals),' from Latin *minari* 'threaten').

a•merce•ment /ə'mərsmənt/ ▶ n. historical a fine.

DERIVATIVES **a•merce v.**

ORIGIN late Middle English: from Anglo-Norman French *amerciment*, based on *estre amercie* 'be at the mercy of another' (with respect to the amount of a fine), from *a merci* 'at (the) mercy.'

a•mi•cus /ə'mēkəs; ə'mī-/ (in full **a•mi•cus cu•ri•ae** /'kyŏŏrē,ī; 'kyŏŏ-rē,ē/) ▶ n. (pl. **a•mi•ci** /ə'mēkē; ə'mīkī/, **amici curiae**) an adviser, often voluntary, to a court of law in a particular case, who is a party to the case: [as adj.] *he was planning to advance this position in an **amicus brief**.*

ORIGIN early 17th cent.: from modern Latin *amicus curiae*, literally 'friend of the court.'

an•swer /'ænsər/ ▶ n. the defendant's reply to the plaintiff's charges: *jury demand is made in defendant's answer.*

▶ v. [trans.] defend oneself against (a charge, accusation, or criticism): *he said he would return to Spain to answer all charges.*

■ [intrans.] (**answer to**) be required to explain or justify oneself to (someone): *you will have the police to answer to.*

PHRASES **answer the description of** correspond to a description, esp. one of a suspect issued by the police: *he answers the description of being slightly taller than his two supposed companions.*

ORIGIN Old English *andswaru* (noun), *andswarian* (verb), of Germanic origin; from a base shared by SWEAR.

an•tic•i•pa•to•ry /æn'tisəpə,tôrē/ ▶ adj. (of a breach of contract) taking the form of an announcement or indication that a contract will not be honored: *the appellants' commencement of the lawsuit constituted anticipatory breach of the contract.*

an•ti•trust /,æntē'trəst; ,æntī-/ ▶ adj. of or relating to legislation preventing or controlling trusts or other monopolies, with the intention of promoting competition in business: *West Virginia joins Massachusetts in its ongoing antitrust battle against Microsoft.*

ap•peal /ə'pēl/ ▶ v. [intrans.] apply to a higher court for a reversal of the decision of a lower court: *he said he would **appeal against** the conviction* | [trans.] *they have 48 hours to appeal the decision.*

▶ n. an application to a higher court for a decision to be reversed: *he has 28 days in which to **lodge an appeal*** | *the right of appeal.*

DERIVATIVES **ap•peal•a•ble** /ə'pēləbəl/ **adj.**

ORIGIN Middle English (in legal contexts): from Old French *apel* (noun), *apeler* (verb), from Latin *appellare* 'to address,' based on *ad-* 'to' + *pellere* 'to drive.'

ap•peals court /ə'pēlz ,kôrt/ ▶ n. a court that hears appeals from a lower court.

ap•pear /ə'pir/ ▶ v. [intrans.] (of an accused person, witness, or lawyer) make an official appearance in a court of law: *he **appeared on** six charges of theft.*

ORIGIN Middle English: from Old French *apareir*, from Latin *apparere*, from *ad-* 'toward' + *parere* 'come into view.'

ap•pel•lant /ə'pelənt/ ▶ n. a person who applies to a higher court for a reversal of the decision of a lower court.

ORIGIN late Middle English: from French *apelant*, literally 'appealing,' from the verb *apeler* (see APPEAL).

ap•pel•late /ə'pelit/ ▶ adj. (typically of a court) concerned with or dealing with applications for decisions to be reversed: *there are two appellate courts in Iowa | rules of appellate procedure.*

ORIGIN late Middle English (originally in the sense 'appealed against, accused'): from Latin *appellatus* 'appealed against,' from the verb *appellare* (see APPEAL). The current sense dates from the mid 18th cent.

ap•pel•lee /ˌæpe'lē/ ▶ n. the respondent in a case appealed to a higher court.

ORIGIN mid 16th cent.: from French *appelé*, past participle of *appeler* 'call,' from Latin *appellare* 'to address' (see APPEAL).

ap•point /ə'point/ ▶ v. [trans.] decide the disposal of (property of which one is not the owner) under powers granted by the owner: *trustees appoint the capital to the beneficiaries.*

DERIVATIVES **ap•point•ee** /ə,poin'tē/ n.; **ap•point•er** n.

ORIGIN late Middle English: from Old French *apointer*, from *a point* 'to a point.'

ar•bi•tral /'ärbitrəl/ ▶ adj. relating to or resulting from the use of an arbitrator to settle a dispute: *the tribunal respects the enforcement of international arbitral awards.*

ORIGIN late 15th cent.: from late Latin *arbitralis*, from *arbiter* 'judge, supreme ruler.'

ar•bi•trar•y /'ärbi,trerē/ ▶ adj. based on unreasonable or capricious exercise of discretion: *Amnesty International condemns the nationwide arbitrary arrests of forty-two journalists | the applicant has failed to demonstrate the judge's decision is arbitrary.*

DERIVATIVES **ar•bi•trar•i•ly** /ˌärbə'trerəlē/ adv.; **ar•bi•trar•i•ness** n.

ORIGIN late Middle English (in the sense 'dependent on one's will or pleasure, discretionary'): from Latin *arbitrarius*, from *arbiter* 'judge, supreme ruler,' perhaps influenced by French *arbitraire*.

ar•bi•trate /'ärbi,trāt/ ▶ v. [intrans.] (of an independent person or body) reach an authoritative judgment or settlement: *by agreeing to arbitrate this dispute, parties give up their legal right to bring a court action and to have a jury trial.*

ORIGIN mid 16th cent.: from Latin *arbitrat-* 'judged,' from *arbitrari*, from *arbiter* 'judge, supreme ruler.'

ar•bi•tra•tion /ˌärbi'trāSHən/ ▶ n. the use of an arbitrator to settle a dispute: *arbitration is generally faster, less expensive, and more informal than going to court.*

PHRASES **go to arbitration** submit a dispute to an arbitrator: *the fifty-seven school districts went to arbitration in sixty-eight separate cases.*

ar•bi•tra•tor /'ärbi‚trātər/ ▶ n. an independent person or body officially appointed to settle a dispute: *the decision of the arbitrator can be enforced by the courts, if necessary.*

ar•raign /ə'rān/ ▶ v. [trans.] (often **be arraigned**) call or bring (someone) before a court to answer a criminal charge: *her sister was arraigned on attempted murder charges.*

DERIVATIVES **ar•raign•ment n.**

ORIGIN late Middle English: from Old French *araisnier*, based on Latin *ad-* 'to' + *ration-* 'reason, account.'

ar•ray /ə'rā/ ▶ n. a list of jurors empaneled.

▶ v. [trans.] empanel (a jury).

ORIGIN Middle English (in the senses 'preparedness' and 'place in readiness'): from Old French *arei* (noun), *areer* (verb), based on Latin *ad-* 'toward' + a Germanic base meaning 'prepare.'

ar•rears /ə'rirz/ ▶ plural n. money that is owed and should have been paid earlier: *he was suing the lessee for the arrears of rent.*

PHRASES **in arrears** (also **in arrear**) behind in paying money that is owed: *two out of three tenants are in arrears.*

DERIVATIVES **ar•rear•age** /ə'ririj/ n.

ORIGIN Middle English (first used in the phrase *in arrear*): from *arrear* (adverb) 'behind, overdue,' from Old French *arere*, from medieval Latin *adretro*, from *ad-* 'toward' + *retro* 'backward.'

ar•rest /ə'rest/ ▶ v. [trans.] seize (someone) by legal authority and take into custody: *the police arrested him for possession of marijuana | two youths aged 16 were arrested.*

▶ n. the action of seizing someone to take into custody: *I have a warrant for your arrest | they placed her under arrest | at least 69 arrests were made.*

ORIGIN late Middle English: from Old French *arester*, based on Latin *ad-* 'at, to' + *restare* 'remain, stop.'

ar•rest•ee /ə‚res'tē/ ▶ n. a person who has been arrested.

ar•son /'ärsən/ ▶ n. the criminal act of deliberately setting fire to property: *police are treating the fire as arson* | [as adj.] *an arson attack.*

DERIVATIVES **ar•son•ist** /'ärsənist/ n.

ORIGIN late 17th cent.: an Anglo-Norman French legal term, from medieval Latin *arsio(n-)*, from Latin *ardere* 'to burn.'

ar•ti•cle /'ärtikəl/ ▶ n. a separate clause or paragraph of a legal document or agreement, typically one outlining a single rule or regulation: [as adj.] *it is an offense under Article 7 of the treaty.*

ORIGIN Middle English (denoting a separate clause of the Apostles' Creed): from Old French, from Latin *articulus* 'small connecting part,' diminutive of *artus* 'joint.'

as•por•ta•tion /‚æspər'tāsHən/ ▶ n. rare the detachment, movement, or carrying away of property, considered an essential component of the crime of larceny.

ORIGIN late 15th cent.: from Latin *asportation-*, from *asportare* 'carry away.'

as•sault /əˈsôlt/ ▸ v. [trans.] make a physical attack on: *he pleaded guilty to assaulting a police officer | she was sexually assaulted as a child.*
▸ n. a physical attack: *his imprisonment for an* **assault on** *the film director | sexual assaults.*
■ an act, criminal or tortious, that threatens physical harm to a person, whether or not actual harm is done: *he appeared in court charged with assault.*
DERIVATIVES **as•sault•er** n.
ORIGIN Middle English: from Old French *asaut* (noun), *assauter* (verb), based on Latin *ad-* 'to' + *saltare*, frequentative of *salire* 'to leap.'

as•sault and bat•ter•y /əˈsôlt ən(d) ˈbæt(ə)rē/ ▸ n. the crime of threatening a person together with the act of making physical contact with them.

as•sign /əˈsīn/ ▸ v. [trans.] transfer (legal rights or liabilities): *they will ask you to assign your rights against the airline.*
▸ n. another term for ASSIGNEE.
DERIVATIVES **as•sign•a•ble** adj.; **as•sign•or** /əˈsīnôr/ n.
ORIGIN Middle English: from Old French *asigner*, *assiner*, from Latin *assignare*, from *ad-* 'to' + *signare* 'to sign.'

as•sign•ee /əˌsīˈnē/ ▸ n. a person to whom a right or liability is legally transferred.
ORIGIN Middle English: from Old French *assigne*, past participle of *assigner* 'allot' (see ASSIGN).

as•sign•ment /əˈsīnmənt/ ▸ n. an act of making a legal transfer of a right, property, or liability: *an assignment of leasehold property.*
■ a document effecting such a transfer.
ORIGIN late Middle English: from Old French *assignement*, from medieval Latin *assignamentum*, from Latin *assignare* 'allot' (see ASSIGN).

as•size /əˈsīz/ ▸ n. (usu. **assizes**) historical a court that formerly sat at intervals in each county of England and Wales to administer the civil and criminal law. In 1972 the civil jurisdiction of assizes was transferred to the High Court, and the criminal jurisdiction to the Crown Court.
ORIGIN Middle English: from Old French *assise*, feminine past participle of *asseeir* 'sit, settle, assess,' from Latin *assidere* (see ASSESS).

at•tach /əˈtæCH/ ▸ v. [trans.] **1** include (a condition) as part of an agreement: *the Commission can attach appropriate conditions to the operation of the agreement.*
2 seize (a person's property) by legal authority: *the court attached his wages for child support.*
DERIVATIVES **at•tach•a•ble** adj.
ORIGIN Middle English (in the sense 'seize by legal authority'): from Old French *atachier* or *estachier* 'fasten, fix.'

at•tach•ment /ə'tæCHmənt/ ▶ n. legal seizure of property.

ORIGIN late Middle English (in the sense 'arrest for contempt of court'): from Old French *attachement*, from *atachier* 'fasten, fix' (see **ATTACH**).

at•tain•der /ə'tāndər/ ▶ n. historical the forfeiture of land and civil rights suffered as a consequence of a sentence of death for treason or felony. See also **BILL OF ATTAINDER**.

ORIGIN late Middle English: from Anglo-Norman French, variant (used as a noun) of Old French *ateindre* in the sense 'convict, bring to justice.'

at•test /ə'test/ ▶ v. [intrans.] declare that something exists or is the case: [with clause] *the deceased's attorney attested that he had been about to institute divorce proceedings.*

■ be a witness to; certify formally: *the witnesses must attest and sign the will in the testator's presence.*

DERIVATIVES **at•tes•ta•tion** /ˌæte'stāSHən/ n.

ORIGIN early 16th cent.: from French *attester*, from Latin *attestari*, from *ad-* 'to' + *testari* 'to witness' (from *testis* 'a witness').

at•tor•ney /ə'tərnē/ ▶ n. (pl. **at•tor•neys**) **1** a person appointed to act for another in business or legal matters.

2 a lawyer.

DERIVATIVES **at•tor•ney•ship** /ə'tərnē,SHip/ n.

ORIGIN Middle English: from Old French *atorne*, past participle of *atorner* 'assign,' from *a* 'toward' + *torner* 'turn.'

at•tor•ney gen•er•al /ə'tərnē 'jen(ə)rəl/ (abbr.: **AG** or **Atty. Gen.**) ▶ n. (pl. **at•tor•neys gen•er•al**) the principal legal officer who represents a country or a state in legal proceedings and gives legal advice to the government.

■ the head of the US Department of Justice.

Atty. ▶ abbr. Attorney.

a•ver /ə'vər/ ▶ v. [trans.] (**a•verred, a•ver•ring**) formal allege as a fact in support of a plea: *they aver that they did not receive any compensation.*

ORIGIN late Middle English (in the sense 'declare or confirm to be true'): from Old French *averer*, based on Latin *ad* 'to' (implying 'cause to be') + *verus* 'true.'

a•ver•ment /ə'vərmənt/ ▶ n. formal a formal statement by a party in a case of a fact or circumstance that the party offers to prove or substantiate.

ORIGIN late Middle English: from Old French *averrement, averement*, from *averer* 'declare true' (see **AVER**).

B

---

bail /bāl/ ▸ n. the temporary release of an accused person awaiting trial, on condition that a sum of money be lodged to guarantee their appearance in court: *he has been released on bail.* See also RECOGNIZANCE.

■ money paid by or for such a person as security.

▸v. [trans.] (usu. **be bailed**) release or secure the release of (a prisoner) on payment of bail: *his son called home to get bailed out of jail.*

PHRASES **jump bail** informal fail to appear for trial after being released on bail: *he jumped bail and was on the run until his arrest.* **go bail** (or **stand bail**) act as surety for an accused person: *before leaving the court, she went bail for four of the strikers | Mr. Harvey's father stood bail for his son.* **post bail** pay a sum of money as bail: *I posted bail for him.*

DERIVATIVES **bail•a•ble adj.**

ORIGIN Middle English: from Old French, literally 'custody, jurisdiction,' from Old French *bailler* 'take charge of,' from Latin *bajulare* 'bear a burden.'

bail•ee /bā'lē/ ▸ n. a person or party to whom goods are delivered for a purpose, such as custody or repair, without transfer of ownership.

bail•iff /'bālif/ ▸ n. an official in a court of law who keeps order, looks after prisoners, etc.

ORIGIN Middle English: from Old French *baillif*, inflected form of *bailli*, based on Latin *bajulus* 'carrier, manager.'

bail•ment /'bālmənt/ ▸ n. an act of delivering goods to a bailee for a particular purpose, without transfer of ownership.

bail•or /'bālər/ ▸ n. a person or party that entrusts goods to a bailee.

bank•rupt /'bæNGkrəpt/ ▸ adj. (of a person or organization) declared in law unable to pay outstanding debts: *the company was declared bankrupt | this editorial explains why the airlines are going bankrupt.*

▸n. a person judged by a court to be insolvent, whose property is taken and disposed of for the benefit of creditors or whose financial affairs are recognized.

▸v. [trans.] reduce (a person or organization) to bankruptcy: *the strike nearly bankrupted the union.*

ORIGIN mid 16th cent.: from Italian *banca rotta* 'broken bench,' from *banca* 'bench' (relating to a money dealer's table) and *rompere* 'to break.' The change in the ending was due to association with Latin *rupt-* 'broken.'

bar /bär/ ▶ n. 1 (**the Bar**) the legal profession.

■ lawyers collectively. ■ Brit. barristers collectively.

2 (**the bar**) a partition in a courtroom, now usually notional, beyond which most persons may not pass and at which an accused person stands: *the prisoner at the bar.*

■ a plea arresting an action or claim in a law case. ■ a particular court of law.

▶ v. (**barred, barring**) [trans.] prevent or delay (an action) by objection.

ORIGIN Middle English: from Old French *barre* (noun), *barrer* (verb), of unknown origin.

bar•ra•try /'berətrē/ ▶ n. vexatious litigation or incitement to it.

DERIVATIVES **bar•ra•tor** /'berətər/ n. (historical); **bar•ra•trous** /'berətrəs/ adj.

ORIGIN from Old French *baraterie*, from *barater* 'deceive,' based on Greek *prattein* 'do, perform, manage' (sometimes dishonestly); perhaps influenced by Old Norse *barátta* 'contest.'

bar•ris•ter /'bærəstər/; 'ber-/ (also **bar•ris•ter-at-law**) ▶ n. chiefly Brit. a lawyer entitled to practice as an advocate, particularly in the higher courts. Compare with ATTORNEY, SOLICITOR.

ORIGIN late Middle English: from the noun BAR, perhaps on the pattern of *minister.*

bat•ter•y /'bæṭərē/ ▶ n. the crime or tort of unconsented harmful or offensive physical contact with another person. See also ASSAULT AND BATTERY.

ORIGIN Middle English: from French *batterie*, from *battre* 'to strike,' from Latin *battuere.*

bel•lig•er•ent /bə'lijərənt/ ▶ adj. engaged in a war or conflict, as recognized by international law: *belligerent military forces are expected to strike by day's end.*

▶ n. a nation or person engaged in war or conflict, as recognized by international law: *Oxfam will refuse money from belligerents during any war.*

DERIVATIVES **bel•lig•er•ent•ly** /bə'lijərəntlē/ adv.

ORIGIN late 16th cent.: from Latin *belligerant-* 'waging war,' from the verb *belligerare*, from *bellum* 'war.'

bench /bencH/ ▶ n. (**the bench**) the office of judge or magistrate: *his appointment to the civil bench.*

■ a judge's seat in a court of law: *approach the bench.* ■ judges or magistrates collectively: *rulings from the bench.*

PHRASES **on the bench** appointed as or in the capacity of a judge or magistrate: *he retired after twenty-five years on the bench.*

ORIGIN Old English *benc*, of Germanic origin; related to Dutch *bank* and German *Bank.*

bench•er /'bencHər/ ▶ n. (in the UK) a senior member of any of the Inns of Court.

ben•e•fi•cial /ˌbenə'fiSHəl/ ▸ **adj.** of or relating to rights, other than legal title: *the beneficiary will be taxed on the value of his beneficial use of the property.*
DERIVATIVES **ben•e•fi•cial•ly adv.**
ORIGIN late Middle English: from late Latin *beneficialis*, from *beneficium.*

ben•e•fi•ci•ar•y /ˌbenə'fisHēˌerē/ ▸ **n.** (pl. **ben•e•fi•ci•ar•ies**) a person who derives advantage from a trust, will, or life insurance policy.
ORIGIN early 17th cent.: from Latin *beneficiarius*, from *beneficium* 'favor, support,' from *bene* 'well' + *facere* 'do.'

be•queath /bi'kwēTH; -'kwēTH/ ▸ **v.** [trans.] leave (a personal estate or one's body) to a person or other beneficiary by a will: *he bequeathed his art collection to the town.*
DERIVATIVES **be•queath•er n.**
ORIGIN Old English *becwethan*, from *be-* 'about' (expressing transitivity) + *cwethan* 'say.'

bet•ter•ment /'beṯərmənt/ ▸ **n.** the enhanced value of real property arising from local improvements: [as adj.] *a betterment charge.*

bi•cam•er•al /bī'kæmərəl/ ▸ **adj.** (of a legislative body) having two branches or chambers.
DERIVATIVES **bi•cam•er•al•ism** /bī'kæmərəˌlizəm/ **n.**
ORIGIN mid 19th cent.: from *bi-* 'two' + Latin *camera* 'chamber' + *-al.*

big•a•my /'bigəmē/ ▸ **n.** the act of going through a marriage ceremony or being married while already married to another person.
DERIVATIVES **big•a•mist** /'bigəmist/ **n.**; **big•a•mous** /'bigəməs/ **adj.**
ORIGIN Middle English: from Old French *bigamie*, from *bigame* 'bigamous,' from late Latin *bigamus*, from *bi-* 'twice' + Greek *-gamos* 'married.'

bill of at•tain•der /'bil əv ə'tāndər/ ▸ **n.** an item of legislation (prohibited by the US Constitution) that inflicts attainder without judicial process: *during the Revolutionary War, bills of attainder were passed to a wide extent.*

bill of in•dict•ment /'bil əv in'dītmənt/ ▸ **n.** a written accusation as presented to a grand jury.

Bill of Rights /'bil əv 'rīts/ ▸ **n.** a statement of the rights of a class of people, in particular:
■ the first ten amendments to the US Constitution, ratified in 1791 and guaranteeing such rights as the freedoms of speech, assembly, and worship. ■ the English constitutional settlement of 1689, confirming the deposition of James II and the accession of William and Mary, guaranteeing the Protestant succession, and laying down the principles of parliamentary supremacy.

bind /bīnd/ ▸ **v.** (past and past part. **bound** /bownd/) [trans.] formal impose a legal or contractual obligation on: *a party who signs a document will normally be bound by its terms.*
■ (**bind oneself**) formal make a contractual or enforceable undertaking:

the government cannot bind itself as to the form of subsequent legislation. ■ secure (a contract), typically with a sum of money: *I have mailed a check to bind the contract.*

▶n. formal a statutory constraint: *the moral bind of the law.*

PHRASES **bind someone over** (usu. **be bound over**) (of a court of law) hold for trial: *he was bound over on a felony charge.*

ORIGIN Old English *bindan*, of Germanic origin; related to Dutch and German *binden*, from an Indo-European root shared by Sanskrit *bandh.*

birth cer•tif•i•cate /'bərTH sər,tifikit/ ▶ n. an official document issued to record a person's birth, including such identifying data as name, gender, date of birth, place of birth, and parentage.

bod•y cor•po•rate /'bädē 'kôrp(ə)rit/ ▶ n. formal term for CORPORATION.

bo•na fide /'bōnə ,fīd; 'bänə/ ▶ adv. sincerely; without intention to deceive: *the court will assume that they have acted bona fide.*

ORIGIN mid 16th cent.: Latin, literally 'with good faith,' ablative singular of BONA FIDES.

bo•na fi•des /'bōnə ,fīdz; 'fīdēz; 'bänə/ ▶ n. [treated as pl.] informal documentary evidence showing a person's legitimacy; credentials: *are you satisfied with my bona fides?*

ORIGIN mid 20th cent.:Latin, literally 'good faith.'

bond /bänd/ ▶ n. an agreement or promise with legal force, in particular: ■ a document by which a person is committed to make payment to another. ■ a promise to pay a sum if a defendant does not appear for trial. ■ a certificate issued by a government or a public company promising to repay borrowed money at a fixed rate of interest at a specified time. ■ (of dutiable goods) a state of storage in a bonded warehouse until the importer pays the duty owing. ■ an insurance policy held by a company, which protects against losses resulting from circumstances such as bankruptcy, failure to perform a contract, or misconduct by employees.

▶v. **1** issue a bond.

2 [usu. as n.] (**bonding**) place (dutiable goods) in bond.

ORIGIN Middle English: variant of *band.*

bond•ed /'bändid/ ▶ adj. [attrib.] **1** (of a person or company) bound by a legal agreement, in particular: ■ (of a debt) secured by bonds: *there are declines in bonded debt being paid by other agencies.* ■ (of a worker or workforce) obliged to work for a particular employer, often in a condition close to slavery: *the bonded workers are always powerless.*

2 (of dutiable goods) placed in bond.

bonds•man /'bändzmən/ ▶ n. (pl. **bonds•men**) a person who stands surety for a bond.

ORIGIN early 18th cent.: from BOND + *man.*

breach /brēCH/ ▶ n. an act of breaking or failing to observe a law, agreement, or code of conduct: *a breach of confidence | I sued for breach of contract.*

▶v. [trans.]

■ break or fail to observe (a law, agreement, or code of conduct): *Australian companies may be breaching the law by deleting business-related e-mail.*

PHRASES **breach of the peace** an act of violent or noisy behavior that causes a public disturbance and is considered a criminal offense.
breach of promise the action of breaking a sworn assurance to do something, formerly esp. to marry someone.

ORIGIN Middle English: from Old French *breche*, ultimately of Germanic origin; related to BREAK.

break /brāk/ ▶ v. [trans.] (past **broke** /brōk/; past part. **brok•en** /'brōkən/) fail to observe (a law, regulation, or agreement): *the district attorney says she will prosecute retailers who break the law | a legally binding contract that can only be broken by mutual consent.*

▶**break in** force entry to a building: *it sounded like someone trying to break in.*

ORIGIN Old English *brecan* (verb), of Germanic origin; related to Dutch *breken* and German *brechen*, from an Indo-European root shared by Latin *frangere* 'to break.'

break-in /'brāk ˌin/ ▶ n. a forced or unconsented entry into a building, car, computer system, etc., typically to steal something.

break•ing and en•ter•ing /'brākiNG ən(d) 'entəriNG/ ▶ n. the crime of entering a building by force so as to commit burglary.

brief /brēf/ ▶ n. a written summary of the facts and legal points supporting one side of a case, for presentation to a court.

■ a written summary of a judicial opinion, typically prepared by law students.

▶v. [intrans.] prepare a summary of a judicial opinion.

ORIGIN Middle English: from Old French *brief*, from Latin *brevis* 'short.' The noun is via late Latin *breve* 'note, dispatch,' hence 'an official letter.'

bring /briNG/ ▶ v. (past and past part. **brought** /brôt/) initiate (legal action) against someone: *riot and conspiracy charges should **be brought against** them.*

ORIGIN Old English *bringan*, of Germanic origin; related to Dutch *brengen* and German *bringen*.

bro•ker /'brōkər/ ▶ n. a person who buys and sells goods or assets for others.

▶v. [trans.] arrange or negotiate (a settlement, deal, or plan): *the ACLU of Maryland brokered the deal.*

ORIGIN Middle English (denoting a retailer or peddler): from Anglo-Norman French *brocour*, of unknown ultimate origin.

bur•glar /'bərglər/ ▶ n. a person who commits burglary.

ORIGIN mid 16th cent.: from legal French *burgler* or Anglo-Latin *burgulator*, *burglator*; related to Old French *burgier* 'pillage.'

bur•glar•ize /'bərgləˌrīz/ ▶ v. [trans.] (often **be burglarized**) enter (a building) illegally with intent to commit a crime, esp. theft: *our summer house has been burglarized.*

bur•gla•ry /'bərglərē/ ▶ n. (pl. **bur•gla•ries**) entry into a building illegally with intent to commit a crime, esp. theft: *a two-year sentence for burglary | a series of burglaries.*

ORIGIN early 16th cent.: from legal French *burglarie*, from *burgler* (see **BURGLAR**).

bur•gle /'bərgəl/ ▶ v. another term for **BURGLARIZE**.

ORIGIN late 19th cent.: originally a humorous and colloquial back-formation from **BURGLAR**.

by•law /'bī,lô/ (also **by-law**) ▶ n. **1** a rule made by a company or society to control the actions of its members.

2 a regulation made by a local authority; an ordinance.

ORIGIN Middle English: probably from obsolete *byrlaw* 'local law or custom,' from Old Norse *býjar*, genitive singular of *býr* 'town.'

CHOOSING A
LAWYER

———————

There are more than a million practicing lawyers in the United States. But it can be hard to find the right lawyer when you need one—a lawyer who is competent, experienced, affordable, and compatible. You have to get names of lawyers or law firms and then discuss your legal needs with them. And to make that discussion productive, you have to prepare.

Getting names
The first step is to find out which lawyers in your area have experience with the particular kind of legal work you need. If you are a member of a prepaid or discount legal services plan, a good starting point is that plan's list of participating lawyers. But explore other options as well.

Most people find their lawyers through word of mouth, so ask around. Talk to friends and coworkers about lawyers they know or have used themselves and been satisfied with. Your union, employer, or clergy may have suggestions. For business or financial matters, your broker, accountant, real estate agent, insurance agent, or any business person you deal with regularly is likely to know an appropriate candidate. You may know someone who has been in a situation similar to yours; if you are looking for a divorce lawyer, for instance, ask your divorced friends. Even learning the name of a lawyer they disliked (often an adversary) can help—either by giving you a name to avoid or because the qualities they disliked are just what you are looking for. Finally, nobody knows more lawyers—or knows them better—than lawyers themselves. The lawyer who helped you when you bought your house might well be able to recommend another for consultation on, say, a medical malpractice issue.

Advertisements on television or in the Yellow Pages can be useful, especially in calling attention to firms that specialize in some very specific area. But since you know nothing about those firms except what they claim about themselves, investigate them very thoroughly.

Legal referral services—especially those found on the Internet—are often just another form of paid advertising. Bar association referral services provide a degree of comfort because they do some screening of their lawyers. The American Bar Association (ABA) maintains a complete list of bar association referral services at www.abanet.org/legalservices/lris/directory.html. Just remember that those services cannot express an opinion on the lawyers who participate; if you get a referral from them, you still have to do your own evaluation.

Some limited legal services for the poor are available in many areas. See the appendix of legal aid organizations in this book (p. 215). See also the ABA's list of volunteer lawyer programs at www.abanet.org/legalservices/probono/directory.html and the list of legal aid programs funded by the Legal Services Corporation at www.lsc.gov/fundprog.htm.

If you are suspected of a crime, you absolutely need a lawyer. Do not talk to the police without one. If you are arrested, you have a right to have a lawyer appointed to represent you for free if you cannot afford to pay. Insist on it.

Homework
Once you have one or more names, do a little research. Check with a state agency to make sure the person is a member of the bar in good standing and learn about any disciplinary rulings against the lawyer. Do what lawyers themselves often do: look up the lawyer or law firm in the *Martindale-Hubbell Law Directory*, available in many libraries and online at www.martindale.com. At a minimum, this publication gives address and

phone information; many lawyers submit additional information about themselves and pay to have it included. (Martindale offers "ratings" of lawyers, but most potential clients find these ratings of modest value, at best.) Many lawyers and law firms these days also have their own Web sites, where you can see in detail what they believe makes them stand out.

Before interviewing a lawyer, collect your thoughts and your documents. Be prepared to summarize your situation clearly and concisely; make a written outline of key points and even practice saying them. If the matter concerns other people, list their names and addresses so that the lawyer can make sure no existing clients are involved. If it concerns estate planning, make a list of your major assets, accounts, and life insurance policies. If it concerns a contract, court paper, or other document, take it with you.

Interview

If it seems worthwhile after a quick inquiry by telephone, most lawyers will be happy to spend twenty minutes or half an hour with you (by phone if necessary), without charge or for a nominal fee, to explore the possibility of working for you. There is much to cover in that short time:

- You will explain why you are looking for a lawyer. Be organized, be open (the information you give is confidential), and above all, be brief. The lawyer can ask follow-up questions if necessary.

- The lawyer will explain whether he or she can be of assistance, and how. Sometimes all the help you need can be given right on the spot.

- This is your opportunity to interview the lawyer about everything you need to know to make the hiring decision—experience with this kind of matter, which lawyers in the firm would do the actual work (e.g., younger and cheaper, or more experienced and more expensive?), how fees will be calculated, what expenses might be charged on top of the fees, and anticipated total cost. Some matters, like a simple will, can be done for a flat fee; some cases can be handled on a contingency basis (you pay expenses but no lawyers' fees unless you win money). Some matters are too complex and open-ended for a definitive estimate.

Feel free to talk to several lawyers before making your choice. Do not sign any agreement until you understand it clearly. And do not neglect the intangibles: in the end, choose a lawyer who seems intelligent, thoughtful, articulate, well organized, and comfortable for you to work with.

C

cal•en•dar /ˈkæləndər/ ▸ n. a list of people or events connected with particular dates, esp. cases for trial; a court schedule.
▸v. [trans.] enter (something) in a calendar: *when a case is calendared, the parties are notified by the court.*
ORIGIN Middle English: from Old French *calendier*, from Latin *kalendarium* 'account book,' from *kalendae*.

cam•er•a /ˈkæm(ə)rə/ ▸ see IN CAMERA.

can•cel•la•tion /ˌkænsəˈlāsHən/ ▸ n. the annulling of a legal document: *the debtor can procure cancellation if satisfied within one month.*

ca•pac•i•ty /kəˈpæsətē/ ▸ n. 1 a person's legal competence: *cases where a patient's testamentary capacity is in doubt.*
2 [in sing.] a specified role or position: *I was engaged in a voluntary capacity* | *writing in his capacity as legal correspondent.*
ORIGIN late Middle English: from French *capacité*, from Latin *capacitas*, from *capax, capac-* 'that can contain,' from *capere* 'take or hold.'

ca•pi•as /ˈkāpēəs/ ▸ n. (pl. **ca•pi•as•es**) a writ ordering the arrest of a named person.
ORIGIN late Middle English: from Latin *capias (ad respondendum)*, literally 'you are to seize (until reply is made),' from *capere* 'take.'

cap•tion /ˈkæpsHən/ ▸ n. a title or brief explanation appended to a pleading document or judicial opinion.
■ the heading of a legal document.
ORIGIN late Middle English: from Latin *caption-*, from *capere* 'take, seize.' Early senses 'arrest' and 'warrant for arrest' gave rise to 'statement of where, when, and by whose authority a warrant was issued' (late 17th cent.): this was usually appended to a legal document, hence the sense 'heading or appended wording' (late 18th cent.).

car•nal knowl•edge /ˈkärnl ˈnälij/ ▸ n. dated sexual intercourse.

case /kās/ ▸ n. 1 an incident or set of circumstances under police investigation: *a murder case.*
2 a legal action, esp. one to be decided in a court of law: *a libel case* | *a former employee brought the case against the council.*
■ a set of facts or arguments supporting one side in such a legal action: *the case for the defense.* ■ a legal action that has been decided and may be cited as a precedent. ■ a reported judicial opinion.

ORIGIN Middle English: from Old French *cas*, from Latin *casus* 'fall,' related to *cadere* 'to fall'; in sense 4 directly from Latin, translating Greek *ptōsis*, literally 'fall.'

case•book /'kās₁bŏŏk/ ▶ n. a book containing a selection of source materials on a particular subject, esp. one used as a reference work or in teaching.

case law ▶ n. (also **case•law**) the law as established by the outcome of former cases. Compare with COMMON LAW, STATUTORY LAW.

cas•u•al•ty /'kæzн(ŏŏ)əltē/ ▶ n. (pl. **cas•u•al•ties**) a person killed or injured in a war or accident.
▪ (chiefly in insurance) an accident, mishap, or disaster. ▪ a loss caused by accident or injury.
ORIGIN late Middle English (in the sense 'chance, a chance occurrence'): from medieval Latin *casualitas*, from *casualis*, from *casus* 'fall,' on the pattern of words such as *penalty*.

cau•sa•tion /kô'zāsнən/ ▶ n. in tort law, the requirement of factual connection between the defendant's conduct and the plaintiff's harm: *this decision has reaffirmed the need to establish causation in cases where a medical practitioner fails to warn the patient of material risks.*
ORIGIN late 15th cent.: from Latin *causatio(n-)* 'pretext' (in medieval Latin 'the action of causing'), from *causare* 'to cause.'

cause /kôz/ ▶ n. **1** a person or thing that gives rise to an action, phenomenon, or condition: *the cause of the accident is not clear.*
2 a matter to be resolved in a court of law.
▪ an individual's case offered at law.
PHRASES **cause of action** a fact or facts that enable a person to bring an action against another.
ORIGIN Middle English: from Old French, from Latin *causa* (noun), *causare* (verb).

ca•ve•at /'kævē₁ät; 'käv-/ ▶ n. a notice, esp. in a probate, that certain actions temporarily may not be taken.
ORIGIN mid 16th cent.: from Latin, literally 'let a person beware.'

ca•ve•at emp•tor /'kævē₁æt 'emp₁tôr; 'käv-/ ▶ n. the principle that the buyer alone is responsible for checking the quality and suitability of goods before a purchase is made.
ORIGIN early 16th cent.: Latin, literally 'let the buyer beware.'

cer•tif•i•cate ▶ n. /sər'tifikit/ an official document attesting a certain fact, in particular:
▪ a document recording a person's birth, marriage, or death. ▪ a document attesting ownership of a certain item: *a stock certificate.*
▶v. /sər'tifə₁kāt/ [trans.] (usu. **be certificated**) provide with or attest in an official document.
ORIGIN late Middle English (in the sense 'certification, attestation'): from French *certificat* or medieval Latin *certificatum*, from *certificare.*

cer•ti•o•ra•ri /₁sersн(ē)ə'rärē; -'rerī/ ▶ n. (usually as **writ of certiorari**) a writ or order from a higher court (especially the US Supreme Court) that it will review a decision of a lower court.

ORIGIN late Middle English: from Law Latin, 'to be informed,' a phrase originally occurring at the start of the writ, from *certiorare* 'inform,' from *certior*, comparative of *certus* 'certain.'

chal•lenge /'CHælinj/ ▶ n. an objection or query as to the truth of something, often with an implicit demand for proof: *a **challenge** to the legality of the order.*
■ an objection regarding the eligibility or suitability of a jury member. See also PEREMPTORY CHALLENGE.
▶v. [trans.] object to (a jury member).
PHRASES **challenge for cause** an objection regarding the eligibility or suitability of a jury member, for which a reason is given.
DERIVATIVES **chal•lenge•a•ble** adj.; **chal•leng•er** n.
ORIGIN Middle English (in the senses 'accusation' and 'accuse'): from Old French *chalenge* (noun), *chalenger* (verb), from Latin *calumnia* 'calumny,' *calumniari* 'calumniate.'

cham•ber /'CHāmbər/ ▶ n. 1 a hall used by a legislative or judicial body.
■ the body that meets in such a hall. ■ any of the houses of a legislature: *the Senate chamber.*
2 (**chambers**) a judge's office.
■ (**chambers**) Brit. rooms used by a lawyer or lawyers.
ORIGIN Middle English (in the sense 'private room'): from Old French *chambre*, from Latin *camera* 'vault, arched chamber,' from Greek *kamara* 'object with an arched cover.'

cham•per•ty /'CHæmpərtē/ ▶ n. an illegal agreement in which a person with no previous interest in a lawsuit finances it with a view to sharing the disputed property if the suit succeeds.
DERIVATIVES **cham•per•tous** /'CHæmpərtəs/ adj.
ORIGIN late Middle English: from Anglo-Norman French *champartie*, from Old French *champart* 'feudal lord's share of produce,' from Latin *campus* 'field' + *pars* 'part.'

chan•cer•y /'CHæns(ə)rē/ ▶ n. (pl. **chan•cer•ies**) 1 a court of equity.
■ equity. ■ (**Chancery**) Brit. the Lord Chancellor's court, a division of the High Court of Justice.
2 a public records office.

charge /CHärj/ ▶ v. [trans.] 1 accuse (someone) of an offense under law: *they were **charged with** assault.*
2 instruct (a jury) as to the law: *after the judge has charged the jury, you will retire to consider your verdict.*
▶n. 1 an accusation, typically one formally made against a prisoner brought to trial: *he appeared in court **on a charge of** attempted murder | three people were arrested but released **without charge**.*
2 an official instruction, esp. one given by a judge to a jury regarding points of law.
PHRASES **press** (or **prefer**) **charges** accuse someone formally of a

crime so that they can be brought to trial: *police decline to press charges against protesters* | *two charges were preferred against the Air Force captain.*
ORIGIN Middle English (in the general senses 'to load' and 'a load'): from Old French *charger* (verb), *charge* (noun), from late Latin *carricare*, *carcare* 'to load,' from Latin *carrus* 'wheeled vehicle.'

char•ter /'CHärtər/ ▶ n. a written grant by a country's legislative or sovereign power, by which an institution such as a company, university, or city is created and its rights and privileges defined.
■ a written constitution or description of an organization's functions.
▶v. [trans.] grant a charter to (a city, university, or other institution): *the company was chartered in 1553.*
ORIGIN Middle English: from Old French *chartre*, from Latin *chartula*, diminutive of *charta* 'paper.'

chat•tel /'CHætl/ ▶ n. (in general use) a personal possession.
■ an item of property other than real estate. See also GOODS AND CHATTELS.
ORIGIN Middle English: from Old French *chatel*, from medieval Latin *capitale*, from Latin *capitalis*, from *caput* 'head.'

chief jus•tice /'CHēf 'jəstis/ ▶ n. (the title of) the presiding judge in a supreme court.
■ **(Chief Justice of the United States)** (the formal title of) the chief justice of the US Supreme Court.

child a•buse /'CHīld ə'byo͞os/ ▶ n. physical maltreatment or sexual molestation of a child.

cir•cuit /'sərkit/ (abbr.: **cir.** or **circ.**) ▶ n. a regular journey made by a judge around a particular district to hear cases in court: [as adj.] *a circuit judge.*
■ a district of this type. ■ a judicial region formerly administered by traveling judges.
ORIGIN late Middle English: via Old French from Latin *circuitus*, from *circuire*, variant of *circumire* 'go around,' from *circum* 'around' + *ire* 'go.'

cir•cum•stan•tial /ˌsərkəm'stænCHəl/ ▶ adj. (of evidence or a legal case) pointing indirectly toward someone's guilt but not conclusively proving it.
DERIVATIVES **cir•cum•stan•ti•al•i•ty** /ˌsərkəmˌstænCHē'æli̯tē/ n.; **cir•cum•stan•tial•ly** adv.
ORIGIN late 16th cent.: from Latin *circumstantia.*

ci•ta•tion /sī'tāsHən/ (abbr.: **cit.**) ▶ n. **1** a reference to a former tried case, used as guidance in the trying of comparable cases or in support of an argument.
2 a summons: *a traffic citation.*
ORIGIN Middle English: from Old French, from Latin *citation-*, from *citare* 'cite.'

cite /sīt/ ▶ v. [trans.] (often **be cited**) **1** induce a former tried case as a guide to deciding a comparable case or in support of an argument: *neither party is able to cite to any case that clarifies the issue | his lawyer cited the ancient case of the Crown vs. Madame X.*

2 summon (someone) to appear in a court of law: *the summons cited four defendants.*

DERIVATIVES **cit•a•ble** adj.

ORIGIN late Middle English (originally with reference to a court of ecclesiastical law): from Old French *citer*, from Latin *citare*, from *ciere*, *cire* 'to call.'

cit•i•zen's ar•rest /'sitəzənz ə'rest/ ▶ n. an arrest by an ordinary person without a warrant, allowable in certain cases.

civ•il /'sivəl/ ▶ adj. relating to private relations between members of a community; noncriminal: *a civil action | a civil court.*

■ of or relating to aspects of the civil (or code) law derived from European systems.

ORIGIN late Middle English: via Old French from Latin *civilis*, from *civis* 'citizen.'

civ•il court /'sivəl 'kôrt/ ▶ n. a court dealing with noncriminal cases.

civ•il dis•o•be•di•ence /'sivəl ˌdisə'bēdēəns/ ▶ n. the refusal to comply with certain laws or to pay taxes and fines, as a peaceful form of political protest.

civ•il law /'sivəl 'lô/ ▶ n. the system of law concerned with private relations between members of a community rather than criminal, military, or religious affairs.Contrasted with CRIMINAL LAW.

■ the system of law predominant on the European continent and of which a form is in force in Louisiana, historically influenced by the codes of ancient Rome.Compare with COMMON LAW.

civ•il lib•er•ty /'sivəl 'libərtē/ ▶ n. the state of being subject only to laws established for the good of the community, esp. with regard to freedom of action and speech.

■ (**civil liberties**) a person's rights to be only so subject.

DERIVATIVES **civ•il lib•er•tar•i•an** /'sivəl ˌlibər'terēən/ n.

civ•il wrong /'sivəl 'rôNG/ ▶ n. an infringement of a person's rights, such as a tort or breach of contract.

claim /klām/ ▶ v. [trans.] formally request or demand; say that one owns or has earned (something): *if no one claims the items, they will become government property.*

■ make a demand for (money) under the terms of an insurance policy: *she could have claimed the cost through her insurance.*

▶ n. a demand or request for something considered one's due: *the court had denied their claims to asylum.*

■ an application for compensation under the terms of an insurance policy. ■ a right or title to something: *they have first claim on the assets of the trust.* ■ (also **mining claim**) a piece of land allotted to or taken by someone in order to be mined.

DERIVATIVES **claim•a•ble** adj.

ORIGIN Middle English: from Old French *claime* (noun), *clamer* (verb), from Latin *clamare* 'call out.'

class ac•tion /'klæs 'ækSHən/ ▸ n. a lawsuit filed or defended by an individual or small group acting on behalf of a large group.

clause /klôz/ ▸ n. a particular and separate article, stipulation, or proviso in a treaty, bill, or contract.

DERIVATIVES **claus•al** /'klôzəl/ **adj.**

ORIGIN Middle English: via Old French *clause*, based on Latin *claus-* 'shut, closed,' from the verb *claudere*.

clerk /klərk/ ▸ n. an official in charge of the records of a local council or court: *a clerk to the court.*

■ a person employed by a judge, or being trained by a lawyer, who does legal research, etc.

▸ v. [intrans.] work as a clerk: *they clerked for several judges at one time.*

ORIGIN Old English *cleric*, *clerc* (in the sense 'ordained minister, literate person'), from ecclesiastical Latin *clericus* 'clergyman'; reinforced by Old French *clerc*, from the same source.

clerk•ship /'klərk,SHip/ ▸ n. the position or status of a clerk, esp. in the legal profession.

code /kōd/ ▸ n. a systematic collection of laws or regulations: *the criminal code.*

PHRASES **bring something up to code** renovate an old building or update its features in line with the latest building regulations.

ORIGIN Middle English: via Old French from Latin *codex*, *codic-*. The term originally denoted a systematic collection of statutes made by one of the later Roman emperors, particularly that of Justinian; (mid 18th cent.), the earliest modern sense.

co•de•fend•ant /,kōdi'fendənt/ ▸ n. a joint defendant.

cod•i•cil /'kädəsil/ ▸ n. an addition or supplement that explains, modifies, or revokes a will or part of one.

DERIVATIVES **cod•i•cil•la•ry** /,kädə'silərē/ **adj.**

ORIGIN late Middle English: from Latin *codicillus*, diminutive of *codex*, *codic-*.

cod•i•fy /'kädə,fī; 'kōd-/ ▸ v. (**cod•i•fies, cod•i•fied**) [trans.] arrange (laws or rules) into a systematic code.

DERIVATIVES **cod•i•fi•ca•tion** /,kädəfi'kāSHən; ,kōd-/ **n.**; **cod•i•fi•er** /'kädə,fīər; 'kōd-/ **n.**

cog•ni•za•ble /'kägnəzəbəl; käg'nīz-/ ▸ **adj.** within the jurisdiction of a court: *a cognizable offense.*

ORIGIN late 17th cent.: from COGNIZANCE + -*able*.

cog•ni•zance /'kägnəzəns/ ▸ n. formal knowledge, awareness, or notice: *he was deputed to bring the affair to the cognizance of the court.*

■ the action of taking jurisdiction. ■ the action of taking judicial notice (of a fact beyond dispute).

ORIGIN Middle English *conisance*, from Old French *conoisance*, based on Latin *cognoscere* 'get to know.' The spelling with *g*, influenced by Latin, arose in the 15th cent. and gradually affected the pronunciation.

col•lu•sion /kə'lōōZHən/ ▶ n. secret or illegal cooperation or conspiracy, esp. between ostensible opponents in a lawsuit.
DERIVATIVES **col•lu•sive** /kə'lōōsiv; -ziv/ adj.; **col•lu•sive•ly** adv.
ORIGIN late Middle English: from Latin *collusion-*, from *colludere* 'have a secret agreement.'

col•or /'kələr/ (Brit. **col•our**) ▶ n. an apparent right or ground.
PHRASES **under color of law** with the apparent authority of the law.
ORIGIN Middle English (as *colo(u)r*): from Old French *colour* (noun), *colourer* (verb), from Latin *color* (noun), *colorare* (verb).

com•mit /kə'mit/ ▶ v. (**com•mit•ted, com•mit•ting**) [trans.] **1** carry out or perpetrate (a mistake, crime, or immoral act): *he committed an uncharacteristic error.*
2 pledge or bind (a person or an organization) to a certain course or policy: *the treaty commits each party to defend the other.*
3 send, entrust, or consign, in particular:
■ consign (someone) officially to prison, esp. on remand: *he was committed to prison for contempt of court.* ■ send (a person or case) for trial. ■ refer (a legislative bill) to a committee.
DERIVATIVES **com•mit•ta•ble** adj.; **com•mit•ter** n.
ORIGIN late Middle English: from Latin *committere* 'join, entrust' (in medieval Latin 'put into custody'), from *com-* 'with' + *mittere* 'put or send.'

com•mon /'kämən/ ▶ adj. (of a crime) of relatively minor importance: *common assault.*
PHRASES **the common good** the benefit or interests of all: *it is time our elected officials stood up for the common good.* **common property** a thing or things held jointly. **in common** See TENANCY IN COMMON.
ORIGIN Middle English: from Old French *comun* (adjective), from Latin *communis.*

com•mon law /'kämən 'lô/ ▶ n. the part of law that is derived from judicial precedent rather than statutes: [as adj.] *this suggests the Supreme Court was invoking the common law notion that the reasonable person standard should not apply to deliberate deception.* Often contrasted with STATUTORY LAW.
■ the body of law originally developed in the English royal courts. Compare with EQUITY, PUBLIC LAW. ■ The body of law in countries that derive their law from England, including the United States, Australia, and New Zealand. ■ [as adj.] denoting a partner in a marriage by common law (which recognized unions created by mutual agreement and public behavior), not by a civil or ecclesiastical ceremony: *a common-law husband.* ■ [as adj.] denoting a partner in a long-term relationship of cohabitation.

Com•mon Pleas /'kämən 'plēz/ (in full **Court of Common Pleas**) (in some jurisdictions) a court for hearing civil cases between citizens.

ORIGIN apart from current limited usage, the term is chiefly historical.

com•mu•ni•ty pro•per•ty /kə'myo͞onitē 'präpərtē/ ▶ n. (in certain US states) property that is owned jointly by a husband and wife, and which is distributed equally on termination of the marriage: *property accumulated by an unmarried couple in a stable relationship is treated like community property.*

com•mu•ni•ty serv•ice /kə'myo͞onitē 'sərvis/ ▶ n. unpaid work, intended to be of social use, that an offender is required to do instead of going to prison: *the vandals were sentenced to 600 hours of community service.*

com•mu•ta•tion /ˌkämyə'tāsHən/ ▶ n. action or the process of commuting a judicial sentence: *there are circumstances concerning the handling of his trial which warrant a commutation of his sentence.*

■ the conversion of a legal obligation or entitlement into another form: *these retirees elected to receive a lump-sum payment in commutation of a monthly annuity.*

ORIGIN late Middle English (in the sense 'exchange, barter,' later 'alteration'): from Latin *commutatio(n-)*, from *commutare* 'exchange, interchange' (see COMMUTE). Usage regarding judicial sentences dates from the late 16th cent.

com•mute /kə'myo͞ot/ ▶ v. [trans.] reduce (a judicial sentence, esp. a sentence of death) to one less severe: *the governor recently commuted the sentences of dozens of women convicted of killing their husbands.*

■ (**commute something for/into**) change one kind of payment or obligation for (another): *monthly income for the remainder of the guaranteed period will be commuted into a lump-sum payment.*

■ replace (an annuity or other series of payments) with a single payment: *if he had commuted some of his pension, he would have received $330,000.*

ORIGIN late Middle English (in the sense 'interchange (two things)'): from Latin *commutare*, from *com-* 'altogether' + *mutare* 'to change.'

com•par•a•tive neg•li•gence /kəm'pæritiv 'neglijəns/ ▶ n. failure of an injured plaintiff to act with reasonable care, thereby reducing the amount recovered from the defendant or preventing the plaintiff from receiving any compensation: *West Dakota has adopted comparative negligence under which the plaintiff's fault reduces recoverable damages but does not bar a cause of action.*

com•pen•sa•ble /kəm'pensəbəl/ ▶ adj. (of a loss or hardship) for which compensation can be obtained: *an on-the-job injury or illness that the Department of Labor determines to be compensable.*

ORIGIN mid 17th cent.: French, from *compenser*, from Latin *compensare* 'weigh (something) against (another).'

com•pe•tence /'kämpitəns/ (also **com•pe•ten•cy** /'kämpitənsē/) ▶ n. the legal authority of a court or other body to deal with a particular matter: *the court's competence has been accepted to cover these matters.*

■ the ability of a participant in a trial, as gauged by their capacity to understand the proceedings: *it is a mental disability that does not affect the competence of the witness to testify.*

com•pe•tent /ˈkämpətənt/ ▶ **adj.** (chiefly of a court or other body) accepted as having legal authority to deal with a particular matter: *the governor was not the* **competent authority** *to deal with the matter.*

■ (of a criminal defendant) able to understand the charges and to aid in defending themselves: *the carjacking suspect was ruled not competent for trial.* ■ (of a witness) capable of testifying.

DERIVATIVES **com•pe•tent•ly adv.**

ORIGIN late Middle English (in the sense 'suitable, adequate'): from Latin *competent-*, from the verb *competere* in its earlier sense 'be fit or proper.'

com•plain•ant /kəmˈplānənt/ ▶ **n.** a plaintiff in certain lawsuits: *the complainant did not have proof of proper service of the notice of hearing.*

ORIGIN late Middle English: from French *complaignant*, present participle of *complaindre* 'to lament.'

com•plaint /kəmˈplānt/ ▶ **n.** the pleading that states the plaintiff's reasons for proceeding in a civil action: *at the time of the collision stated in the complaint, the plaintiff was driving home from work.*

ORIGIN late Middle English: from Old French *complainte*, feminine past participle of *complaindre* 'to lament.'

com•po•si•tion /ˌkämpəˈziSHən/ ▶ **n.** a legal agreement to pay an amount of money in lieu of a larger debt or other obligation: *he never made a composition with his creditors in satisfaction of his debts.*

■ an amount of money paid in this way.

ORIGIN late Middle English: via Old French from Latin *composition-*, from *componere* 'put together.'

com•pound ▶ **v.** /kəmˈpownd; kämˈpownd; ˈkämˌpownd/ [trans.] forbear from prosecuting (a felony) in exchange for money or other consideration.

■ settle (a debt or other matter) in this way: *he compounded the case with the defendant for a cash payment.*

DERIVATIVES **com•pound•a•ble** /kəmˈpowndəbəl; käm-/ **adj.**

ORIGIN late Middle English *compoune* (verb), from Old French *compoun-*, present tense stem of *compondre*, from Latin *componere* 'put together.' The final *-d* was added in the 16th cent. on the pattern of *expound* and *propound.*

com•pur•ga•tion /ˌkämpərˈgāSHən/ ▶ **n.** historical acquittal from a charge or accusation, obtained by statements of innocence given by witnesses under oath.

ORIGIN mid 17th cent.: from medieval Latin *compurgation-*, from Latin *compurgare*, from *com-* (expressing intensive force) + *purgare* 'purify' (from *purus* 'pure').

com•pur•ga•tor /ˈkämpərˌgātər/ ▶ **n.** historical a sworn witness to the innocence or good character of an accused person: *the reservation would enable the compurgator to escape the charge of false swearing.* ORIGIN mid 16th cent.: medieval Latin, from Latin *com-* 'together with' + *purgator*, from *purgare* 'purify' (see **COMPURGATION**).

con•cert ▸ n. /'kän‚sərt; 'känsərt/ formal agreement, accordance, or harmony.

▸v. /kən'sərt/ [trans.] formal arrange (something) by mutual agreement or coordination: *they could be liable for concerting their behavior in order to deter entry into the market.*

PHRASES **in concert** acting jointly: *he made his decision **in concert with** his son and son-in-law.*

ORIGIN late 16th cent. (in the sense 'unite, cause to agree'): from French *concerter*, from Italian *concertare* 'harmonize.'

con•demn /kən'dem/ ▸ v. [trans.] sentence (someone) to a particular punishment, esp. death: *the rebels had been **condemned to death** |* [as adj.] (**condemned**) *the condemned men.*

■ (usu. **be condemned**) officially declare (something, esp. a building) to be unfit for use: *the pool has been condemned as a health hazard.*

DERIVATIVES **con•dem•na•ble** /kən'dem(n)əbəl/ **adj.**; **con•dem•na•tion** /‚kändəm'nāsHən; -dem-/ **n.**; **con•dem•na•to•ry** /kən'demnə‚tôrē/ **adj.**

ORIGIN Middle English: from Old French *condemner*, from Latin *condemnare*, from *con-* (expressing intensive force) + *damnare* 'inflict loss on.'

con•di•tion•al sale /kən'disHənl 'sāl/ ▸ n. the sale of goods according to a contract containing conditions, typically that ownership does not pass to the buyer until after a set time, usually after payment of the last installment of the purchase price, although the buyer has possession and is committed to acquiring ownership.

con•do•min•i•um /‚kändə'minēəm/ ▸ n. (pl. **con•do•min•i•ums**) **1** a building or complex of buildings containing a number of individually owned apartments or houses: *a lakeshore condominium*

■ each of the individual apartments or houses in such a building or complex: *they're thinking of selling their Florida condominium.* ■ the system of ownership by which these operate, in which owners have full title to the individual apartment or house and an undivided interest in the shared parts of the property: *all the other buildings on the block have **gone condominium**.*

2 the joint control of a country's or territory's affairs by other countries: *the Western part of the district was ruled in condominium between Trier and Luxembourg.*

■ a state so governed.

ORIGIN early 18th cent.: modern Latin, from *con-* 'together with' + *dominium* 'right of ownership' (see **DOMINION**). Sense 1 dates from the 1960s.

con•ju•gal rights /'känjəgəl 'rīts; kən'jŏŏgəl/ ▸ **plural n.** the rights, especially to sexual relations, regarded as exercisable in law by each partner in a marriage: *in certain cases, spouses have withdrawn conjugal rights from each other and continue to live under the same roof.*

con•ju•gal vis•it /'känjəgəl 'vizit/ ▸ **n.** a visit by the spouse of a prisoner, especially for sexual relations.

con•science clause /'känsHəns ˌklôz/ ▸ **n.** a clause that makes concessions to the consciences of those affected by a law: *Congress passed a "conscience clause" bill, which permitted any individual opposed to abortion to refuse to perform the procedure.*

con•sent /kən'sent/ ▸ **n.** permission for something to happen or agreement to do something: *no change may be made without the consent of all the partners.*

▸ **v.** [intrans.] give permission for something to happen: *he consented to a search by a detective.*

■ [with infinitive] agree to do something: *he had consented to serve on the panel.*

PHRASES **by common consent** with the agreement of all: *the parties may by common consent agree to replace any conciliator.* **informed consent** permission granted in the knowledge of the possible consequences, typically that which is given by a patient to a doctor for treatment with full knowledge of the possible risks and benefits.

ORIGIN Middle English: from Old French *consente* (noun), *consentir* (verb), from Latin *consentire*, from *con-* 'together' + *sentire* 'feel.'

con•sent•ing a•dult /kən'sentiNG ə'dəlt; ˈædˌəlt/ ▸ **n.** an adult who willingly agrees to engage in an act, esp. a sexual act: *socially acceptable and lawful activities between consenting adults.*

con•se•quen•tial /ˌkänsə'kwenCHəl/ ▸ **adj.** resulting from an act, but not immediately and directly: *consequential damages.*

DERIVATIVES **con•se•quen•ti•al•i•ty** /ˌkänsəˌkwenCHē'ælitē/ **n.**; **con•se•quen•tial•ly** adv.

ORIGIN early 17th cent.: from Latin *consequentia.*

con•sid•er•a•tion /kənˌsidə'rāsHən/ ▸ **n. 1** (in a contractual agreement) anything given or promised or forborne by one party in exchange for the promise or undertaking of another: *in consideration of the services provided under this Agreement, the company will pay the agent a commission on all sales.*

2 archaic importance; consequence.

ORIGIN late Middle English: via Old French from Latin *consideration-*, from *considerare* 'examine.'

con•sol•i•date /kən'säliˌdāt/ ▸ **v.** [trans.] combine (two or more legal actions involving similar or related questions) into one for action by a court: *the husband moved the trial court to dismiss the action on the note or, in the alternative, to consolidate the action with the pending divorce proceedings.*

DERIVATIVES **con•sol•i•da•tion** /kənˌsäli'dāsHən/ **n.**

ORIGIN early 16th cent. (in the sense 'combine into a single whole'): from Latin *consolidare*, from *con-* 'together' + *solidare* 'make firm' (from *solidus* 'solid').

con•sor•ti•um /kən'sôrSH(ē)əm; -'sôrtēəm/ ▶ n. (pl. **con•sor•ti•a** /kən'sôrSH(ē)ə; -'sôrtēə/ or **con•sor•ti•ums**) the right of association and companionship with one's husband or wife.

PHRASES **loss of consortium** damage to a spouse for loss of companionship (often including sexual relations) due to injury to their spouse: *the extent to which a spouse may apply for loss of consortium damages in a wrongful death claim.*

ORIGIN early 19th cent. (in the sense 'partnership'): from Latin, from *consors* 'sharing, partner.'

con•sta•ble /'känstəbəl; 'kən-/ ▶ n. a peace officer with limited policing authority, typically in a small town.

■ Brit. a police officer.

ORIGIN Middle English: from Old French *conestable*, from late Latin *comes stabuli* 'count (head officer) of the stable.'

con•stab•u•lar•y /kən'stæbyə,lerē/ ▶ n. (pl. **con•stab•u•lar•ies**) the constables of a district, collectively.

■ an armed police force organized as a military unit. ■ Brit. a police force covering a particular area or city: *the Durham Constabulary.*

▶ adj. [attrib.] of or relating to a constabulary.

ORIGIN late 15th cent. (denoting the district under the charge of a constable): from medieval Latin *constabularia (dignitas)* '(rank) of constable,' from *constabulus*, based on Latin *comes stabuli* (see CON-STABLE).

con•stit•u•ent /kən'sticHo͞oənt/ ▶ adj. [attrib.] being a voting member of a community or organization and having the power to appoint or elect: *the constituent body has a right of veto.*

■ able to make or change a political constitution: *a constituent assembly.*

▶ n. a member of a constituency: *Senator Kyle offers many services to his constituents.*

ORIGIN late 15th cent. (in the legal sense of the noun): from Latin *constituent-* (partly via French *constituant*) 'establishing, appointing,' from the verb *constituere* (see CONSTITUTE).

con•sti•tute /'känsti,t(y)o͞ot/ ▶ v. [trans.] (usu. **be constituted**) give legal or constitutional form to (an institution); establish by law: *the committee delegation was constituted by written procedure on November 28th, 2000.*

ORIGIN late Middle English: from Latin *constitut-* 'established, appointed,' from the verb *constituere*, from *con-* 'together' + *statuere* 'set up.'

con•sti•tu•tion•al•ize /,känsti't(y)o͞osHənl-,īz/ ▶ v. [trans.] make subject to explicit provisions of a country's constitution: *divorce is not constitutionalized.*

con•struc•tion•ist /kən'strəksHənist/ ▶ n. a person who puts a particular construction upon a legal document, esp. the US Constitution.
DERIVATIVES **con•struc•tion•ism** n.

con•struc•tive /kən'strəktiv/ ▶ adj. derived by inference; implied by operation of law; not obvious or explicit: *constructive notice.*
ORIGIN mid 17th cent.: from late Latin *constructivus*, from Latin *construct-* 'heaped together,' from the verb *construere*, from *con* 'together' + *struere* ' pile, build.'

con•sul /'känsəl/ ▶ n. **1** an official appointed by a government to live in a foreign city and protect and promote the government's citizens and interests there: *the Colombian consul in San Francisco.*
2 (in ancient Rome) one of the two annually elected chief magistrates who jointly ruled the republic.
■ any of the three chief magistrates of the first French republic (1799–1804).
DERIVATIVES **con•su•lar** /'käns(y)ələr/ adj.; **con•sul•ship** /'känsəl ˌsHip/ n.
ORIGIN late Middle English (denoting an ancient Roman magistrate): from Latin, related to *consulere* 'take counsel.'

con•su•late /'känsəlit/ ▶ n. **1** the place or building in which a consul's duties are carried out: *the American Consulate in Strasbourg.*
■ the office, position, or period of office of a consul.
2 historical the period of office of a Roman consul.
■ **(the consulate)** the system of government by consuls in ancient Rome.
3 **(the Consulate)** the government of the first French republic (1799–1804) by three consuls.
ORIGIN late Middle English (denoting the government of Rome by consuls, or their office or dignity): from Latin *consulatus*, from *consul* (see **CONSUL**).

con•tem•pla•tion /ˌkäntəm'plāsHən/ ▶ n. the state of being thought about or planned; anticipation: *Mr. Truman's gift was made in contemplation of death.*
ORIGIN Middle English: from Old French, from Latin *contemplatio(n-)*, from the verb *contemplari*, based on *templum* 'place for observation.'

con•tempt /kən'tem(p)t/ ▶ n. (also **contempt of court**) the offense of being disobedient to or disrespectful of a court of law and its officers: *several unions were **held** to be **in contempt** and were fined.*
■ the offense of being similarly disobedient to or disrespectful of the lawful operation of a legislative body (e.g., its investigations): *what are the consequences of being cited in contempt of Congress?*
ORIGIN late Middle English: from Latin *contemptus*, from *contemnere*, from *con-* (expressing intensive force) + *temnere* 'despise.'

con•test ▶ n. /'känˌtest/ the act of disputing or challenging the validity of

a will: *if a contest is successful, a portion of the estate may descend by intestate succession.*
▶**v.** /kən'test; 'kän‚test/ [trans.] dispute or challenge the validity of (a will): *what are legitimate grounds for contesting the will?*
PHRASES **no contest** another term for **NOLO CONTENDERE**: *he pleaded no contest to two misdemeanor counts.*
DERIVATIVES **con•test•a•ble** /kən'testəbəl/ **adj.**; **con•test•er** /kən 'testər; 'kän‚tes-/ **n.**
ORIGIN late 16th cent.: from Latin *contestari* 'call upon to witness, initiate an action (by calling witnesses),' from *con-* 'together' + *testare* 'to witness.'

con•test•ant /kən'testənt/ ▶ **n.** a person who takes part in a legal contest: *a contestant is trying to establish that the testator was inebriated at the time when the testamentary instruments were signed.*
ORIGIN mid 17th cent.: from French, present participle of *contester*, from Latin *contestari* 'call upon to witness' (see **CONTEST**).

con•tin•u•ance /kən'tinyo͞oəns/ ▶ **n.** a postponement or adjournment: *if this man's testimony is important, I will grant a continuance.*
ORIGIN late Middle English: from Old French, from *continuer* 'continue,' from Latin *continuare*, from *continuus* 'uninterrupted,' from *continere* 'hang together' (from *con-* 'together with' + *tenere* hold) + *-ous*.

con•tin•ue /kən'tinyo͞o/ ▶ **v.** [trans.] (**con•tin•ues, con•tin•ued, con•tin• u•ing**) postpone or adjourn (a legal proceeding): *the case was continued without a finding until August 2.*
ORIGIN Middle English: from Old French *continuer*, from Latin *continuare*, from *continuus* (see **CONTINUANCE**).

con•tract ▶ **n.** /'kän‚trækt/ a written or spoken agreement that is intended to be enforceable by law: *both parties must sign employment contracts | a network of doctors and hospitals are **under contract** to provide services.*
■ the branch of law concerned with the making and observation of such agreements. ■ dated a formal agreement to marry.
▶**v.** [intrans.] **1** /'kän‚trækt; kən'trækt/ enter into a formal and legally binding agreement: *the local authority will **contract with** a wide range of agencies to provide services.*
■ secure specified rights or undertake specified obligations in a formal and legally binding agreement: *a buyer may **contract for** the right to withhold payment | the paper had **contracted to** publish extracts from the diaries.* ■ [trans.] impose an obligation on (someone) to do something by means of a formal agreement: *health authorities contract a hospital to treat a specific number of patients.* ■ [trans.] (**contract something out**) arrange for work to be done by another organization: *local authorities will have to contract out waste management.* ■ [trans.] dated formally enter into (a marriage): *before Fanny met him, he had contracted a disastrous liaison and marriage.*

2 /kən'trækt/ [trans.] become liable to pay (a debt): *he contracted a debt of $3,300.*
DERIVATIVES **con•tract•ee** /ˌkäntræk'tē/ n.; **con•trac•tive** /kən'træktiv; 'kän͵træktiv/ **adj.**
ORIGIN Middle English: via Old French from Latin *contractus,* from *contract-* 'drawn together, tightened,' from the verb *contrahere,* from *con-* 'together' + *trahere* 'draw.'

con•tra pro•fer•en•tem /'käntrə ͵präfə'rentem/ ▶ **adv.** (of the interpretation of a contract) against the party that proposed (or, more usually, drafted) the contract or a provision in the contract: *Intel argued that a decision in the district court made a mistake because it applied contra proferentum.*
▶ **n.** The rule that a contract must be construed most strictly against the drafter: *the drafting history will establish through extrinsic evidence that Nestle's interpretation is correct and that contra proferentum applies.*
ORIGIN Latin, 'against (the person) mentioning.'

con•trib•u•to•ry /kən'tribyə͵tôrē/ ▶ **adj.** (of or relating to a pension or insurance plan) operated by means of a fund into which people pay: *contributory benefits.*
ORIGIN late Middle English: from medieval Latin *contributorius,* from Latin *contribut-* 'added.'

con•trib•u•to•ry neg•li•gence /kən'tribyə͵tôrē 'neglijəns/ ▶ **n.** failure of an injured plaintiff to act with reasonable care, considered to be a contributory factor in the injury suffered, thereby barring the plaintiff from compensation by the defendant.

con•tu•ma•cious /ˌkänt(y)ə'māsHəs/ ▶ **adj.** (esp. of a defendant's behavior) stubbornly or willfully disobedient to authority; in contempt: *a clear record of delay or contumacious conduct.*
DERIVATIVES **con•tu•ma•cious•ly** adv.
ORIGIN late 16th cent.: from Latin *contumax, contumac-* (perhaps from *con-* 'with' + *tumere* 'to swell') + *-ious.*

con•tu•ma•cy /kən't(y)o͞oməsē; 'känt(y)əməsē/ ▶ **n.** stubborn refusal to obey or comply with authority, esp. a court order or summons: *his refusal to comply with the Court Order is based upon contumacy rather than inability.*
ORIGIN Middle English: from Latin *contumacia* 'inflexibility,' from *contumax* (see CONTUMACIOUS).

con•ver•sion /kən'vərzHən/ ▶ **n.** the action of wrongfully dealing with goods or money in a manner inconsistent with the owner's rights: *he was found guilty of the fraudulent conversion of clients' monies.*
ORIGIN Middle English: via Old French from Latin *conversio(n-),* from *convers-* 'turned around,' from the verb *convertere* (see CONVERT).

con•vert ▶ **v.** [trans.] /kən'vərt/ wrongfully deal with (goods or money) in a manner inconsistent with the owner's rights: *the defendant converted the plaintiff's construction materials to his own use.*

ORIGIN Middle English (in the sense 'turn around, send in a different direction'): from Old French *convertir*, based on Latin *convertere* 'turn around,' from *con-* 'altogether' + *vertere* 'turn.'

con•vey /kən'vā/ ▸ v. [trans.] transfer the title to (property): *the cabin was conveyed to her by inheritance.*
DERIVATIVES **con•vey•a•ble adj.**
ORIGIN Middle English: from Old French *conveier*, from medieval Latin *conviare*, from *con-* 'together' + Latin *via* 'way.'

con•vey•ance /kən'vāəns/ ▸ n. the legal process of transferring property from one owner to another: *protective measures that might be taken before the conveyance is concluded.*
■ a legal document effecting such a process.

con•vey•anc•ing /kən'vāənsiNG/ ▸ n. the branch of law concerned with the preparation of documents for the transferring of property.
■ the action of preparing documents for the transfer of property: *settlement costs include transfer tax, recording fees, documentary stamps, and conveyancing.*
DERIVATIVES **con•vey•anc•er n.**

con•vict ▸ v. /kən'vikt/ [trans.] (often **be convicted**) declare (someone) to be guilty of a criminal offense by the verdict of a jury or the decision of a judge in a court of law: *her former boyfriend was **convicted of** assaulting her* | [as adj.] (**convicted**) *a convicted murderer.*
▸n. /'kän,vikt/ a person found guilty of a criminal offense and serving a sentence of imprisonment.
ORIGIN Middle English: from Latin *convict-* 'demonstrated, refuted, convicted,' from the verb *convincere*, from *con-* 'with' + *vincere* 'conquer.' The noun is from obsolete *convict* 'convicted.'

con•vic•tion /kən'viksHən/ ▸ n. a formal declaration that someone is guilty of a criminal offense, made by the verdict of a jury or the decision of a judge in a court of law: *she had a previous conviction for a similar offense.*
ORIGIN late Middle English: from Latin *convictio(n-)*, from the verb *convincere* (see **CONVICT**).

cop•y•right /'käpē,rīt/ ▸ n. the exclusive legal right, given to a creator or an assignee for a fixed number of years, to reproduce, distribute, or perform literary, artistic, or musical material, and to authorize others to do the same: *they bought the copyright to the whole film archive.*
▸v. [trans.] secure copyright for (such material): *is the book copyrighted in the name of the author or the publisher?*

co-re•spond•ent /,kō ris'pändənt/ (also **co•re•spond•ent**) ▸ n. 1 a joint defendant in a lawsuit, esp. one on appeal: *the bank is a co-respondent in the case, but is not being represented legally.*
2 a person cited in a divorce case as having committed adultery with the respondent.

cor•po•rate /'kôrp(ə)rət/ ▸ adj. (of a company or group of people) authorized to act as a single entity and recognized as such in law: *the historical development of corporate rights in America.*

▶n. a corporate company or group.

DERIVATIVES **cor•po•rate•ly** adv.

ORIGIN late 15th cent.: from Latin *corporatus*, past participle of *corporare* 'form into a body,' from *corpus, corpor-* 'body.'

cor•po•ra•tion /ˌkôrpəˈrāSHən/ ▶ n. a company or group of people authorized to act as a single entity (legally a person) in which the individuals who make up the corporation have limited liability.

■ (also **municipal corporation**) a group of people elected to govern a city, town, or borough.

ORIGIN late Middle English: from late Latin *corporatio(n-)*, from Latin *corporare* 'combine in one body' (see **CORPORATE**).

cor•po•re•al /kôrˈpôrēəl/ ▶ adj. consisting of material objects; tangible: *corporeal property.*

DERIVATIVES **cor•po•re•al•i•ty** /kôrˌpôrēˈælitē/ n.; **cor•po•re•al•ly** adv.

ORIGIN late Middle English (in the sense 'material'): from late Latin *corporealis*, from Latin *corporeus* 'bodily, physical,' from *corpus, corpor-* 'body.'

cor•pus de•lic•ti /ˈkôrpəs dəˈliktī; dəˈliktē/ ▶ n. the facts and circumstances constituting a breach of a law.

■ concrete evidence of a crime, such as a corpse: *it isn't necessary to rely upon a corpus delicti to gain a murder conviction.*

ORIGIN Latin, literally 'body of offense.'

cor•rupt prac•tice /kəˈrəpt ˈpræktis/ ▶ n. (often **corrupt practices**) a fraudulent activity, especially an attempt to rig an election or bribe an official.

Co•sa Nos•tra /ˌkōsə ˈnōstrə; ˌkōzə/ a US criminal organization resembling and related to the Mafia.

ORIGIN Italian, literally 'our affair.'

costs /kôsts/ ▶ plural noun legal expenses, esp. those allowed in favor of the winning party or against the losing party in a suit: *the plaintiff was awarded $7,500 general damages, plus costs.*

ORIGIN Middle English: from Old French *coust* (noun), *couster* (verb), based on Latin *constare* 'stand firm, stand at a price.'

coun•sel /ˈkownsəl/ ▶ n. (pl. same) the lawyer or lawyers conducting a case: *the counsel for the defense.*

ORIGIN Middle English: via Old French *counseil* (noun), *conseiller* (verb), from Latin *consilium* 'consultation, advice,' related to *consulere* 'take counsel.'

count /kownt/ ▶ n. a separate charge in an indictment: *he pleaded guilty to five counts of murder.*

ORIGIN Middle English (as a noun): from Old French *counte* (noun), *counter* (verb), from the verb *computare* 'calculate.'

coun•ter•claim /ˈkowntərˌklām/ ▶ n. a claim made to rebut a previous

claim: *the employer made a counterclaim, affirming that there would be no hearing in the case.*
■ a claim made by a defendant against the plaintiff: *the defendant's counterclaim may demand money from the plaintiff.*
▶v. [intrans.] make a counterclaim for something: *Century counterclaimed for the difference between the amount the Association had paid and its statutory coverage limit.*

coun•ter•mand /ˌkowntər'mænd; 'kowntərˌmænd/ ▶ v. [trans.] revoke (an order): *an order to arrest the strike leaders had been countermanded.*
■ declare (voting) invalid: *the election commission has countermanded voting on the grounds of intimidation.*
ORIGIN late Middle English: from Old French *contremander* (verb), *contremand* (noun), from medieval Latin *contramandare*, from *contra-* 'against' + *mandare* 'to order.'

coun•ter•part /'kowntərˌpärt/ ▶ n. one of two or more copies of a legal document: *everyone ensures that the unsigned headers are identical to their signed counterparts.*

coun•ty court /'kowntē 'kôrt/ ▶ n. a court in some states with civil and criminal jurisdiction for a given county.

court /kôrt/ ▶ n. (also **court of law**) a tribunal presided over by a judge, judges, or a magistrate: *a settlement was reached during the first sitting of the court* | *she will **take** the matter **to court*** | [as adj.] *a court case.*
■ any of various other tribunals, such as military courts. ■ the place where such a tribunal meets: *reporters and photographers were waiting in front of the court.* ■ **(the court)** the judge or judges presiding at such a tribunal:
PHRASES **go to court** take legal action. **in court** appearing as a party or an attorney in a court of law: *Ms. Webber is in court every day this week.* **out of court** before a legal hearing can take place: *they are trying to settle the squabble out of court* | [as adj.] *an out-of-court settlement.*
ORIGIN Middle English: from Old French *cort*, from Latin *cohors*, *cohort-* 'yard or retinue.' The verb is influenced by Old Italian *corteare*, Old French *courtoyer*.

court•house /'kôrtˌhows/ ▶ n. **1** a building in which a judicial court is held.
2 a building containing the administrative offices of a county.

court-mar•tial /'kôrt ˌmärsHəl/ ▶ n. (pl. **courts-mar•tial** or **court-mar•tials**) a judicial court for trying members of the armed services accused of offenses against military law: *they appeared before a court-martial* | *he was found guilty by court-martial.*
▶v. (**court-mar•tialed, court-mar•tial•ing**; Brit **court-mar•tialled, court-mar•tial•ling**) [trans.] try (someone) by such a court: *two Army officers were court-martialed for the security breach.*

court of ap•peals /'kôrt əv ə'pēls/ ▶ n. a court to which appeals are taken in a federal circuit or a state.

court of claims /'kôrt əv 'klāmz/ ▸ **n.** a court in which claims against the government are adjudicated.

court of in•quir•y /'kôrt əv in'kwīrē; 'inkwīrē; 'iNGkwərē/ ▸ **n.** a tribunal appointed in the armed forces to investigate a matter and decide whether a court-martial is called for: *the Navy will convene a court of inquiry to determine whether disciplinary action should be taken against senior officers.*

court of rec•ord /'kôrt əv 'rekərd/ ▸ **n.** a court whose proceedings are recorded and available as evidence of fact.

court or•der /'kôrt 'ôrdər/ ▸ **n.** a direction issued by a court or a judge requiring a person to do or not do something: *a court order banning her from being within three blocks of the White House.*

court rec•ord /'kôrt 'rekərd/ ▸ **n.** see RECORD (sense 1).

court•room /'kôrt,rōōm; -,rōōm/ ▸ **n.** the place or room in which a court of law meets.

cov•e•nant /'kəvənənt/ ▸ **n.** a contract drawn up by deed: *it is agreed in the covenant that the municipalities will make these requirements known to the operators.*

■ a clause in a contract.

▸**v.** [intrans.] agree, esp. by lease, deed, or other legal contract: *the landlord covenants to repair the property* | *the county shall covenant that the real property tax assessment will reflect the fair market value.*

DERIVATIVES **cov•e•nan•tal** /ˌkəvə'næntl/ **adj.**; **cov•e•nan•tor** /'kəvənəntər/ (also **cov•e•nan•ter**) **n.**

ORIGIN Middle English: from Old French, present participle of *covenir* 'agree,' from Latin *convenire* 'assemble, agree, fit,' from *con-* 'together' + *venire* 'come.'

cov•e•nan•tee /ˌkəvənən'tē; -næn-/ ▸ **n.** the person to whom a promise by covenant is made.

co•vert ▸ **adj.** /'kōvərt; kō'vərt; 'kəvərt/ (of a woman) married and under the authority and protection of her husband. See also FEME COVERT.

ORIGIN Middle English (in the general senses 'covered' and 'a cover'): from Old French, 'covered,' past participle of *covrir,* from Latin *cooperire,* from *co-* (expressing intensive force) + *operire* 'to cover.'

cov•er•ture /'kəvər,CHŏŏr; -CHər/ ▸ **n.** historical the legal status of a married woman, considered to be under her husband's protection and authority.

ORIGIN Middle English: from Old French, from *covrir* 'to cover.' It originally denoted a coverlet or a garment, later various kinds of covering or shelter.

cri•er /'krīər/ ▸ **n.** an officer who makes public announcements in a court of justice.

ORIGIN late Middle English: from Old French *criere,* from *crier* 'to shout.'

crime /krīm/ ▸ **n.** an action or omission that constitutes an offense that may be prosecuted by the state and is punishable by law: *shoplifting was a serious crime.*

■ illegal activities: *the victims of crime.*
ORIGIN Middle English (in the sense 'wickedness, sin'): via Old French from Latin *crimen* 'judgment, offense,' based on *cernere* 'to judge.'

crim•i•nal /ˈkrimənl/ ▶ n. a person who has committed a crime: *these men are dangerous criminals.*
▶adj. of or relating to a crime: *he is charged with conspiracy to commit criminal damage.*
■ of or relating to crime as opposed to civil matters: *a criminal court.*
DERIVATIVES **crim•i•nal•i•ty** /ˌkriməˈnælitē/ n.; **crim•i•nal•ly adv.** *criminally negligent*
ORIGIN late Middle English (as an adjective): from late Latin *criminalis*, from Latin *crimen, crimin-* (see **CRIME**).

crim•i•nal con•ver•sa•tion /ˈkrimənl ˌkänvərˈsāsHən/ ▶ n. historical adultery, esp. as formerly constituting grounds for the recovery of legal damages by a husband from his adulterous wife's partner: *causes of action for breach of promise, alienation of affections, and criminal conversation.*

crim•i•nal•is•tics /ˌkrimənlˈistiks/ ▶ plural n. [treated as sing.] another term for **forensics** (see **forensic**).
DERIVATIVES **crim•i•nal•ist** n.

crim•i•nal law /ˈkrimənl ˈlô/ ▶ n. a system of law concerned with the punishment of those who commit crimes.Contrasted with **CIVIL LAW**.
■ a law belonging to this system.

crim•i•nal li•bel /ˈkrimənl ˈlībəl/ ▶ n. historical a malicious, defamatory statement in a permanent form, rendering the maker liable to criminal prosecution: *it is the question of whether the publication of anything with a malicious intention to cause a breach of the peace constitutes criminal libel.*

crim•i•nal re•cord /ˈkrimənl ˈrekərd/ ▶ n. a history of being convicted for crime: *he admits he has a criminal record.*
■ a list of a person's previous criminal convictions: *the court said his criminal record would be expunged at the end of the year.*

crim•i•nol•o•gy /ˌkriməˈnäləjē/ ▶ n. the scientific study of crime and criminals.
DERIVATIVES **crim•i•no•log•i•cal** /ˌkrimənlˈäjikəl/ adj.; **crim•i•nol•o•gist** /ˌkriməˈnäləjist/ n.
ORIGIN late 19th cent.: from Latin *crimen, crimin-* 'crime' + *-logy.*

cross-claim /ˈkrôs ˈklām/ ▶ a claim brought by one defendant against another in the same proceeding.

cross-ex•am•ine /ˈkrôs igˈzæmin/ ▶ v. [trans.] question (a witness called by the other party) in a court of law to discredit or undercut testimony already given. *the approach to cross-examining the defense medical expert varies on a case-to-case basis.* Compare with **DIRECT EXAMINATION**.
DERIVATIVES **cross-ex•am•i•na•tion** /ˈkrôs igˌzæməˈnāsHən/ n.; **cross-ex•am•in•er** n.

cru•el•ty /'krōōəltē/ ▶ n. (pl. **cru•el•ties**) behavior that causes physical or mental harm to another, esp. a spouse, whether intentionally or not: *the mother, 18, was charged with cruelty and attempted murder.*
ORIGIN Middle English: from Old French crualte, based on Latin *crudelitas,* from *crudelis.*

cui bo•no? /kwē 'bōnō/ ▶ exclam. who stands, or stood, to gain (from a crime, and so might have been responsible for it)?
ORIGIN early 17th cent.: Latin, literally 'to whom (is it) a benefit?'

cur•te•sy /'kərtəsē/ ▶ n. (pl. **cur•te•sies**) historical a tenure by which a husband, after his wife's death, held certain kinds of property that she had inherited.

cur•ti•lage /'kərtl-ij/ ▶ n. an area of land attached to a house and forming one enclosure with it: *the roads **within the curtilage of** the development site.*
ORIGIN Middle English: from Anglo-Norman French, variant of Old French *courtillage,* from *courtil* 'small court,' from *cort* 'court.'

cus•to•dy /'kəstədē/ ▶ n. the protective care or guardianship of someone or something: *the property was placed in the custody of a trustee.*
■ imprisonment: *my father was being **taken into custody.*** ■ parental responsibility, esp. as allocated to one of two divorcing parents: *he was trying to get **custody of** their child.*
DERIVATIVES **cus•to•di•al** /kə'stōdēəl/ adj. *the custodial parent | custodial sentences.*
ORIGIN late Middle English: from Latin *custodia,* from *custos* 'guardian.'

cy-pres /sē'prā/ ▶ adv. & adj. as near as possible to the testator's or donor's intentions when these cannot be precisely followed: [as adj.] *these are the cy-pres options for distributions of pecuniary penalties.*
ORIGIN early 19th cent.: from a late Anglo-Norman French variant of French *si près* 'so near.'

D

DA ▸ **abbr.** district attorney: *the DA for the Third Judicial Circuit.*

dam•ages /'dæmijiz/ ▸ **plural noun** a sum of money claimed or awarded in compensation for a loss or an injury: *she was awarded $284,000 in damages.*

ORIGIN Middle English: from Old French, from *dam, damne* 'loss or damage,' from Latin *damnum* 'loss or hurt.'

date rape /'dāt ‚rāp/ ▸ **n.** rape committed by the victim's escort: *a former UM student was accused of a 1994 date rape.*

dead hand /'ded 'hænd/ ▸ **n.** an undesirable persisting influence, especially concerning property after the death of a prior owner: *the purposes behind the rule against remoteness are to curtail dead hand domination and to facilitate marketability.*

■ see **MORTMAIN.**

death cer•tif•i•cate /'deTH sər‚tifikit/ ▸ **n.** an official statement, signed by a physician, of the cause, date, and place of a person's death.

death pen•al•ty /'deTH ‚penltē/ ▸ **n.** the punishment of execution, administered to someone convicted of a capital crime.

death tax /'deTH ‚tæks/ ▸ **n. 1** another term for **ESTATE TAX.**

2 another term for **INHERITANCE TAX.**

death war•rant /'deTH ‚wôrənt; ‚wärənt/ ▸ **n.** an official order for the execution of a condemned person: *the motion to stay execution was denied as premature as the governor has not yet signed a death warrant.*

de•cease /di'sēs/ ▸ **n.** [in sing.] death: *he left no property at the time of his decease.*

ORIGIN Middle English: from Old French *deces,* from Latin *decessus* 'death,' past participle (used as a noun) of *decedere* 'to die.'

de•ceased /di'sēst/ formal ▸ **n.** (**the deceased**) a person who has died: *you should present any evidence you have that shows your relationship to the deceased.*

▸ **adj.** dead; no longer living: *the vehicle title of the deceased owner was transferred to the spouse's name.*

de•ce•dent /di'sēdnt/ ▸ **n.** a person who has died: *measures to make sure the decedent's property passes to his children.*

ORIGIN late 16th cent.: from Latin *decedent-* 'dying,' from the verb *decedere* (see **DECEASE**).

de•ci•sion /di'sizHən/ ▸ n. a formal judgment: *last year's Supreme Court decision.*
ORIGIN late Middle English: from Latin *decisio(n-)*, from *decidere* 'determine.'

de•clar•ant /di'klerənt/ ▸ n. a person or party who makes a formal declaration: *the statement was made while the declarant was under the stress of excitement.*
■ an alien who has signed a declaration of intent to become a US citizen: *the form contains little more than the declarant's name and native country.*
▸adj. making or having made a formal declaration.
ORIGIN late 17th cent.: from French *déclarant*, present participle of *déclarer*, from Latin *declarare* 'make quite clear.'

dec•la•ra•tion /ˌdeklə'rāsHən/ ▸ n. a statement asserting or protecting a legal right: *the Universal Declaration of Human Rights.*
■ a written public announcement of intentions or of the terms of an agreement: *authors are required to submit this declaration of competing financial interests form.* ■ a plaintiff's statement of claims in proceedings: *in a declaration, the plaintiff speaks of much more than an affiliation with the Association.* ■ an affirmation made instead of taking an oath.
ORIGIN late Middle English: from Latin *declaratio(n-)*, from *declarare* 'make quite clear.'

de•cree /di'krē/ ▸ n. an official order issued by a legal authority: *an interlocutory decree of divorce.*
■ the issuing of such an order: *the king ruled by decree.* ■ a judgment or decision of certain courts of law: *a consent decree.*
▸v. (**de•crees, de•creed, de•cree•ing**) [trans.] order (something) by decree: *the government decreed a ban on any contact with the guerrillas* | [with clause] *the president decreed that the military was to be streamlined.*
ORIGIN Middle English (denoting an edict issued by an ecclesiastical council to settle a point of doctrine or discipline): from Old French *decre, decret*, from Latin *decretum* 'something decided,' from *decernere* 'decide.'

de•crim•i•nal•ize /dē'krimənlˌīz/ ▸ v. [trans.] cease to treat (something) as illegal, typically by legislation: *a battle to decriminalize drugs.*
DERIVATIVES **de•crim•i•nal•i•za•tion** /dēˌkrimənli'zāsHən/ n.

deed /dēd/ ▸ n. a legal document that is signed and delivered, esp. one regarding the ownership of property or legal rights. See also TITLE DEED.
▸v. [trans.] convey or transfer (property or rights) by legal deed: *they deeded their property to their children.*
ORIGIN Old English *dēd, dǣd*, of Germanic origin; related to Dutch *daad* and German *Tat*, from an Indo-European root shared by *do.*

deed of trust /'dēd əv 'trəst/ ▸ n. another term for TRUST DEED.

de fac•to /di 'fæktō; dā/ ▸ adv. in fact, whether by right or not: *assume he is de facto stateless if he says he is stateless but cannot establish he is de jure stateless.*Often contrasted with DE JURE.

▸ **adj.** [attrib.] denoting someone or something that is such in fact: *evidence that the child has been cared for by a de facto custodian.*

ORIGIN early 17th cent.: Latin, literally 'of fact.'

de fac•to seg•re•ga•tion /di 'fæktō segri'gāsHən/ ▸ n. segregation that exists as a consequence of social, economic, and political circumstances, and not as the result of legislation: *busing was ordered as a way to deal with de facto segregation brought about by housing patterns.*

de•fal•cate /di'fælkāt; -'fôl-/ ▸ v. [trans.] misappropriate or fail to turn over (funds with which one has been entrusted): *the officials were charged with defalcating government money.* Compare with EMBEZZLE.

DERIVATIVES **de•fal•ca•tion** /ˌdēfæl'kāsHən; -fôl-/ n.; **de•fal•ca•tor** n.

ORIGIN mid 16th cent. (in the sense 'deduct, subtract'): from medieval Latin *defalcat-* 'lopped,' from the verb *defalcare,* from *de-* 'away from, off' + Latin *falx, falc-* 'sickle.'

def•a•ma•tion /ˌdefə'māsHən/ ▸ n. the modern form of the action for slander or libel: *defamation of character | the group was initially organized to speak out against defamation and hate crimes.*

ORIGIN see DEFAME.

de•fame /di'fām/ ▸ v. [trans.] damage the good reputation of (someone); slander or libel: *he claimed that the article defamed his family.*

DERIVATIVES **de•fam•a•to•ry** /di'fæməˌtôrē/ adj.; **de•fam•er** n.

ORIGIN Middle English: from Old French *diffamer,* from Latin *diffamare* 'spread evil report,' from *dis-* (expressing removal) + *fama* 'report.'

de•fault /di'fôlt/ ▸ n. failure to fulfill an obligation, esp. to repay a loan or appear in a court of law: *it will have to restructure its debts to avoid default.*

▸ v. [intrans.] fail to fulfill an obligation, esp. to repay a loan or to appear in a court of law: *some had defaulted on student loans.*

■ [trans.] declare (a party) in default and give judgment against that party: *the possibility that cases would be defaulted and defendants released.*

PHRASES **by default** through lack of positive action rather than conscious choice: *legislation dies by default if the governor fails to act on it.* **in default** guilty of failing to repay a loan or appear in a court of law: *the company is already in default on its loans.* **in default of** in the absence of: *in default of agreement, the rent was to be determined by a surveyor.*

ORIGIN Middle English: from Old French *defaut,* from *defaillir* 'to fail,' based on Latin *fallere* 'disappoint, deceive.'

de•fault judg•ment /di'fôlt ˌjəjmənt/ ▸ n. judgment awarded to the plaintiff on the defendant's failure to plead.

de•fea•sance /di'fēzəns/ ▸ n. the action or process of rendering something null and void: *riparian rights held by the United States under California law are subject to defeasance by subsequent appropriators.*
■ a clause or condition which, if fulfilled, renders a deed or contract null and void.
ORIGIN late Middle English (as a legal term): from Old French *defesance*, from *defaire, desfaire* 'undo.'

de•fea•si•ble /di'fēzəbəl/ ▸ adj. (especially of an interest in land) subject to being defeated or extinguished: *in the typical mortgage relationship a mortgagee holds defeasible legal title to the mortgaged property interest.*
DERIVATIVES **de•fea•si•bil•i•ty** /di,fēzə'bilitē/ n.; **de•fea•si•bly** /di'fēzəblē/ adv.
ORIGIN Middle English: via Anglo-Norman French from the stem of Old French *desfesant* 'undoing' (see also **DEFEASANCE**).

de•feat /di'fēt/ ▸ v. [trans.] reject or block (a motion or proposal): *the amendment was defeated.*
■ render null and void; annul: *title to goods may be defeated under certain conditions involving irregularities in warehousing and freight forwarding.*
▸ n. an instance of defeating or being defeated.
ORIGIN late Middle English (in the sense 'undo, destroy, annul'): from Old French *desfait* 'undone,' past participle of *desfaire*, from medieval Latin *disfacere* 'undo.'

de•fend /di'fend/ ▸ v. [trans.] conduct the case for (the party being accused or sued) in a lawsuit: *their lawyer had defended dozens of indigent clients.*
DERIVATIVES **de•fend•a•ble** adj.
ORIGIN Middle English: from Old French *defendre*, from Latin *defendere*, from *de-* 'off' + *-fendere* 'to strike.'

de•fend•ant /di'fendənt/ ▸ n. an individual or entity sued or accused in a court of law. *this defendant identifies himself in his deposition as Timothy E. Nickel.* Compare with **PLAINTIFF**.
ORIGIN Middle English (as an adjective in the sense 'defending'): from Old French, 'warding off,' present participle of *defendre* (see **DEFEND**).

de•fense /di'fens; 'dēfens/ (Brit. **de•fence**) ▸ n. 1 the case presented by or on behalf of the party being accused or sued in a lawsuit.
2 one or more defendants in a trial.
■ (usu. **the defense**) [treated as sing. or pl.] the counsel for the defendant in a lawsuit: *the defense requested more time to prepare their case.*
ORIGIN Middle English: from Old French *defens*, from late Latin *defensum* (neuter), *defensa* (feminine), past participles of *defendere* 'defend.'

de•gree /di'grē/ ▸ n. [in combination] a legal grade of crime or offense, esp. murder: *second-degree murder.*

ORIGIN Middle English (in the senses 'step,' 'tier,' 'rank,' or 'relative state'): from Old French, based on Latin *de-* 'down' + *gradus* 'step or grade.'

de ju•re /di ˈjo͝orē; dā ˈjo͝orā/ ▸ **adv.** according to rightful entitlement or law; by right: *if the product configuration is not de jure functional, the mark may be registered on the Supplemental Register.* Often contrasted with **DE FACTO**.

▸ **adj.** denoting something or someone that is such by law: *he has been the de jure president of the company since his father's death.*

ORIGIN mid 16th cent.: Latin, literally 'of law.'

de•lict /diˈlikt/ ▸ **n.** a violation of the law; a tort or crime: *an international delict.*

DERIVATIVES **de•lict•u•al** /diˈlikSHo͞oəl/ **adj.**

ORIGIN late Middle English: from Latin *delictum* 'something showing fault,' neuter past participle of *delinquere*, from *de-* 'away' + *linquere* 'to leave.'

de•liv•er /diˈlivər/ ▸ **v.** [trans.] **1** transfer (property), acknowledging that one intends to be bound by a deed, either explicitly by declaration or implicitly by formal handover.

2 (of a judge or court) give (a judgment or verdict): *the judge delivered his verdict.*

ORIGIN Middle English: from Old French *delivrer*, based on Latin *de-* 'away' + *liberare* 'set free.'

de•liv•er•y /diˈlivərē/ ▸ **n.** (pl. **de•liv•er•ies**) the formal or symbolic handing over of property, esp. by deed, to a grantee or third party.

ORIGIN late Middle English: from Anglo-Norman French *delivree*, feminine past participle of *delivrer* (see **DELIVER**).

de•mand /diˈmænd/ ▸ **n.** a formal request, as a right: *there is no fee in federal court for filing a jury demand.*

▸ **v.** [trans.] **1** call into court; summon.

2 make a formal request: *the court demanded that the FDA support its claims with evidence.*

DERIVATIVES **de•mand•er n.**

ORIGIN Middle English (as a noun): from Old French *demande* (noun), *demander* (verb), from Latin *demandare* 'hand over, entrust' (in medieval Latin 'demand'), from *de-* 'formally' + *mandare* 'to order.'

de•mise /diˈmīz/ ▸ **v.** [trans.] convey or grant (an estate) by will or lease: *the premises hereby demised may be used for any lawful retail purpose.*

▸ **n.** [in sing.] conveyance or transfer of property or a title by demising: *documents that confirm any demise of title to real estate are fully taxable.*

ORIGIN late Middle English (as a legal term): from Anglo-Norman French, past participle (used as a noun) of Old French *desmettre* 'dismiss,' (in reflexive) 'abdicate,' based on Latin *dimittere* (see **DISMISS**).

de•mon•stra•tive ev•i•dence /di'mänstrətiv 'evidns/ ▶ n. evidence that makes use of a demonstration or display or an addition to testimony: *computer-generated demonstrative evidence.*

de•mur /di'mər/ ▶ v. (**de•murred, de•mur•ring**) [intrans.] dated put forward a demurrer.

▶ n. [usu. with negative] the action or process of objecting to or hesitating over something: *they accepted this ruling **without demur**.*

ORIGIN Middle English (in the sense 'linger, delay'): from Old French *demourer* (verb), *demeure* (noun), based on Latin *de-* 'away, completely' + *morari* 'delay.'

de•mur•rage /di'mərij/ ▶ n. a charge payable to the owner of a chartered ship in the event of failure to load or discharge the ship within the time agreed.

ORIGIN mid 17th cent. (also in the general sense 'procrastination, delay'): from Old French *demourage*, from the verb *demourer* (see **DEMUR**).

de•mur•rer /di'mərər/ ▶ n. an objection that a plaintiff's claim is irrelevant or invalid, while granting the factual basis of the point: *on **demurrer** it was held that the plaintiff's claim succeeded.*

ORIGIN early 16th cent.: from Anglo-Norman French (infinitive used as a noun), from Old French *demourer* 'remain, stay' (see **DEMUR**).

de•po•nent /di'pōnənt/ ▶ n. a person who makes a deposition or affidavit under oath: *the attorney may instruct the deponent not to answer a question.*

ORIGIN late Middle English: from Latin *deponent-* 'laying aside, putting down' (in medieval Latin 'testifying'), from the verb *deponere*, from *de-* 'down' + *ponere* 'place.'

de•port /di'pôrt/ ▶ v. [trans.] expel (a foreigner) from a country, typically on the grounds of illegal status or for having committed a crime: *he was deported for violation of immigration laws.*

■ exile (a native) to another country or territory.

DERIVATIVES **de•port•a•ble** adj.; **de•por•ta•tion** /,dēpôr'tāsHən/ n. *deportation proceedings.*

ORIGIN late 16th cent.: from French *déporter*, from Latin *deportare*, from *de-* 'away' + *portare* 'carry.'

de•pose /di'pōz/ ▶ v. [trans.] **1** remove from office suddenly and forcefully: *he had been deposed by a military coup.*

2 testify to or give (evidence) on oath, typically in a written statement: *every affidavit shall state which of the facts **deposed to** are within the deponent's knowledge.*

3 question (a witness) in deposition: *we conclude that deposing the accused's mother-in-law would provide no conceivable benefit.*

ORIGIN Middle English: from Old French *deposer*, from Latin *deponere* (see **DEPONENT**), but influenced by Latin *depositus* and Old French *poser* 'to place.'

dep•o•si•tion /,depə'zisHən/ ▶ n. the process of giving sworn testimony out of court, typically as part of discovery: *claimants and representatives have the same rights during deposition that they have during hearings.*

■ the record of such a process: *his deposition stated he intended to use the product for business purposes.*

ORIGIN late Middle English: from Latin *depositio(-n)*, from the verb *deponere* 'lay aside.'

der•e•lict /'derə,likt/ ▶ **adj.** in a very poor condition as a result of disuse and neglect: *derelict buildings.*

■ (of a person) shamefully negligent in not having done what one should have done: *he was* **derelict in** *his duty to conduct the review process.*

▶ **n.** a person without a home, job, or property: *streets lined with derelicts.*

■ a piece of property, esp. a ship, abandoned by the owner or crew: *the government determined her a derelict and a menace* | [as adj.] *a derelict orchard.*

ORIGIN mid 17th cent.: from Latin *derelictus* 'abandoned,' past participle of *derelinquere*, from *de-* 'completely' + *relinquere* 'forsake.'

der•e•lic•tion /ˌderə'likʃən/ ▶ **n.** the state of having been abandoned and become dilapidated: *the neighborhood already shows signs of dereliction.*

■ (usu. **dereliction of duty**) the willful failure to fulfill one's obligations: *their dereliction of duty in refusing to cooperate with him in lifting the easement.*

ORIGIN late 16th cent.: from Latin *derelictio(n-)*, from the verb *derelinquere* (see **DERELICT**).

de•re•strict /ˌdēri'strikt/ ▶ **v.** [trans.] remove restrictions from: *the reports were put in final form and derestricted for public distribution later in the year.*

DERIVATIVES **de•re•stric•tion** /ˌdēri'strikʃən/ n.

der•mat•o•glyph•ics /ˌdərmətə'glifiks; dər,mætə-/ ▶ **plural n.** [treated as sing.] the study of skin markings or patterns on fingers, hands, and feet, and its application, esp. in criminology.

DERIVATIVES **der•mat•o•glyph** /dər'mætə,glif/ n.; **der•mat•o•glyph•ic** adj.; **der•mat•o•glyph•i•cal•ly** adv.

ORIGIN 1920s: from **DERMATO-**'skin' + Greek *gluphikos* 'carved' (from *gluphē* 'carving').

de•scend•i•ble /di'sendəbəl/ ▶ **adj.** (of property) able to be inherited by a descendant: *the property rights are freely transferable and descendible.*

de•scent /di'sent/ ▶ **n.** the transmission of qualities, property (in the case of intestacy), or privileges by inheritance: *the legislature regulates the descent and distribution of property.*

ORIGIN Middle English: from Old French *descente*, from *descendre* 'to descend.'

de•tain /di'tān/ ▶ v. [trans.] keep (someone) in official custody, typically for questioning about a crime or in politically sensitive situations: *she was detained without trial for two years.*
DERIVATIVES **de•tain•ment** n.
ORIGIN late Middle English (in the sense 'be afflicted with sickness or infirmity'): from Old French *detenir*, from a variant of Latin *detinere*, from *de-* 'away, aside' + *tenere* 'to hold.'

de•tain•er /di'tānər; dē-/ ▶ n. **1** the action of detaining or withholding property: *detainer of the premises was part of the drug investigation.*
■ the detention of a person in custody: *a charge of unlawful detainer.*
■ an order authorizing the continued detention of a person in custody: *the federal prosecutor handling this case has lodged a detainer against Thorpe with the Florida authorities.*
2 a person who detains someone or something.
ORIGIN early 17th cent.: from Anglo-Norman French *detener* 'detain' (used as a noun), variant of Old French *detenir* (see DETAIN).

de•ten•tion /di'tensHən/ ▶ n. the action of detaining someone or the state of being detained in official custody: *he committed suicide while in police detention.*
ORIGIN late Middle English (in the sense 'withholding of what is claimed or due'): from late Latin *detentio(n-)*, from Latin *detinere* 'hold back' (see DETAIN).

de•ten•tion cen•ter /di'tensHən ˌsentər/ ▶ n. an institution where people are held in detention, usually for short periods, in particular illegal immigrants, refugees, people awaiting trial or sentence, or young offenders.

de•ter•mi•na•ble /di'tərmənəbəl/ ▶ adj. capable of being brought to an end under given conditions; terminable.
ORIGIN late Middle English: via Old French from late Latin *determinabilis* 'finite,' from the verb *determinare* (see DETERMINE).

de•ter•mi•na•tion /diˌtərməˈnāsHən/ ▶ n. **1** the settlement of a dispute by the authoritative decision of a judge or arbitrator.
■ a judicial decision or sentence: *the secretary shall file in the court the record of the proceedings on which he based his determination as provided in this section.*
2 the cessation of an estate or interest.
ORIGIN late Middle English: via Old French from Latin *determinatio(n-)*, from the verb *determinare* (see DETERMINE).

de•ter•mine /di'tərmin/ ▶ v. [trans.] archaic bring or come to an end.
ORIGIN late Middle English: from Old French *determiner*, from Latin *determinare* 'limit, fix,' from *de-* 'completely' + *terminare* 'terminate.'

det•i•nue /'detnˌ(y)o͞o/ ▶ n. a common-law claim or action to recover wrongfully detained goods or possessions.
ORIGIN late Middle English: from Old French *detenue*, past participle (used as a noun) of *detenir* 'detain.'

de•vise /di'vīz/ ▶ v. [trans.] leave (property, especially real estate) to

someone by the terms of a will: *the court determined that the decedent had not devised the property to the petitioner.*
▶**n.** a clause in a will leaving property, especially real estate, to someone: *they are authorized to receive donations of money, lands, goods, chattels and the like, either by gift or devise.*
DERIVATIVES **de•vi•see** /di‚vī'zē/ **n.**; **de•vi•sor** n.; **de•vis•er** n.
ORIGIN Middle English: the verb from Old French *deviser,* from Latin *divis-* 'divided,' from the verb *dividere* (this sense being reflected in the original English sense of the verb); the noun is a variant of *device* (in the early sense 'will, desire').

dev•o•lu•tion /‚devə'lo͞osHən/ ▶ **n.** the transfer or delegation of power to a lower level, esp. by central government to local or regional administration: *the devolution of housing programs from federal housing resources closer to communities.*
■ the transfer of property from one owner to another.
DERIVATIVES **dev•o•lu•tion•ar•y** /‚devə'lo͞osHə‚nerē/ **adj.**; **dev•o•lu•tion•ist** /‚devə'lo͞osHənist/ n.
ORIGIN late 15th cent. (in the sense 'transference by default'): from late Latin *devolutio(n-),* from Latin *devolvere* 'roll down' (see DEVOLVE).

de•volve /di'välv/ ▶ **v.** [trans.] transfer or delegate (power) to a lower level, esp. from central government to local or regional administration: *measures to **devolve** power to the provinces* | [as adj.] (**devolved**) *devolved and decentralized government.*
■ [intrans.] (**devolve on/upon/to**) (of duties or responsibility) pass to (a body or person at a lower level): *his duties devolved on a comrade.*
DERIVATIVES **de•volve•ment** n.
ORIGIN late Middle English (in the sense 'roll down'): from Latin *devolvere,* from *de-* 'down' + *volvere* 'to roll.'

dic•tum /'diktəm/ ▶ **n.** (pl. **dic•ta** /'diktə/ or **dic•tums**) a formal pronouncement from an authoritative source: *the Politburo's dictum that the party will become a "left-wing parliamentary party."*
■ short for OBITER DICTUM.
ORIGIN late 16th cent.: from Latin, literally 'something said,' neuter past participle of *dicere.*

di•es non /‚dēāz 'nän/ ▶ **n.** (pl. same) a day on which no court is in session or which does not count for legal or other purposes.
ORIGIN Latin, short for *dies non juridicus* 'nonjudicial day.'

di•gest ▶ **n.** /'dī‚jest/ a methodical summary of a body of laws, decided cases, legal rules, etc.
ORIGIN late Middle English: from Latin *digest-* 'distributed, dissolved, digested,' from the verb *digerere,* from *di-* 'apart' + *gerere* 'carry'; the noun from Latin *digesta* 'matters methodically arranged,' from *digestus* 'divided,' from *digerere.*

di•min•ished ca•pac•i•ty /di'minisHt kə'pæsitē/ ▶ **n.** an unbalanced mental state that is considered to make a person unable to act with the intent necessary for a particular crime and is recognized as grounds to reduce the charge: *she had wished to convince the court that she suffered from diminished capacity at the time of the murder.*

di•rect ex•am•i•na•tion /dəˈrekt igˌzæməˈnāsHən/ ▸ n. the questioning of a witness by the party that has called that witness to give evidence, in order to support the case that is being made: *on direct examination of Airman TJ, trial counsel sought to explain these circumstances.* Compare with CROSS-EXAMINE.

dis•a•bil•i•ty /ˌdisəˈbilit̬ē/ ▸ n. (pl. **dis•a•bil•i•ties**) a disadvantage or handicap, esp. one imposed or recognized by the law.
■ welfare income provided because of this: *he had to quit his job and go on disability.*
■ an incapacity to perform all one's legal rights.

dis•af•firm /ˌdisəˈfərm/ ▸ v. [trans.] repudiate; declare void: *to disaffirm a contract is to say it never existed.*
DERIVATIVES **dis•af•fir•ma•tion** /disˌæfərˈmāsHən/ n.

dis•bar /disˈbär/ ▸ v. (**dis•barred, dis•bar•ring**) [trans.] (usu. **be disbarred**) expel (a lawyer) from the Bar, so that they no longer have the right to practice law: *he was unable to show cause why he should not be disbarred.*
DERIVATIVES **dis•bar•ment** n.

dis•charge ▸ v. /disˈCHärj/ [trans.] **1** (often **be discharged**) tell (someone) officially that they can or must leave, in particular:
■ release (someone) from the custody or restraint of the law: *he ordered that 1,671 prisoners of war be **discharged from** prison.* ■ relieve (a juror or jury) from serving in a case: *the district court discharged the jury over the objections of defense counsel.* ■ relieve (a bankrupt) of liability. ■ release (a party) from a contract or obligation: *the insurer is discharged from liability from the day of breach.*
2 pay off (a debt or other financial claim): *her membership was suspended until such time as she could discharge her debts.*
3 dated (of a judge or court) cancel (an order of a court).
■ cancel (a contract) because of completion or breach: *the existing mortgage will be discharged on completion.*
▸ n. /ˈdisˌCHärj/ **1** an act of releasing someone from the custody or restraint of the law: *four days in jail and one year conditional discharge.*
■ the action of relieving a bankrupt from residual liability: *the debtor may be entitled to a discharge.*
2 the payment of a debt or other financial claim: *money paid in discharge of a claim.*
3 dated the action of canceling an order of a court.
DERIVATIVES **dis•charge•a•ble** /disˈCHärjəbəl/ adj.; **dis•charg•er** /disˈCHärjər/ n.
ORIGIN Middle English (in the sense 'relieve of (an obligation)'): from Old French *descharger*, from late Latin *discarricare* 'unload,' from *dis-* (expressing reversal) + *carricare* 'to load' (see CHARGE).

dis•claim /disˈklām/ ▸ v. [trans.] renounce a legal claim to (a property or

title): *a statement disclaiming any interest in a specifically described aircraft may be recorded upon payment of a $5 recording fee.*
ORIGIN late Middle English (in legal contexts): from Anglo-Norman French *desclamer*, from *des-* (expressing reversal) + *clamer* 'to claim' (see CLAIM).

dis•claim•er /dis'klāmər/ ▶ n. a statement that denies something, esp. responsibility: *Amtrak's disclaimer of liability is printed on the ticket.*
■ an act of repudiating another's claim or renouncing one's own: *the court concluded that her disclaimer constituted a taxable gift.*
ORIGIN late Middle English (as a legal term): from Anglo-Norman French *desclamer* (infinitive used as noun: see DISCLAIM).

dis•clo•sure /dis'klōzHər/ ▶ n. the action of making new or secret information known: *a judge ordered the disclosure of the government documents.*
ORIGIN late 16th cent.: from *disclose*, on the pattern of *closure.*

dis•cov•er•y /dis'kəvərē/ ▶ n. (pl. **dis•cov•er•ies**) the compulsory disclosure, by a party to a civil or criminal action, of relevant documents referred to by the other party: *material obtained by discovery or otherwise.*
■ the process by which parties to an action investigate facts prior to trial, including depositions, interrogatories, and examinations: *counsel should take advantage of the potential for discovery offered by a hearing.*
ORIGIN mid 16th cent.: from *discover*, on the pattern of the pair *recover, recovery.*

dis•en•fran•chise /ˌdisen'frænCHīz/ (also **dis•fran•chise** /dis'frænCHīz/) ▶ v. [trans.] deprive (someone) of the right to vote: *the law disenfranchised some 3,000 voters on the basis of a residence qualification.*
■ deprive (someone) of a right or privilege: *the move would disenfranchise the disabled from using the transit system.* ■ archaic deprive (someone) of the rights and privileges of a free inhabitant of a borough, city, or country.
DERIVATIVES **dis•en•fran•chise•ment** n.

dis•miss /dis'mis/ ▶ v. [trans.] refuse further hearing to (a case): *the judge dismissed the case for lack of evidence.*
■ revoke an order of a court: *the writ of certiorari is dismissed as improvidently granted.*
DERIVATIVES **dis•miss•al** /dis'misəl/ n.; **dis•miss•i•ble** /dis'misəbəl/ adj.
ORIGIN late Middle English: from medieval Latin *dismiss-*, variant of Latin *dimiss-* 'sent away,' from the verb *dimittere.*

dis•or•der•ly /dis'ôrdərlē/ ▶ adj. involving or contributing to a breakdown of peaceful and law-abiding behavior: *they had no intention of staging a disorderly protest.*
DERIVATIVES **dis•or•der•li•ness** n.

dis•or•der•ly con•duct /dis'ôrdərlē 'kändəkt/ ▶ n. unruly behavior constituting a minor offense: *McDonald was arrested and charged with assault in the fourth degree and convicted of disorderly conduct.*

dis•or•der•ly house /dis'ôrdərlē ˌhows/ ▶ n. archaic a brothel.

dis•pose /dis'pōz/ ▶ v. [intrans.] (**dispose of**) make a final resolution of: *there was no heritable property to be disposed of* | *most cases are disposed of by motion or settlement.*

ORIGIN late Middle English: from Old French *disposer*, from Latin *disponere* 'arrange,' influenced by *dispositus* 'arranged' and Old French *poser* 'to place.'

dis•po•si•tion /ˌdispə'zisHən/ ▶ n. 1 conclusive action on a matter by a court or other tribunal: *they'll stay the schedule for record preparation and briefing pending the court's disposition of the motion.*
2 the action of distributing or transferring property or money to someone, in particular by bequest: *this is a tax that affects the disposition of assets on death.*

ORIGIN late Middle English: via Old French from Latin *dispositio(n-)*, from *disponere* 'arrange' (see DISPOSE).

dis•pos•i•tive /dis'päzitiv/ ▶ adj. relating to or bringing about the settlement of an issue or the disposition especially of property: *such litigation will rarely be dispositive of any question.*
■ dealing with the disposition of property by deed or will: *the testator had to make his signature after making the dispositive provisions.*
■ dealing with the settling of international conflicts by an agreed disposition of disputed territories: *a peace settlement in the nature of a dispositive treaty.*

ORIGIN late Middle English (in the sense 'contributory, conducive'): from Old French, or from medieval Latin *dispositivus*, from Latin *disposit-* 'arranged, disposed,' from the verb *disponere* (see DISPOSE).

dis•qual•i•fy /dis'kwäləˌfī/ ▶ v. (**dis•qual•i•fies, dis•qual•i•fied**) [trans.] (often **be disqualified**) pronounce (someone) ineligible for an office or activity because of an offense, infringement, or conflict of interest: *he was **disqualified from** driving for six months.*

dis•train /dis'trān/ ▶ v. [trans.] seize (someone's property) to obtain payment of rent or other money owed: *legislation has restricted the right to distrain goods found on the premises.*
■ seize the property of (someone) for this purpose: *the government applied political pressure by distraining debtors.*

DERIVATIVES **dis•train•er** n.; **dis•train•ment** n.

ORIGIN Middle English: from Old French *destreindre*, from Latin *distringere* 'stretch apart,' from *dis-* 'apart' + *stringere* 'tighten.'

dis•traint /dis'trānt/ ▶ n. the seizure of someone's property in order to obtain payment of money owed, esp. rent: *many faced heavy fines and the distraint of goods.*

ORIGIN mid 18th cent.: from DISTRAIN, on the pattern of *constraint.*

dis•tress /dis'tres/ ▶ n. 1 (esp. as **emotional distress**) extreme anxiety, sorrow, or pain: *damages for emotional distress have been permitted.*

2 another term for **DISTRAINT**.

ORIGIN Middle English: from Old French *destresce* (noun), *destrecier* (verb), based on Latin *distringere* 'stretch apart.'

dis•trict at•tor•ney /ˈdistrikt əˈtərnē/ (abbr.: **DA**) ▶ n. a public official who acts as prosecutor for the state or the federal government in court in a particular district.

dis•trict court /ˈdistrikt ˈkôrt/ ▶ n. a state or federal trial court.

dis•tur•bance /disˈtərbəns/ ▶ n. the interruption of a settled and peaceful condition, specifically:

■ a breakdown of peaceful and law-abiding behavior; a riot: *the disturbances were precipitated when four men were refused bail.* ■ interference with rights or property: *the field party shall assure the landowner that every effort will be made to minimize disturbance or disruption to the property.*

ORIGIN Middle English: from Old French *destourbance*, from *destourber*, from *dis-* 'utterly' + *turbare* 'disturb' (from *turba* 'tumult').

di•vorce /diˈvôrs/ ▶ n. the legal dissolution of a marriage by a court or other competent body: *her **divorce from** her first husband* | *one in three marriages ends in divorce* | [as adj.] *divorce proceedings.*

■ a legal decree dissolving a marriage: *the wife obtained a divorce in a Mexican court.*

▶ v. [trans.] legally dissolve one's marriage with (someone): *he divorced his first wife after 10 months* | [as adj.] (**divorced**) *a divorced couple* | [intrans.] *they divorced eight years later.*

DERIVATIVES **di•vorce•ment** n.

ORIGIN late Middle English: the noun from Old French *divorce*, from Latin *divortium*, based on *divertere*, from *di-* 'aside' + *vertere* 'to turn'; the verb from Old French *divorcer*, from late Latin *divortiare*, from *divortium*.

dock /däk/ ▶ n. (usu. **the dock**) the enclosure in a criminal court where a defendant is placed.

PHRASES **in the dock** (of a defendant) on trial in court.

ORIGIN late 16th cent.: probably originally slang and related to Flemish *dok* 'chicken coop, rabbit hutch,' of unknown origin.

dock•et /ˈdäkit/ ▶ n. a calendar or list of cases for trial or people having cases pending: *orders and opinions appear here for only sixty days after the date of entry on the court's docket.*

■ an abridged account of legal proceedings.

▶ v. (**dock•et•ed, dock•et•ing**) [trans.] (usu. **be docketed**) enter (a case or suit) onto a list of those due to be heard: *the case will go to the Supreme Court, and may be docketed for the fall term.*

ORIGIN late 15th cent. The word originally denoted a short summary or abstract; hence, in the early 18th cent., 'a document giving particulars of a consignment.'

doc•trine /ˈdäktrin/ ▶ n. a rule or standard of law; the body of such rule: *the doctrine of the separation of powers.*

DERIVATIVES **doc•tri•nal** /'däktrənl/ **adj.**; **doc•tri•nal•ly adv.**
ORIGIN late Middle English: from Old French, from Latin *doctrina* 'teaching, learning,' from *doctor* 'teacher,' from *docere* 'teach.'

dom•i•cile /'dämə͵sīl; 'dō-; 'däməsəl/ (also **dom•i•cil** /'däməsəl/) ▶ n. the state or country that a person treats as their permanent home, or lives in and has a substantial connection with: *his wife has a **domicile of origin** in Germany.*
■ a person's residence or home: *he is a financially independent student who has had a domicile in the state of Washington for the period of one year.* ■ the place at which a corporation or other body is registered, esp. for tax purposes.
▶ v. [with adverbial of place] (**be domiciled**) formal or treat a specified country as a permanent home: *the tenant is domiciled in the United States.*
■ reside; be based: *he was domiciled in a frame house on the outskirts of town.*
ORIGIN late Middle English: via Old French from Latin *domicilium* 'dwelling,' from *domus* 'home.'

do•nee /dō'nē/ ▶ n. a person who receives a gift: *the third party was a donee of the 20 shares.*
■ a person who is given a power of appointment.
ORIGIN early 16th cent.: from *donor* + *-ee.*

dou•ble jeop•ard•y /'dəbəl 'jepərdē/ ▶ n. the prosecution of a person twice for the same offense.

dow•er /'dow(-ə)r/ ▶ n. historical a widow's share for life of her husband's estate: *W expressly waived all right to alimony, dower, and future interest in R's property.*
■ archaic a dowry.
▶ v. [trans.] archaic give a dowry to.
ORIGIN late Middle English: from Old French *douaire*, from medieval Latin *dotarium*, from Latin *dotare* 'endow,' from *dos, dot-* 'dowry'; related to *dare* 'give.'

drunk driv•ing /'drəNGk 'drīviNG/ (also **drunk•en driv•ing** /'drəNGkən 'drīviNG/) ▶ n. the crime of driving a vehicle with an excess of alcohol in the blood.
DERIVATIVES **drunk driv•er n.**

due dil•i•gence /'d(y)o͞o 'diləjəns/ ▶ n. reasonable steps taken by a person in order to satisfy a legal requirement, esp. in performing a professional duty: *any person can file a petition challenging the due diligence of an applicant for patent.*

due proc•ess /'d(y)o͞o 'präses/ (also **due proc•ess of law**) ▶ n. fair treatment through the normal judicial system, esp. as a citizen's entitlement. Due process is guaranteed by the Fifth and Fourteenth Amendments to the US Constitution: *plaintiff claims that defendants violated his due process rights when he was discharged from his employment.*

DUI ▶ abbr. driving under the influence (of drugs or alcohol): *the charge was originally filed as a DUI* | [as adj.] *a DUI program.*

du•plic•i•tous /d(y)oo'plisitəs/ ▸ **adj.** (of a charge or plea) containing more than one allegation: *the risk behind a duplicitous charge is that a jury may convict the defendant without unanimous agreement on a particular offense.*

du•ress /d(y)oo'res/ ▸ **n.** constraint illegally exercised to force someone to perform an act: *the question is whether the defendant acted in self-defense or was* **under duress.**

■ archaic forcible restraint or imprisonment.

ORIGIN Middle English (in the sense 'harshness, severity, cruel treatment'): via Old French from Latin *duritia*, from *durus* 'hard.'

dwell•ing house /'dweliNG ˌhows/ ▸ **n.** a house used as a residence and not for business purposes: *distilled spirits plants shall not be located in any dwelling house.*

DWI ▸ **abbr.** driving while intoxicated: *Holden has vowed that drivers charged with DWI will face stiffer penalties.*

HOW TO UNDERSTAND
A CONTRACT

A contract is a legally recognized promise or set of promises. Usually, contracts involve exchanges; in a contract for the sale of a house, the seller promises to deliver the house and the buyer promises to pay for it. Some promises lacking an exchange are enforceable, too; if you pledge a donation to a charity, most states will hold you to it.

Contracts can be made orally, with a few exceptions, such as land transactions and sales of goods above a certain dollar amount. Complex contracts are usually made in writing. Written contracts range from a few words on the back of a ticket stub to hundreds of pages. Common examples include apartment leases, auto financing or rental agreements, credit card agreements, employment contracts, and insurance policies.

For the most part, you are on you own when it comes to entering into a contract. For very important transactions, consult a lawyer. But you should understand the principal terms of common contracts, and if a problem arises, it is helpful to be able to make sense out of some of the more obscure clauses as well.

Getting the main points
When reading a contract, think first about its primary purposes and what will be expected of each party. Is this a home improvement contract? If so, you (the homeowner) expect to pay for the contractor's work. What work is to be done, when, and to what standard of quality? How much do you have to

pay, and on what schedule? Is this a homeowner's insurance policy? Look for clauses that identify the property covered, the kinds of damage or loss covered, and how compensation is determined—and on the other side, how much you have to pay, how and when to make payments, and how to file claims.

Second, think about what could go wrong and look for clauses that address that. What happens if the contractor is late in starting the work, or if your new roof leaks? In your insurance policy, what happens if you miss a payment? Is there a grace period? A late payment charge? Will the policy be canceled? What if the insurance company refuses to pay a claim?

Additional terms

If you look through the entire contract, you are likely to find not only those basic provisions, but also a number of more or less standard clauses—often called *boilerplate*—such as the following:

■ *Definitions.*
Crucial words, like "the premises," "the insured," or even "you," are often defined in a special section.

■ *Representations.*
These are statements by one party that the other is relying upon in entering into the contract. For example, applicants for life insurance are screened for health problems and thus are required to "represent" (state as true) that all requested information about their medical history has been fully disclosed. Representations are very important; a false representation can render a contract void.

■ *Notice.*
This clause will spell out what each side must do to notify the other of a problem or other matter relating to the contract. For example, it might require written notice by certified mail to a particular address.

- *Choice of forum and consent to jurisdiction.*
  The contract may specify that any dispute will be submitted to a particular court, usually a court in one party's home state. A companion clause will state explicitly that the other party agrees to submit to the jurisdiction of that court.

- *Arbitration clause.*
  In an increasing number of contracts, companies prevent consumers or employees from suing by providing that any dispute over a contract must be submitted to an arbitration panel rather than to a court. Sometimes this is quicker and cheaper than suing, but it means that you must use the arbitration system of the company's choosing, you will not have a judge or jury, you may have to pay fees, and you are denied certain ordinary remedies.

- *Choice of law.*
  The contract may require that, in any dispute over the contract, it will be interpreted according to the law of a particular state—even if the case is brought in a different state.

- *Merger clause* (also called *integration clause*).
  This says something like "This constitutes the entire agreement of the parties." The purpose of this is to keep either party from later claiming that there was a side agreement or an additional contract term that was not written into the final contract. If there are other such agreements, get them in writing.

How do courts interpret contracts?

If you think contracts are hard to understand, you are not alone. Courts are regularly called upon to settle disputes about what a contract means.

The first thing a court does is look at the document itself. Many of the contracts we agree to every day are *adhesion contracts*, presented on a take-it-or-leave-it basis with no opportunity to negotiate the terms. If you want to get a credit card, you have to agree to its standard terms. Few people even bother to read the fine print that makes up most of these contracts. A court will usually hold you to the terms, even if you did not read them and would not have understood them if you had read them. But there are limits; the law requires some contract terms to be disclosed prominently, such as interest rate and annual fee on credit card solicitations, and courts will strike down some provisions that are *unconscionable*, or grossly unfair.

Beyond the words of the contract, the court tries to determine how the parties reasonably should have expected the contract to be understood in light of its purposes and all the circumstances. In a famous case, the issue was what a contract meant by "chicken," and the court looked at understandings in the poultry trade and Department of Agriculture regulations to figure out what reasonable commercial buyers and sellers of chicken would have meant. It is impossible to state everything in a contract—you would have to include an unabridged dictionary to define every word—but contract drafters (especially lawyers) try to avoid major problems by not leaving too much to the court's interpretation.

E

ear•nest /ˈərnist/ ▶ n. [in sing.] earnest money
ORIGIN Middle English *ernes*, literally 'installment paid to confirm a contract,' based on Old French *erres*, from Latin *arra*, shortened form of *arrabo* 'a pledge.' The spelling was influenced by words ending in *-ness*; the final *-t* is probably by association with the adjective *earnest*.

ear•nest mon•ey /ˈərnist ˈmənē/ ▶ n. money paid to confirm a contract: *there are discrepancies in the amount of earnest money on deposit.*

ease•ment /ˈēzmənt/ ▶ n. a right to cross or otherwise use someone else's land for a specified purpose: *an agricultural conservation easement.*
ORIGIN late Middle English: from Old French *aisement*, from *aisier*, from the phrase *a aise* 'at ease.'

e•ject /iˈjekt/ ▶ v. [trans.] (often **be ejected**) dispossess (a tenant or occupant) by legal process: *after interrogating the organizers, casino security guards again ejected them from the property.*
DERIVATIVES **e•jec•tion** /iˈjekSHən/ n.
ORIGIN late Middle English: from Latin *eject-* 'thrown out,' from the verb *eicere*, from *e-* (variant of *ex-*) 'out' + *jacere* 'to throw.'

e•ject•ment /iˈjektmənt/ ▶ n. the action or process of evicting a tenant from property: *the landlord shall serve a **writ in ejectment**.*
■ the action or process in which a person evicted from property seeks to recover possession and damages.

e•man•ci•pate /iˈmænsəˌpāt/ ▶ v. [trans.] set free, esp. from legal, social, or political restrictions: *it was the first effort of an infant community to assert its individuality and emancipate itself from the tutelage of Oregon.*
■ set (a child) free from the authority of its parents: *attaining the age of majority does not automatically emancipate the child.* ■ free from slavery: *it is estimated that he emancipated 8,000 slaves.*
DERIVATIVES **e•man•ci•pa•tion** /iˌmænsəˈpāSHən/ n.; **e•man•ci•pa•tor** /iˈmænsəˌpātər/ n.; **e•man•ci•pa•to•ry** /iˈmænsəpəˌtôrē/ adj.
ORIGIN early 17th cent.: from Latin *emancipat-* 'transferred as property,' from the verb *emancipare*, from *e-* (variant of *ex-*) 'out' + *mancipium* 'slave.'

em•bez•zle /emˈbezəl/ ▶ v. [trans.] steal or misappropriate (money or property placed in one's trust or belonging to the organization for which one works): *she had embezzled $5,600,000 in company funds.* Compare with DEFALCATE.

DERIVATIVES **em•bez•zle•ment** n.; **em•bez•zler** /em'bezlər/ n.

ORIGIN late Middle English (in the sense 'steal'): from Anglo-Norman French *embesiler*, from *besiler* in the same sense (compare with Old French *besillier* 'maltreat, ravage'), of unknown ultimate origin. The current sense dates from the late 16th cent.

em•i•nent do•main /'emənənt dō'mān/ ▶ n. the right of a government or its agent to expropriate private property for public use, with payment of compensation.

em•pan•el /im'pænl/ ▶ v. variant spelling of IMPANEL.

en•a•bling act /en'ābliNG 'ækt/ ▶ n. a statute empowering a person or body to take certain action, esp. to make regulations, rules, or orders: *a statehood enabling act.*

en•act•ment /en'æktmənt/ ▶ n. the process of passing legislation: *within 90 days after the enactment of the bill, the FCC is directed to adopt waiver procedures.* ■ a law that is passed.

DERIVATIVES **en•ac•tive** /en'æktiv/ adj.

en•cum•brance /en'kəmbrəns/ ▶ n. a burden or impediment: *plaintiff's easement by way of necessity does not constitute an encumbrance.* ■ a mortgage or other charge on property or assets: *a motor vehicle or trailer may be subject to a lien or encumbrance.* ■ archaic a person, esp. a child, who is dependent on someone else for support.

ORIGIN Middle English (denoting an encumbered state; formerly also as *incumbrance*): from Old French *encombrance*, from *encombrer* 'block up.'

en•dorse /en'dôrs/ (also dated **in•dorse** /in'dôrs/) ▶ v. [trans.] sign (a check or bill of exchange) on the back to make it payable to someone other than the stated payee or to accept responsibility for paying it: *the claimant endorsed this check over to the City.* ■ (usu. **be endorsed on**) write (a comment) on the front or back of a document: *the court shall endorse on the reverse side of the license that the person was ordered not to drive.*

DERIVATIVES **en•dors•a•ble** adj.; **en•dors•er** n.

ORIGIN late 15th cent. (in the sense 'write on the back of'; formerly also as *indorse*): from medieval Latin *indorsare*, from Latin *in-* 'in, on' + *dorsum* 'back.'

en•dorse•ment /en'dôrsmənt/ (also dated **in•dorse•ment** /in'dôrsmənt/) ▶ n. **1** a clause in an insurance policy detailing an exemption from or change in coverage: *carriers often include endorsements that waive exclusions and offer coverages additional to those included in a standard policy.* **2** the action of endorsing a check or bill of exchange.

en•force /en'fôrs/ ▶ v. [trans.] compel observance of or compliance with (a law, rule, or obligation): *evidence indicates that the ordinance is rarely enforced.*

DERIVATIVES **en•force•a•bil•i•ty** /enˌfôrsəˈbilitē/ n.; **en•force•a•ble** /enˈfôrsəbəl/ adj.; **en•forc•ed•ly** /enˈfôrsidlē/ adv.; **en•force•ment** n.; **en•forc•er** n.

ORIGIN Middle English (in the senses 'strive' and 'impel by force'; formerly also as *inforce*): from Old French *enforcir, enforcier,* based on Latin *in-* 'in' + *fortis* 'strong.'

en•gross /enˈgrōs/ ▸ v. [trans.] produce (a legal document) in its final or definitive form: *the judge may direct the appellant to engross the statement or transcript, or both, as settled.*

DERIVATIVES **en•gross•ment** n.

ORIGIN late Middle English (formerly also as *ingross*): based on *en-, in-* 'in' + late Latin *grossus* 'large.'

en•join /enˈjoin/ ▸ v. [trans.] (**enjoin someone from**) prohibit someone from performing (a particular action) by issuing an injunction: *Judge Sessions has enjoined USDA from implementing milk market order reform.*

DERIVATIVES **en•join•er** n.; **en•join•ment** n.

ORIGIN Middle English (formerly also as *injoin*): from Old French *enjoindre,* from Latin *injungere* 'join, attach, impose,' from *in-* 'in, toward' + *jungere* 'to join.'

en•ter /ˈentər/ ▸ v. submit (a statement) in an official capacity, usually in a court of law: *an attorney entered a plea of guilty on her behalf.*

▸**enter into** undertake to bind oneself by (an agreement or other commitment): *the council entered into an agreement with a private firm.*

enter on/upon (as a legal entitlement) go freely into property as or as if the owner: *you are not allowed to enter upon railroad property.*

ORIGIN Middle English: from Old French *entrer,* from Latin *intrare,* from *intra* 'within.'

en•try /ˈentrē/ ▸ n. (pl. **-ies**) the action of taking up the legal right to property.

ORIGIN Middle English: from Old French *entree,* based on Latin *intrata,* feminine past participle of *intrare* (see ENTER).

e•qual /ˈēkwəl/ ▸ adj. (of people) having the same status, rights, or opportunities.

■ uniform in application or effect; without discrimination on any grounds: *a dedicated campaigner for equal rights.*

ORIGIN late Middle English: from Latin *aequalis,* from *aequus* 'even, level, equal.'

eq•ui•ta•ble /ˈekwitəbəl/ ▸ adj. valid in equity as distinct from law: *the beneficiaries have an equitable interest in the property.*

DERIVATIVES **eq•ui•ta•bil•i•ty** /ˌekwitəˈbilitē/ n.; **eq•ui•ta•ble•ness** n.; **eq•ui•ta•bly** /ˈekwitəblē/ adv.

ORIGIN mid 16th cent.: from French *équitable,* from *équité* (see EQUITY).

eq•ui•ty /'ekwitē/ ▶ n. (pl. **eq•ui•ties**) **1** a branch of law that developed alongside common law in order to remedy some of its defects in fairness and justice, formerly, and still in some jurisdictions, administered in special courts.
2 the value of a mortgaged property after deduction of charges against it: *negative equity arises from plummeting house prices.*
ORIGIN Middle English: from Old French *equité*, from Latin *aequitas*, from *aequus* 'equal.'

eq•ui•ty of re•demp•tion /'ekwitē əv ri'dempSHən/ ▶ n. the right of a mortgagor over the mortgaged property, esp. the right to redeem the property on payment of the principal, interest, and costs.

er•ror /'erər/ ▶ n. a mistake of fact or of law in a court's opinion, judgment or order: *the District Court's procedural errors.*
ORIGIN Middle English: via Old French from Latin *error*, from *errare* 'to stray, err.'

es•cape clause /i'skāp ˌklôz/ ▶ n. a clause in a contract that specifies the conditions under which one party can be freed from an obligation: *OMSF left itself many escape clauses that could have important effects on the scientific program.*

es•cheat /es'CHēt/ ▶ n. the reversion of property to the state, or (in feudal law) to the owner's dying without legal heirs: *if it appears that there may be an escheat, notice of hearing and a copy of the petition must be sent to the Attorney General.*
■ an item of property affected by this.
▶ v. [intrans.] (of land) revert to a lord or the state by escheat: *probate of estates in which property escheated to Indian tribes.*
■ [trans.] [usu. as adj.] (**escheated**) hand over (land) as an escheat.
ORIGIN Middle English: from Old French *eschete*, based on Latin *excidere* 'fall away,' from *ex-* 'out of, from' + *cadere* 'to fall.'

es•crow /'eskrō/ ▶ n. a bond, other document, or payment kept in the custody of a third party, taking effect only when a specified condition has been fulfilled: *a mechanism for the escrow of digital signature keys is desirable.*
■ [usu. as adj.] a deposit or fund held in trust or as a security: *an escrow account.* ■ the state of being kept in custody or trust in this way: *the board holds funds in escrow.*
▶ v. [trans.] place in custody or trust in this way: *the cooperative has received and escrowed the amount of $75,016.22.*
ORIGIN late 16th cent.: from Old French *escroe* 'scrap, scroll,' from medieval Latin *scroda*, of Germanic origin; related to *shred.*

es•quire /'eskwīr; i'skwīr/ ▶ n. (**Es•quire**) (abbr.: **Esq.**) a title appended to a lawyer's surname.
ORIGIN late Middle English: from Old French *esquier*, from Latin *scutarius* 'shield-bearer,' from *scutum* 'shield.'

es•tate /i'stāt/ ▶ n. the interest that a person possesses in land or other property.

■ all the money and property owned by a particular person, esp. at death: *in his will, he divided his estate between his wife and daughter.* ORIGIN Middle English (in the sense 'state or condition'): from Old French *estat*, from Latin *status* 'state, condition,' from *stare* 'to stand.'

es•tate tax /i'stāt ˌtæks/ ▶ n. a tax levied on the net value of the estate of a deceased person before distribution to the heirs. Also called DEATH TAX.

es•top /e'stäp/ ▶ v. (**es•topped, es•top•ping**) [trans.] (usu. **be estopped from**) bar or preclude by estoppel: *estopping the government from enforcing the laws disserves the public interest.* ORIGIN late Middle English (in the sense 'stop up, dam, plug'): from Old French *estopper* 'stop up, impede,' from late Latin *stuppare*, from Latin *stuppa* 'tow, oakum.'

es•top•pel /e'stäpəl/ ▶ n. the principle that precludes a person from asserting something contrary to what is implied by a previous action or statement of that person or by a previous pertinent judicial determination: *estoppel could not be invoked to prevent recoupment of an overpayment to a medical provider under Part A of Medicare.* ORIGIN mid 16th cent.: from Old French *estouppail* 'bung,' from *estopper* (see ESTOP).

Eu•ro•pe•an Com•mis•sion for Hu•man Rights /ˌyoŏrə'pēən kə 'misHən fər '(h)yoōmən 'rīts/ an institution of the Council of Europe, set up to examine complaints of alleged breaches of the European Convention on Human Rights (an international agreement set up by the Council of Europe in 1950 to protect human rights). It is based in Strasbourg, France.

Eu•ro•pe•an Court of Jus•tice /ˌyoŏrə'pēən 'kôrt əv 'jəstis/ an institution of the European Union, with thirteen judges appointed by its member governments, meeting in Luxembourg. Established in 1958, it exists to safeguard the law in the interpretation and application of Community treaties.

eu•tha•na•sia /ˌyoŏTHə'nāzHə/ ▶ n. the painless killing of a patient suffering from an incurable and painful disease or in an irreversible coma. The practice is illegal in most countries. ORIGIN early 17th cent. (in the sense 'easy death'): from Greek, from *eu* 'well' + *thanatos* 'death.'

e•vade /i'vād/ ▶ v. escape or avoid, in particular:

■ avoid giving a direct answer to (a question): *he denied evading the question.* ■ avoid dealing with or accepting; contrive not to do (something morally or legally required): *these are difficulties to be faced and not evaded.* ■ escape paying (tax or duty), esp. by illegitimate presentation of one's finances: *he allegedly evaded payment of property taxes.* ■ defeat the intention of (a law or rule), esp. while complying with its letter. DERIVATIVES **e•vad•a•ble** adj.; **e•vad•er** n. ORIGIN late 15th cent.: from French *évader*, from Latin *evadere*, from *e-* (variant of *ex-*) 'out of' + *vadere* 'go.'

e•ven date /'ɛvən 'dāt/ ▸ **phrase** (**of even date**) of the same date: *please refer to our attached report of even date.*

e•vict /i'vikt/ ▸ v. [trans.] expel (someone, usually a tenant) from a property, esp. with the support of the law: *he had court orders to evict the trespassers from three camps.*

DERIVATIVES **e•vic•tion** /i'vikSHən/ n.; **e•vic•tor** /i'viktər/ n.

ORIGIN late Middle English (in the sense 'recover property, or the title to property, by legal process'): from Latin *evict-* 'overcome, defeated,' from the verb *evincere,* from *e-* (variant of *ex-*) 'out' + *vincere* 'conquer.'

ev•i•dence /'evədəns/ ▸ n. information given personally, drawn from a document, or in the form of material objects, tending or used to establish facts in a legal investigation or as testimony in a court of law: *without evidence, they can't bring a charge.*

PHRASES **give evidence** give information formally and in person in a law court or at an inquiry. **turn state's** (or Brit. **King's** or **Queen's**) **evidence** (of a criminal) give information in court against one's partners in order to receive a less severe punishment oneself.

ORIGIN Middle English: via Old French from Latin *evidentia,* from *evident-* 'obvious to the eye or mind.'

ev•i•den•tial /ˌevi'denCHəl/ ▸ adj. another term for EVIDENTIARY.

DERIVATIVES **ev•i•den•ti•al•i•ty** /ˌeviˌdenCHē'æliṯē/ n.; **ev•i•den•tial•ly** adv.

ORIGIN early 17th cent.: from medieval Latin *evidentialis,* from Latin *evidentia* (see EVIDENCE).

ev•i•den•tia•ry /ˌevi'denCHərē/ ▸ adj. of or providing evidence: *the evidentiary value of the record.*

ex•am•i•na•tion /igˌzæmə'nāSHən/ ▸ n. the formal questioning of a witness in court: *attorneys may move about the courtroom as they like during examination of witnesses.*

ORIGIN late Middle English (also in the sense 'testing (one's conscience) by a standard'): via Old French from Latin *examinatio(n-),* from *examinare* 'weigh, test' (see EXAMINE).

ex•am•ine /ig'zæmin/ ▸ v. [trans.] formally question (a defendant or witness) in court. Compare with CROSS-EXAMINE.

DERIVATIVES **ex•am•in•a•ble** adj.; **ex•am•i•nee** /igˌzæmə'nē/ n.; **ex•am•in•er** n.

ORIGIN Middle English: from Old French *examiner,* from Latin *examinare* 'weigh, test,' from *examen.*

ex•clude /ik'sklo͞od/ ▸ v. [trans.] prevent the occurrence of; preclude: *clauses seeking to exclude liability for loss or damage.*

ORIGIN late Middle English: from Latin *excludere,* from *ex-* 'out' + *claudere* 'to shut.'

ex•clu•sion /ik'sklo͞oZHən/ ▸ n. the process or state of excluding or being excluded: *drug users are subject to exclusion from the military.*

■ an item or risk specifically not covered by an insurance policy or other contract: *exclusions can be added to your policy.*
DERIVATIVES **ex•clu•sion•ar•y** /ik'sklo͞oZHə͟,nerē/ **adj.**
ORIGIN late Middle English: from Latin *exclusio(n-)*, from *excludere* 'shut out.'

ex•cul•pate /'ekskəl,pāt/ ▶ v. [trans.] show or declare that (someone) is not guilty of wrongdoing: *he used this evidence to exculpate himself.*
DERIVATIVES **ex•cul•pa•tion** /͟ekskəl'pāSHən/ n.; **ex•cul•pa•to•ry** /iks'kəlpə͟,tôrē/ **adj.**
ORIGIN mid 17th cent.: from medieval Latin *exculpat-* 'freed from blame,' from the verb *exculpare*, from *ex-* 'out, from' + Latin *culpa* 'blame.'

ex•e•cute /'eksi,kyo͞ot/ ▶ v. [trans.] 1 carry out or put into effect (a plan, order, or course of action), in particular:
■ make (a legal instrument) valid by signing or sealing it: *the documents were executed before a notary public.* ■ carry out (a judicial sentence, the terms of a will, or other order): *police executed a search warrant.*
2 (often **be executed**) carry out a sentence of death on (a legally condemned person): *he was convicted of treason and executed.*
ORIGIN late Middle English: from Old French *executer*, from medieval Latin *executare*, from Latin *exsequi* 'follow up, carry out, punish,' from *ex-* 'out' + *sequi* 'follow.'

ex•e•cu•tion /͟eksi'kyo͞oSHən/ ▶ n. 1 the carrying out or putting into effect of a plan, order, or course of action, in particular:
■ the putting into effect of a legal instrument or order. ■ seizure of the property or person of a debtor in default of payment.
2 short for WRIT OF EXECUTION.
3 the carrying out of a sentence of death on a condemned person: *the place of execution* | *executions of convicted murderers.*

ex•e•cu•tion•er /͟eksi'kyo͞oSH(ə)nər/ ▶ n. an official who carries out a sentence of death on a legally condemned person.

ex•ec•u•tive ses•sion /ig'zekyətiv 'seSHən/ ▶ n. a private meeting of a legislative body: *the Committee met today in executive session.*

ex•ec•u•tor ▶ n. /ig'zekyətər/ a person or institution appointed by a testator to carry out the terms of their will: *the brother she appointed as executor predeceased her.*
DERIVATIVES **ex•ec•u•to•ri•al** /ig͟,zekyə'tôrēəl/ adj. (rare); **ex•ec•u•tor•ship** /ig'zikyətər͟,SHip/ n.; **ex•ec•u•to•ry** /ig'zekyə͟,tôrē/ adj.
ORIGIN Middle English: via Anglo-Norman French from Latin *execut-* 'carried out,' from *exsequi* (see EXECUTE).

ex•em•pla•ry /ig'zemplərē/ ▶ adj. (of a punishment) serving as a warning or deterrent: *exemplary sentencing may discourage the ultraviolent minority.*
■ (of damages) exceeding the amount needed for simple compensa-

tion, and intending to mark disapproval of the defendant's conduct; punitive. See also PUNITIVE DAMAGES.

DERIVATIVES **ex•em•pla•ri•ly** /igˈzemplərəlē/ adv.; **ex•em•pla•ri• ness** n.; **ex•em•plar•i•ty** /ˌegzemˈplæritē; -ˈpler-/ n.

ORIGIN late 16th cent.: from late Latin *exemplaris*, from Latin *exemplum* 'sample, imitation.'

ex•hib•it /igˈzibit/ ▶ n. a document or other object produced in a court as evidence.

ORIGIN late Middle English (in the sense 'submit for consideration,' also specifically 'present a document as evidence in court'): from Latin *exhibit-* 'held out,' from the verb *exhibere*, from *ex-* 'out' + *habere* 'hold.'

ex par•te /eks ˈpärtē/ ▶ adj. & adv. with respect to or in the interests of one side only, without notice to the other party: *the petitions included are for the ex parte order as well as the 150-day order.*

■ one-sided; partial.

PHRASES **ex parte contact** contact with a judge made by only one party to a proceeding: *a telephone call to the judge would be a prohibited ex-parte contact.*

ORIGIN late 17th cent.: Latin, literally 'from a side.'

ex•pert wit•ness /ˈekspərt ˈwitnis/ ▶ n. a person who is permitted to testify at a trial because of their special knowledge or proficiency in a particular field that is relevant to the case: *Bachman was hired as an expert witness because she had assisted in more than 100 similar surgical procedures.*

ex post fac•to /ˌeks ˌpōst ˈfæktō/ ▶ adj. & adv. with retroactive effect or force: [as adj.] *ex post facto laws.*

ORIGIN erroneous division of Latin *ex postfacto* 'in the light of subsequent events.'

ex•pro•pri•ate /eksˈprōprēˌāt/ ▶ v. [trans.] (esp. of the state) take away (property) from its owner: *they were protesting government plans to expropriate farmland.*

■ dispossess (someone) of property: *the land reform expropriated the Irish landlords.*

DERIVATIVES **ex•pro•pri•a•tion** /eksˌprōprēˈāSHən/ n.; **ex•pro•pri•a• tor** /eksˈprōprēˌātər/ n.

ORIGIN late 16th cent.: from medieval Latin *expropriat-* 'taken from the owner,' from the verb *expropriare*, from *ex-* 'out, from' + *proprium* 'property,' neuter singular of *proprius* 'own.'

ex•tin•guish /ikˈstiNGgwiSH/ ▶ v. [trans.] render (a right or obligation) void: *rights of common pasture were extinguished.*

■ (often **be extinguished**) cancel (a debt) by full payment: *the debt was absolutely extinguished.*

DERIVATIVES **ex•tin•guish•a•ble** adj.; **ex•tin•guish•ment** n.

ORIGIN mid 16th cent.: from Latin *exstinguere*, from *ex-* 'out' + *stinguere* 'quench.'

ex•tra•dit•a•ble /'ekstrə,dīṯəbəl/ ▸ **adj.** (of a crime) making a criminal liable to extradition: *possession of explosives will be an extraditable offense.*
■ (of a criminal) liable to extradition.

ex•tra•dite /'ekstrə,dīt/ ▸ **v.** [trans.] hand over (a person accused or convicted of a crime) to the jurisdiction of another state or country: *Greece refused to extradite him to Italy.*
ORIGIN mid 19th cent.: back-formation from EXTRADITION.

ex•tra•di•tion /,ekstrə'disHən/ ▸ **n.** the action of extraditing a person accused or convicted of a crime: *they fought to prevent his extradition to the US* | *extraditions of drug suspects.*
ORIGIN mid 19th cent.: from French, from *ex-* 'out, from' + *tradition* 'delivery.'

ex•tra•ju•di•cial /,ekstrəjo͞o'disHəl/ ▸ **adj.** (of a sentence) not legally authorized: *there have been reports of extrajudicial executions.*
■ (of a settlement, statement, or confession) not made in court; out-of-court: *lawyers involved must abstain from making any extrajudicial statement about the case.*
DERIVATIVES **ex•tra•ju•di•cial•ly** adv.

ex•tra•le•gal /,ekstrə'lēgəl/ ▸ **adj.** (of an action or situation) beyond the authority of the law; not regulated by the law: *the president has extensive legal and estralegal powers.*

ex•tra•ter•ri•to•ri•al /,ekstrə,terə'tôrēəl/ ▸ **adj.** (of a law or decree) valid outside a country's territory.
■ denoting the freedom of an ambassador or other embassy staff from the jurisdiction of the territory of residence: *foreign embassies have extraterritorial rights.* ■ situated outside a country's territory: *extraterritorial industrial zones.*
DERIVATIVES **ex•tra•ter•ri•to•ri•al•i•ty** /,ekstrə,terə,tôrē'ælite/ n.
ORIGIN mid 19th cent.: from Latin *extra territorium* 'outside the territory' + *-al.*

eye•wit•ness /'ī'witnəs/ ▸ **n.** [often as adj.] a person who has personally seen something happen and so can give a firsthand description of it: *eyewitness accounts of the robbery.*

F

fact /fækt/ ▶ n. the truth about events as opposed to interpretation: *there was a question of fact as to whether they had received the letter.*

PHRASES **before** (or **after**) **the fact** before (or after) the committing of a crime: *an accessory before the fact.*

ORIGIN late 15th cent.: from Latin *factum,* neuter past participle of *facere* 'do.' The original sense was 'an act or feat,' later 'bad deed, a crime,' surviving in the phrase *before (or after) the fact.* The earliest of the current senses ('truth, reality') dates from the late 16th cent.

fair use /'fer 'yo͞os/ ▶ n. the doctrine that, under certain conditions, copyright material may be quoted verbatim without need for permission from or payment to the copyright holder: *the court is trying to address whether parody can constitute fair use.*

fault /fôlt/ ▶ n. responsibility for an accident or misfortune: *it was his fault she had died.*
■ responsibility for an act or omission, usually intentional and leading to liability. Compare with **NEGLIGENCE**.

PHRASES **at fault** responsible for an undesirable situation or event; in the wrong, sometimes legally liable: *we recover compensation from the person at fault.*

ORIGIN Middle English *faut(e)* 'lack, failing,' from Old French, based on Latin *fallere* 'deceive.' The -*l*- was added (in French and English) in the 15th cent. to conform with the Latin word, but did not become standard in English until the 17th cent., remaining silent in pronunciation until well into the 18th.

fee /fē/ ▶ n. **1** a payment made to a professional person or to a professional or public body in exchange for advice or services: *all land transfers require the payment of a recording fee.*
2 an inheritable estate of land, either absolute (see **FEE SIMPLE**) or conditional.
■ historical an estate held on condition of feudal service.
▶v. (**fees, fee'd** or **feed, fee•ing**) [trans.] rare make a payment to (someone) in return for services.

PHRASES **hold something in fee** hold an estate in land, especially absolutely.■ historical hold an estate in return for feudal service to a superior.

ORIGIN Middle English: from an Anglo-Norman French variant of Old French *feu, fief,* from medieval Latin *feodum, feudum,* ultimately of Germanic origin.

fee sim•ple /'fē 'simpəl/ ▶ n. (pl. **fees sim•ple**) a permanent and absolute tenure of an estate in land with freedom to dispose of it at will, esp. (in full **fee simple absolute**) a freehold tenure, which is the main type of land ownership.

fee tail /'fē 'tāl/ ▶ n. (pl. **fees tail**) historical a former type of tenure of an estate in land with restrictions or entailment regarding the line of heirs to whom it may be willed.

ORIGIN late Middle English: from Anglo-Norman French *fee tailé.*

fel•on /'felən/ ▶ n. a person who has been convicted of a felony: *fugitive felons.*

▶ **adj.** [attrib.] archaic cruel; wicked: *the felon undermining hand of dark corruption.*

ORIGIN Middle English: from Old French, literally 'wicked, a wicked person' (oblique case of *fel* 'evil'), from medieval Latin *fello, fellon-,* of unknown origin.

fe•lo•ni•ous /fə'lōnēəs/ ▶ **adj.** of, relating to, or involved in a felony or felonies: *they turned their felonious talents to the smuggling trade.*

■ relating to or of the nature of felony: *his conduct was felonious.*

DERIVATIVES **fe•lo•ni•ous•ly** adv.

fel•o•ny /'felənē/ ▶ n. (pl. **fel•o•nies**) a crime, often one involving violence, regarded as more serious than a misdemeanor, and usually punishable by imprisonment for more than one year or by death: *he pleaded guilty to six felonies | an accusation of felony.*

The distinction between felonies and misdemeanors usually depends on the penalties or consequences attaching to the crime, felonies typically involving prison sentences of at least one year. In English common law, felony originally comprised those offenses (murder, wounding, arson, rape, and robbery) for which the penalty included forfeiture of land and goods.

ORIGIN Middle English: from Old French *felonie,* from *felon* (see **FELON**).

feme cov•ert /'fem 'kəvərt; 'fēm/ ▶ n. historical a married woman.

ORIGIN early 16th cent.: from Anglo-Norman French, literally 'a woman covered (i.e., protected by marriage).'

feme sole /'fem 'sōl; 'fēm/ ▶ n. historical a woman without a husband, esp. one who is divorced.

ORIGIN early 16th cent.: from Anglo-Norman French *feme soule* 'a woman alone.'

fi•du•ci•ar•y /fə'dooSHē,erē; -SHərē/ ▶ **adj.** involving trust, esp. with regard to the relationship between a trustee and a beneficiary: *the company has a fiduciary duty to shareholders.*

■ archaic held or given in trust: *fiduciary estates.*

▶**n.** (pl. **fi•du•ci•ar•ies**) a trustee.

ORIGIN late 16th cent. (in the sense 'something inspiring trust; credentials'): from Latin *fiduciarius*, from *fiducia* 'trust,' from *fidere* 'to trust.'

fi•e•ri fa•ci•as /ˌfīərē ˈfāSH(ē)əs/ ▶ **n.** a writ commanding a sheriff to seize and sell a debtor's goods in executing a judgment.

ORIGIN late Middle English: Latin, 'you shall make happen.'

Fifth /fi(f)TH/ ▶ **n.** (**the Fifth**) the Fifth Amendment to the US Constitution, used in particular reference to the amendment's provision that no person "shall be compelled in any criminal case to be a witness against himself."

PHRASES **take** (or **plead**) **the Fifth** exercise the right guaranteed by the Fifth Amendment of refusing to answer questions in order to avoid incriminating oneself.

fight•ing words /ˈfītiNG ˈwərdz/ ▶ **plural n.** informal words, such as those expressing an insult, esp. of an ethnic, racial, or sexist nature, which are considered likely to provoke a violent response: *Mr. Posson allegedly shouted fighting words at the others in the group.*

file /fīl/ ▶ **v.** [trans.] submit (a legal document, application, or charge) to be placed on record by the appropriate authority: *criminal charges were **filed against** the firm* | [intrans.] *the company had **filed for** bankruptcy.*

ORIGIN late Middle English (as a verb meaning 'string documents on a thread or wire to keep them in order'): from French *filer* 'to string,' *fil* 'a thread,' both from Latin *filum* 'a thread.'

find /fīnd/ ▶ **v.** (past and past part. **found** /fownd/) [trans.] (often **be found**) (of a court) officially declare to be the case: *he was found guilty of speeding* | [with clause] *the court found that a police lab expert had fabricated evidence.*

PHRASES **find in favor of** see **find for** below.

▶**find against** (of a court) make a decision against or judge to be guilty: *the panel found against the United States on three of the five principal claims.*

find for (or **find in favor of**) (of a court) make a decision in favor of or judge to be innocent: *a jury found for the plaintiff.*

ORIGIN Old English *findan*, of Germanic origin; related to Dutch *vinden* and German *finden*.

fine /fīn/ ▶ **n.** a sum of money exacted as a penalty by a court of law or other authority: *a parking fine.*

▶**v.** [trans.] (often **be fined**) punish (someone) by making them pay a sum of money, typically as a penalty for breaking the law: *he was fined $600 and sentenced to one day in jail.*

DERIVATIVES **fine•a•ble** /ˈfīnəbəl/ **adj.**

ORIGIN Middle English: from Old French *fin* 'end, payment,' from Latin *finis* 'end' (in medieval Latin denoting a sum paid on settling a lawsuit). The original sense was 'conclusion'; also used in the medieval

Latin sense, the word came to denote a penalty of any kind, later specifically a monetary penalty.

fine print /'fīn 'print/ ▶ **n.** inconspicuous details or conditions printed in an agreement or contract, esp. ones that may prove unfavorable: *read the fine print of whatever loan document is shoved under your nose.*

first-de•gree /'fərst də'grē/ ▶ **adj.** [attrib.] denoting the most serious category of a crime, esp. murder.

first of•fend•er /'fərst ə'fendər/ ▶ **n.** a person who is convicted of a criminal offense for the first time: *a first offender prostitution program.*

fix•tures /'fiksCHərz/ ▶ **plural n.** articles attached to a house or land and considered legally part of it so that they normally remain in place when an owner moves: *the hotel retains many original fixtures.*
ORIGIN late 16th cent. (in the sense 'fixing, becoming fixed'): alteration (first found in Shakespeare) of obsolete *fixure* (from late Latin *fixura*, from Latin *figere* 'to fix'), with *t* inserted on the pattern of *mixture.*

force ma•jeure /ˌfôrs mä'zHər/ ▶ **n.** unforeseeable circumstances that prevent someone from fulfilling a contract: *the company may suspend bargaining agreements if required by force majeure or economic conditions.*
PHRASES **force majeure clause** a contract provision excusing performance in the event of unforeseeable circumstances.
ORIGIN late 19th cent.: French, literally 'superior strength.'

fore•close /fôr'klōz/ ▶ **v.** [intrans.] take possession of a mortgaged property as a result of someone's failure to keep up their mortgage payments: *the bank was threatening to **foreclose** on his mortgage.*
■ [trans.] take away someone's power of redeeming (a mortgage) and take possession of the mortgaged property.
ORIGIN Middle English: from Old French *forclos*, past participle of *forclore*, from *for-* 'out' (from Latin *foras* 'outside') + *clore* 'to close.' The original sense was 'bar from escaping,' in late Middle English 'shut out,' and 'bar from doing something', hence specifically 'bar someone from redeeming a mortgage' (early 18th cent.).

fore•clo•sure /fôr'klōzHər/ ▶ **n.** the process of taking possession of a mortgaged property as a result of someone's failure to keep up mortgage payments.

fore•man /'fôrmən/ ▶ **n.** (pl. **fore•men**) (in a court of law) a person, esp. a man, who presides over a jury and speaks on its behalf.

fo•ren•sic /fə'renzik; -sik/ ▶ **adj.** of, relating to, or denoting the application of scientific methods and techniques to the investigation of crime: *forensic evidence.*
■ of or relating to courts of law.
▶ **n.** (**forensics**) scientific tests or techniques used in connection with the detection of crime.
■ (also **forensic**) [treated as sing. or pl.] informal a laboratory or department responsible for such tests.
DERIVATIVES **fo•ren•si•cal•ly** /fə'renziklē; -sik-/ **adv.**

ORIGIN mid 17th cent.: from Latin *forensis* 'in open court, public,' from *forum* (see **FORUM**).

fo•ren•sic med•i•cine /fə'renzik 'medisən; fə'rensik/ ▸ n. the application of medical knowledge to the investigation of crime, particularly in establishing the causes of injury or death.

fore•per•son /'fôr,pərsən/ ▸ n. (in a court of law) a person who presides over a jury and speaks on its behalf (used as a neutral alternative to **FOREMAN**).

for•feit /'fôrfit/ ▸ v. (**for•feit•ed, for•feit•ing**) [trans.] lose or be deprived of (property or a right or privilege) as a penalty for wrongdoing: *those unable to meet their taxes were liable to forfeit their property.*
■ (of a court or other authority) cause or order (property, a right, etc,) to be lost or surrendered.
▸ n. a fine or penalty for wrongdoing or for a breach of the rules in a club or game.
■ an item of property or a right or privilege lost as a legal penalty.
▸ adj. [predic.] lost or surrendered as a penalty for wrongdoing or neglect: *the lands which he had acquired were automatically forfeit.*
DERIVATIVES **for•feit•a•ble** adj.; **for•feit•er** /'fôrfitər/ n.; **for•fei•ture** /'fôrfəCHər/ n.
ORIGIN Middle English (originally denoting a crime or transgression, hence a fine or penalty for this): from Old French *forfet, forfait*, past participle of *forfaire* 'transgress,' from *for-* 'out' (from Latin *foris* 'outside') + *faire* 'do' (from Latin *facere*).

forge /fôrj/ ▸ v. [trans.] produce a copy or imitation of (a document, signature, banknote, or work or art) for the purpose of deception: *Walton admitted that he had forged the initials on the painting.*
DERIVATIVES **forge•a•ble** adj.; **forg•er** n.
ORIGIN Middle English (also in the general sense 'make, construct'): from Old French *forger*, from Latin *fabricare* 'fabricate,' from *fabrica* 'manufactured object, workshop.' The noun is via Old French from Latin *fabrica*.

for•ger•y /'fôrjərē/ ▸ n. (pl. **for•ger•ies**) the action of forging or producing a copy of a document, signature, banknote, or work of art.
■ a forged or copied document, signature, banknote, or work of art.

fo•rum /'fôrəm/ ▸ n. (pl. **fo•rums**) a court or tribunal.
ORIGIN from Latin, literally 'what is out of doors,' originally denoting an enclosure surrounding a house; related to *fores* '(outside) door.'

fran•chise /'fræn,CHīz/ ▸ n. **1** an authorization granted by a government or company to an individual or group enabling them to carry out specified commercial activities, e.g., providing a broadcasting service or acting as an agent for a company's products: *the use of franchises to sell foreign goods and supplies has been growing rapidly.*
■ a business or service given such authorization to operate.
2 (usu. **the franchise**) the right to vote.
■ the rights of citizenship.

▶**v.** [trans.] grant a franchise to (an individual or group): *the state franchises the various power companies to operate in different areas.*
■ grant a franchise for the sale of (goods) or the operation of (a service): *all the catering was **franchised** out.*
DERIVATIVES **fran•chi•see** /ˌfrænCHīˈzē/ **n.**; **fran•chis•er** (also **fran•chi•sor** /ˌfrænCHəˈzôr/) **n.**
ORIGIN Middle English (denoting a grant of legal immunity): from Old French, based on *franc, franche* 'free.' Sense 2 dates from the late 18th cent. and sense 1 from the 20th cent.

fraud /frôd/ ▶ **n.** wrongful or criminal deception intended to result in unjust advantage, especially financial or personal gain: *he was convicted of fraud* | *prosecutions for social security frauds.*
■ a person or thing intended to deceive others, typically by unjustifiably claiming or being credited with accomplishments or qualities: *mediums exposed as tricksters and frauds.*
ORIGIN Middle English: from Old French *fraude*, from Latin *fraus, fraud-* 'deceit, injury.'

fraud•u•lent /ˈfrôjələnt/ ▶ **adj.** obtained, done by, or involving deception, esp. criminal deception: *the fraudulent copying of American software.*
■ unjustifiably claiming or being credited with particular accomplishments or qualities: *he unmasked fraudulent psychics.*
DERIVATIVES **fraud•u•lence n.; fraud•u•lent•ly adv.**
ORIGIN late Middle English: from Old French, or from Latin *fraudulentus*, from *fraus, fraud-* 'deceit, injury.'

free•hold /ˈfrēˌhōld/ ▶ **n.** permanent and absolute tenure of land or property with freedom to dispose of it at will. Often contrasted with LEASEHOLD.
■ (**the freehold**) the ownership of a piece of land or property by such tenure. ■ a piece of land or property held by such tenure.
▶**adj.** held by or having the status of freehold: *a freehold interest in a property.*
DERIVATIVES **free•hold•er n.**

friend of the court /ˈfrend əv T͟Hə ˈkôrt/ ▶ **n.** See AMICUS.

fun•gi•ble /ˈfənjəbəl/ ▶ **adj.** (of goods contracted for without an individual specimen being specified) able to replace or be replaced by another identical item; mutually interchangeable: *money is fungible—money that is raised for one purpose can easily be used for another.*
DERIVATIVES **fun•gi•bil•i•ty** /ˌfənjəˈbilətē/ **n.**
ORIGIN late 17th cent.: from medieval Latin *fungibilis*, from *fungi* 'perform, enjoy,' with the same sense as *fungi vice* 'serve in place of.'

THE COMMON LAW AND THE CIVIL LAW: TWO APPROACHES TO JUSTICE

Origins

Like the world's languages, the world's legal systems can be divided into families linked by common origins. The two most widespread families of law originated in England and western Europe.

The English legal system emerged after the Norman Conquest of 1066. The former patchwork of Anglo-Saxon law was gradually replaced by royal judges who dispensed justice throughout the countryside, applying the same general principles everywhere. The result was a shared body of law—the *common law* of the realm. England's language and legal system spread to its colonial empire, including most of Canada and what was to become the United States.

The other leading legal system in the world today comes from across the English Channel. It is modeled upon the law of ancient Rome, which was revived by Italian scholars in the 11th century and then spread to the rest of continental Europe. In English it is called the *civil law*, from Latin *jus civile*, meaning 'the law of the state'.

The heart of most civil law systems is a civil code—a unified, organized, comprehensive code of law that encompasses contract, tort, property, family, and inheritance law. The most influential modern civil code was prepared in France at the direction of Napoleon Bonaparte at the beginning of the 19th century. Its elegance and simplicity found favor in many other countries, and even in Louisiana (originally colonized by the French)—the only U.S. state with a legal system grounded in civil law. Subsequent codes, notably in Germany, were also influential, and ultimately the European model was followed—to a greater or lesser extent by most other countries in the world apart from those once controlled by Britain or the U.S., making it by a large margin the world's predominant legal system. During the mid-19th century, a movement arose to incorporate civil law principles into American law. Several states adopted civil codes, but America's common law tradition proved too strong and the movement died out.

Approaching the same goal from opposite directions
Although every nation's law is unique, certain characteristic philosophies and features distinguish common law from civil law. The central figure in the common law tradition is the judge. Most of the common law was not enacted; it *evolved* through case-by-case decision-making over the centuries. The "rules" of law—what a contract is, when one party to an accident is liable for another's injury, what constitutes larceny—are generalizations derived from countless specific cases. Until modern times, statutes were viewed as supplemental. Since there is no comprehensive written code, adherence to judicial precedent is crucial; otherwise there would be no consistency to the law. At the same time, judges must expand, and even at times overrule, earlier cases so that the law can keep up as social conditions change. Judgeship is a prestigious and often highly political position; judges are either elected or politically appointed. Because every nonroutine decision "makes law," judges write elaborate opinions showing how their decisions follow from earlier cases, some of which go back centuries.

In the civil law tradition, the source of the law is not cases but codes. Codes derived from those of Napoleon are worded briefly and simply; Napoleon was codifying the egalitarian ideals of the French Revolution and believed that the law should be accessible to all. The job of the civil law judge is to apply the code to the facts. In contrast to the *inductive* logic of the common law (general principles derived from individual decisions), the civil law is *deductive* (individual decisions derived from general principles). Judgeship is an important but basically administrative position; judges are highly trained civil service employees selected and promoted for their skill and objectivity and not for their ideology or popularity. Since judges are applying codified legal rules to particular facts, decisions by other judges in cases with different facts are irrelevant. Judicial opinions are perfunctory and cite little precedent.

Yet both systems reach the same general results. They enforce contracts, compensate injured parties, punish criminals. And despite their theoretical differences, in practice the requirements of modern life have driven the two systems closer together. Common law countries make extensive use of statutes; in the United States, major areas of the law have been organized into comprehensive codes such as the Uniform Commercial Code and the state penal codes. In civil law countries, the generally worded codes have been supplemented by narrower statutes and judges have developed a body of precedents interpreting the codes.

The real differences

There are some differences in substantive law between civil and common law systems, but for the most part they are minor. For example, property law is simpler in the civil law, which is not burdened by convoluted principles of common law passed down from feudal times. The sometimes bizarre concept of a trust (see *Understanding Wills, Trusts, and Intestate Succession,* p. 197) is unknown in the civil law, but the purposes served by trusts are accomplished through other means. Conversely, the civil law concept of *community property* (in which each spouse's earnings during marriage belong equally to both) is foreign to the common law—although that principle was inherited from Spanish law by territories in the American Southwest and ultimately adopted in nine states.

The truly significant legal differences between the United States and continental Europe lie in the realm of trial procedure. The protracted drama, the elaborate fencing, the great winner-take-all game that is American litigation does not exist on the continent. Noncriminal cases are usually dealt with in a series of meetings over a period of time, during which relevant information is collected, analyzed, and followed up on. Whereas American lawyers have total control over what evidence is offered in a trial, in Europe the panel of judges (sometimes including some lay judges) exercises a high degree of control. Witnesses are usually not prepared by the lawyers; they simply tell their stories in their own words and without interruption. Judges prompt them with questions as needed, and at the end the lawyers may pose additional questions in case anything was left out. Because there is usually no lay jury to be confused by extraneous information, there are virtually no rules of evidence; there are no objections; the panel considers whatever the witness has to say. The object is not to decide which side's story is more plausible, but to find out the actual truth—even if it is not quite what either party contends. In some systems the public prosecutor may even appear in a private case to make sure that facts affecting the public interest are not concealed or overlooked. If an expert witness would be helpful, instead of hosting an inconclusive shootout between opposing experts paid to support one side or the other, the court retains a neutral expert acceptable to both sides.

Criminal cases are exhaustively investigated before prosecution begins. Defendants do not have all the constitutional protections they have in the United States, but they have other protections, which on balance are regarded by advocates of the system as producing a more reliable result. For example, unlike American defendants, defendants in Europe typically have full access to the evidence against them in advance. The judge is less a neutral referee and more an active participant in the trial, and the prosecutor's job is not simply to fight for one side, taking advantage of any oversight by the opposing attorney, but rather to help the court in finding the truth, wherever it may lie. In some countries, the victims of a crime may claim damages in the criminal case instead of having to file a separate action. And sometimes a victim may even institute a criminal case personally if the public prosecutor fails to do so.

G

gar•nish /ˈgärnisʜ/ ▸ v. [trans.] serve notice of garnishment.
  ■ seize (money, esp. part of a person's salary) to settle a debt or claim: *the IRS garnished his earnings.*
  ORIGIN Middle English (in the sense 'equip, arm'): from Old French *garnir*, probably of Germanic origin and related to *warn.*
gar•nish•ee /ˌgärniˈsʜē/ ▸ n. a third party who is served notice by a court to surrender money in settlement of a debt or claim: [as adj.] *a garnishee order.*
▸ v. (**gar•nish•ees, gar•nish•eed**) another term for GARNISH.
  gar•nish•ment /ˈgärnisʜmənt/ ▸ n. a court order directing that money or property of a third party (usually wages paid by an employer), be seized to satisfy a debt owed by a debtor to a plaintiff creditor.
GBH ▸ abbr. grievous bodily harm.
gen•er•al jur•is•dic•tion /ˈjen(ə)rəl ˌjo͝orisˈdiksʜən/ ▸ n. the authority of a court to hear civil or criminal cases within its geographic area: *Alabama's trial courts of general jurisdiction are the circuit courts.*
  ■ the authority of a court to hear a defendant's claims within the geographic area in which the defendant resides, when there is no connection between this area and the claims.
goods and chat•tels /ˈgo͝odz ən(d) ˈcʜætlz/ ▸ plural n. all kinds of personal possessions.
grace /grās/ ▸ n. (also **grace period**) a period officially allowed for payment of a sum due or for compliance with a law or condition, esp. an extended period granted as a special favor: *another three days' grace.*
  ORIGIN Middle English: via Old French from Latin *gratia*, from *gratus* 'pleasing, thankful'; related to *grateful.*
grand /grænd/ ▸ adj. (of a crime) involving money or items with a value over a statutorily defined amount; serious: *grand theft.* Compare with PETTY.
  ORIGIN Middle English: from Old French *grant*, *grand*, from Latin *grandis* 'full-grown, big, great.' The original uses were to denote family relationships and as a title (*the Grand*, translating Old French *le Grand*); hence the senses 'of the highest rank,' 'of great importance.'
grand•fa•ther clause /ˈgræn(d)ˌfäтʜər ˌklôz/ ▸ n. informal a clause exempting certain classes of people or things from the requirements of

a piece of legislation affecting their previous rights, privileges, or practices.

ORIGIN early 20th cent.: so called because under constitutional clauses in some southern states, permitting whites to vote and disenfranchising blacks, the descendants of those voting before 1867 were permitted to vote without having to meet certain stringent conditions.

grand ju•ry /ˈgrænd ˈjʊ͝orē/ ▶ n. a jury, typically of twenty-three jurors, selected to examine whether the evidence supporting a criminal accusation is sufficient for an indictment and trial by (petty) jury: *the grand jury returned a 21-count indictment.*

grand lar•ce•ny /ˈgrænd ˈlärsənē/ ▶ n. (in many US states and formerly in Britain) theft of personal property having a value above a legally specified amount.

grant /grænt/ ▶ v. [trans., with two objs.] give (a right, power, property, etc.) formally or legally to: *the amendment that granted women the right to vote.*

▶ n. a legal conveyance or formal conferment: *a grant of land* | *a grant of probate.*

DERIVATIVES **grant•a•ble adj.; grant•er n.**

ORIGIN Middle English: from Old French *granter* 'consent to support,' variant of *creanter* 'to guarantee,' based on Latin *credere* 'entrust.'

gran•tee /grænˈtē/ ▶ n. a person or institution to whom a grant or conveyance is made.

gran•tor /grænˈtôr; ˈgræntər/ ▶ n. a person or institution that makes a grant or conveyance.

gra•va•men /grəˈvāmən/ ▶ n. (pl. **gra•va•mi•na** /grəˈvæmənə/) the essence or most serious part of a complaint or accusation: *the gravamen of a conspiracy charge is the agreement to commit an illegal act.*

■ a grievance.

ORIGIN early 17th cent. (as an ecclesiastical term denoting formal presentation of a grievance): from late Latin, literally 'physical inconvenience,' from Latin *gravare* 'to load,' from *gravis* 'heavy.'

griev•ous bod•i•ly harm /ˈgrēvəs ˈbädəlē ˈhärm/ (abbr.: **GBH**) ▶ n. serious physical injury inflicted on a person by the deliberate action of another.

guar•an•tee /ˌgerənˈtē/ ▶ n. a formal promise or assurance (typically in writing) that certain conditions will be fulfilled, esp. that a product will be repaired or replaced if not of a specified quality and durability: *we offer a 10-year guarantee against rusting.*

■ variant spelling of GUARANTY. ■ less common term for GUARANTOR.

▶v. (**guar•an•tees, guar•an•teed, guar•an•tee•ing**) [intrans.] provide a formal assurance or promise, esp. that certain conditions shall be fulfilled relating to a product, service, or transaction.

■ [trans.] provide such an assurance regarding (something, esp. a product): *the repairs will be guaranteed for three years* | [as adj.] (**guaran-**

teed) *the guaranteed bonus is not very high.* ■ [trans.] provide financial security for; underwrite: *a demand that $100,000 be deposited to guarantee their costs.*
ORIGIN late 17th cent. (in the sense 'guarantor'): perhaps from Spanish *garante*, corresponding to French *garant* (see WARRANT), later influenced by French *garantie* 'guaranty.'

USAGE: **Guarantee** and **guaranty** are interchangeable for both noun and verb, although the latter is now rare as a verb. **Warranty** is widely used in their place.

guar•an•tor /ˌgerənˈtôr; ˈgerəntər/ ▶ n. a person or organization that provides a guaranty.
guar•an•ty /ˈgerənˌtē/ (also **guar•an•tee**) ▶ n. (pl. **guar•an•ties**) a formal pledge to pay another person's debt or to perform another person's obligation in the case of default.
■ a thing serving as security for a such a pledge.
ORIGIN early 16th cent.: from Old French *garantie*, from *garantir*; related to WARRANT.
guard•i•an /ˈgärdēən/ ▶ n. a person who looks after and is legally responsible for someone who is unable to manage their own affairs, esp. an incompetent or disabled person or a child whose parents have died.
DERIVATIVES **guard•i•an•ship** /ˈgärdē,ən,SHip/ n.
ORIGIN late Middle English: from Old French *garden*, of Germanic origin; compare with WARD. The ending was altered by association with *-ian.*
guilt•y /ˈgiltē/ ▶ adj. (**guilt•i•er, guilt•i•est**) culpable of or responsible for a specified wrongdoing: *the police will soon discover who the guilty party is* | *he was found guilty of manslaughter* | *he found them guilty on a lesser charge.* See also FIND, PLEAD.
DERIVATIVES **guilt•i•ness** n.

H

ha•be•as cor•pus /ˈhābēəs ˈkôrpəs/ ▶ n. a writ requiring a person under custody to be brought before a judge or into court, esp. to secure the person's release unless lawful grounds are shown for their detention. ■ the legal right to apply for such a writ.

ORIGIN late Middle English: Latin, literally 'you shall have the body (in court).'

ha•ben•dum /həˈbendəm/ ▶ n. the part of a deed or conveyance that states the estate or quantity of interest to be granted: [as adj.] *a habendum clause.*

ORIGIN early 17th cent.: Latin, literally '(that is) to be had'.

half•way house /ˈhæf,wā ˌhows/ ▶ n. a center for helping former drug addicts, prisoners, psychiatric patients, or others to adjust to life in general society.

head•note /ˈhed,nōt/ ▶ n. a summary of a decided case prefixed to the case report, setting out the principles behind the decision and an outline of the facts.

hear /hir/ ▶ v. (past and past part. **heard** /hərd/) [trans.] listen to and judge (a case, appeal, etc.): *an all-woman jury heard the case.*

ORIGIN Old English *hīeran*, *hēran*, of Germanic origin; related to Dutch *hooren* and German *hören*.

hear•ing /ˈhiriNG/ ▶ n. an act of listening to evidence or arguments in a court of law or before an official, esp. a trial before a judge without a jury.

hear•say /ˈhir,sā/ ▶ n. the report of another person's words by a witness, usually disallowed as evidence in a court of law: *everything they had told him would have been ruled out as hearsay* | [as adj.] *hearsay evidence.*

heir /er/ ▶ n. a person legally entitled to the property or rank of another on that person's death: *his eldest son and heir* | *she aspired to marry the heir to the throne.*

DERIVATIVES **heir•dom** /ˈerdəm/ n.; **heir•less** adj.; **heir•ship** /ˈer,SHip/ n.

ORIGIN Middle English: via Old French from Latin *heres*.

heir•ess /ˈeris/ ▶ n. a female heir, esp. to vast wealth: *the heiress to the Postum Cereal Company.*

her•e•dit•a•ment /ˌherə'ditəmənt/ ▶ n. dated any item of inheritable property, either a **corporeal hereditament** (such as land or a building) or an **incorporeal hereditament** (such as a rent or a right of way).
■ an item of inheritance.
ORIGIN late Middle English: from medieval Latin *hereditamentum*, from ecclesiastical Latin *hereditare* 'inherit,' from Latin *heres, hered-* 'heir.'

here•in•af•ter /ˌhirin'æftər/ ▶ adv. formal further on in this document: *the Cincinnati Gas & Electric Company (hereinafter CG&E).*

here•in•be•fore /ˌhirinbə'fôr/ ▶ adv. formal before this point in this document: *defendant denies each and every allegation of the petition not hereinbefore specifically admitted.*

her•it•a•ble /'heritəbəl/ ▶ adj. (of property) capable of being inherited.
DERIVATIVES **her•it•a•bil•i•ty** /ˌheritə'bilitē/ n.; **her•it•a•bly** /'heritəblē/ adv.
ORIGIN late Middle English: from Old French *heriter* 'inherit,' from ecclesiastical Latin *hereditare*, from Latin *heres, hered-* 'heir.'

high court /'hī 'kôrt/ ▶ n. the court of final appeal in a state or national judicial system.
■ the US Supreme Court. ■ (in the US) the supreme court in a state.
■ a higher court, such as an appeals court in relation to a trial court.
■ (in full **High Court of Justice**) (in England and Wales) the court of unlimited civil jurisdiction forming part of the Supreme Court and comprising three divisions: Queen's Bench, Chancery, and the Family Division.

high•er court /'hīər 'kôrt/ ▶ n. a court that can overrule the decision of another.

high seas /'hī 'sēz/ ▶ plural n. (**the high seas**) the open ocean, esp. that not within any country's territorial jurisdiction but governed by maritime law: *they commited the crime of piracy on the high seas.*

hold /hōld/ ▶ v. (past and past part. **held** /held/) 1 [trans.] keep or detain (someone): *the police were holding him on a murder charge* | *she was held prisoner for two days.*
2 [trans.] have in one's possession: *the managing director still holds fifty shares in the company.*
■ [intrans.] informal be in possession of illegal drugs: *he was holding, and the police hauled him off to jail.* ■ [with clause] (of a judge or court) rule; decide: *the Court of Appeals held that there was no evidence to support the judge's assessment.*
PHRASES **hold someone/something harmless** indemnify.
ORIGIN Old English *haldan, healdan*, of Germanic origin; related to Dutch *houden* and German *halten*; the noun is partly from Old Norse *hald* 'hold, support, custody.'

home•stead /'hōmˌsted/ ▶ n. **1** a person's or family's residence, which comprises the land, house, and outbuildings, and in most states is exempt from forced sale for collection of debt.

2 historical (as provided by the federal Homestead Act of 1862) an area of public land in the West (usually 160 acres) granted to any US citizen willing to settle on and farm the land for at least five years.
DERIVATIVES **home•stead•er** n.
ORIGIN Old English *hāmstede* 'a settlement.'

hom•i•cide /'hämə‚sīd; 'hōmə-/ ▶ n. the killing of one person by another: *he was charged with homicide* | *two thirds of homicides in the county were drug-related.* Compare with MANSLAUGHTER, MURDER.
■ **(Hom•i•cide)** the police department that deals with such crimes: *a detective from Homicide.* ■ dated a murderer.
ORIGIN Middle English: from Old French, from Latin *homicidium*, from *homo, homin-* 'man.'

hon•or /'änər/ (Brit. **honour**) ▶ n. **(His, Your,** etc., **Honor)** a title of respect given to or used in addressing a judge or a mayor.
ORIGIN Middle English: from Old French *onor* (noun), *onorer* (verb), from Latin *honor.*

horn•book /'hôrn‚bŏŏk/ ▶ n. historical a one-volume treatise summarizing the law in a specific field: [as adj.] *the hornbook explanation of the rule of reason is that it calls for balancing of pro- and anticompetitive effects.*

hos•tile wit•ness /'hästl ‚witnis; 'hästīl/ ▶ n. a witness who is antagonistic to the party calling them, and who may, if the judge permits, be cross-examined by that party.

house•break•ing /'hows‚brākiNG/ ▶ n. the action of breaking into a building, esp. in daytime, to commit a felony.
DERIVATIVES **house•break•er** /'hows‚brākər/ n.

hy•poth•e•cate /hə'päTHi‚kāt; hī-/ ▶ v. [trans.] pledge (money) by law to a specific purpose: *No beneficiary shall have any right to alienate, encumber, or hypothecate his or her interest in the principal.*
■ pledge (property) as security without handing over possession; mortgage: *you need the landlord's permission to hypothecate the property to guarantee a loan.*
DERIVATIVES **hy•poth•e•ca•tion** /hə‚päTHi'kāSHən; hī-/ n.
ORIGIN early 17th cent.: from medieval Latin *hypothecat-* 'given as a pledge,' from the verb *hypothecare*, based on Greek *hypothēkē.*

MAKING A
LIVING WILL

According to surveys, most people do not want their life prolonged through extreme or invasive measures, and by common law tradition, most people have the right to refuse unwanted medical procedures. As the great American judge Benjamin Cardozo wrote in 1914, "Every human being of adult years and sound mind has a right to determine what shall be done with his own body."

But in many cases, by the time this issue arises, the underlying medical condition has rendered the patient mentally incompetent or unable to communicate. This problem gave rise to the idea of a *living will*. A regular will concerns the treatment of your property after your death; a living will concerns the treatment of *you* while you are alive. It states your wishes with respect to medical care in the event of terminal illness or irreversible coma. Although living wills initially had no special legal status, they could help doctors and relatives in deciding whether to start and when to terminate life-support measures.

Starting with California in 1976, states adopted statutes recognizing living wills, sometimes under other names such as *advance medical directive* or *declaration of a desire for a natural death*. At about the same time, the concept of a *durable power of attorney* was gaining ground (see *What Is a Power of Attorney?*, p. 108), and it became clear that, just as it is useful to have a trusted representative making financial decisions for us when we can no longer handle our own affairs, we should be allowed to designate someone to speak for us in medical matters when we cannot speak for ourselves. Thus was born the concept of a *durable power of attorney for health care*, also referred to as *heath care proxy* or *medical power of attorney*. The person empowered by that document to make medical decisions for the principal is identified by a variety of names, including *attorney-in-fact*, *health care agent*, and *health care proxy*. Living wills and medical powers of attorney are collectively referred to as *advance directives*.

The movement for advance directives took on added urgency in 1990, when the U.S. Supreme Court issued its ruling in the case of Missouri resident Nancy Cruzan. Cruzan was a young woman who had been lying in a persistent vegetative state ever since an automobile accident seven and a half years earlier, kept alive by nutrients and fluids passed into her stomach through a tube (so-called *artificial nutrition and hydration*). Cruzan's parents—agreed by all to be caring parents—asked to have the tube removed. By a vote of five to four, the Supreme Court held that the state of Missouri was within its rights to refuse the request. The state could disregard the parents' views of what Cruzan would want and require "clear and convincing evidence" of Cruzan's own views. A housemate had testified to conversations in which Cruzan said she would not want to be kept alive as a "vegetable," but since there was no testimony that Cruzan had referred to artificial nutrition and hydration, the Missouri Supreme court did not see this as "clear and convincing."

A formally executed advance directive provides the best chance of having one's wishes respected. All states now have statutes specifically authorizing advance directives. Each state has its own forms of directives, its own requirements for executing directives, its own rules as to what medical steps may or may not be governed by a living will, and what medical decisions may or may not be made by a health care agent—and the laws are still evolving. A lawyer knowledgeable about estate planning or elder law can be helpful, but you can make advance directives on your own:

- Get current forms and instructions for your state from a reliable source. State and national organizations concerned with the elderly or the right to die are good starting places. A major organization that provides forms for all states is Partnership for Caring (www.partnershipforcaring.org).

■ Most people will be content to fill in the blanks and check various options. But if the form does not adequately express your deeply held beliefs, you can add to it—for example, by including additional instructions for your doctors or extending greater authority to your health care agent. A request the law does not allow might not be enforced; but at least your feelings will be on record, and by the time the instrument is required the law might have changed.

■ Most forms will have specific clauses concerning artificial nutrition and hydration (tube feeding). If you would not want your body kept alive in this way when all other hope is gone, be sure that your advance directive specifically says so.

■ Try not to rely solely on a living will: appoint a health care agent as well, with broad power to interpret your living will and make decisions according to the circumstances. Hospitals do not always obey living wills. Your agent can speak for you and demand your rights.

■ Give copies of your advance directives to family, friends, and doctors, and discuss them. Make sure your doctor and his or her hospital understand and will abide by your wishes. If they might not, consider switching.

■ Reread the documents at least every five years and either update them or make a notation that the contents still represent your beliefs.

There are at least two related documents that you may want to attend to at the same time. One is an organ donation (or *anatomical gift*) card, authorized in all states as a means for expressing one's willingness to have bodily organs used for transplantation or other purposes after death. Another, now authorized in most states, is a *non-hospital* (or *out-of-hospital*) *Do Not Resuscitate Order*, which is appropriate for certain patients who are staying at home but would not want to be subjected to resuscitation efforts by emergency personnel.

il•le•gal /i(l)'lēgəl/ ▸ **adj.** contrary to or forbidden by law, esp. criminal law: *illegal drugs.*
▸**n.** an illegal immigrant: *five of the illegals carried base clearance cards.*
DERIVATIVES **il•le•gal•i•ty** /ˌi(l)li'gælitē/ **n.** (pl. **il•le•gal•i•ties**); **il•le•gal•ly adv.**
ORIGIN early 17th cent.: from French *illégal* or medieval Latin *illegalis*, from Latin *in-* 'not' + *legalis* 'according to the law.'

il•le•git•i•mate ▸ **adj.** /ˌi(l)lə'jitəmit/ not authorized by the law; not in accordance with accepted standards or rules: *an illegitimate exercise of power by the military.*
■ (of a child) born of parents not lawfully married to each other.
▸**n.** a person who is illegitimate by birth.
DERIVATIVES **il•le•git•i•ma•cy** /ˌi(l)lə'jitəməsē/ **n.**; **il•le•git•i•mate•ly adv.**
ORIGIN mid 16th cent.: from late Latin *illegitimus* (from *in-* 'not' + *legitimus* 'lawful'), suggested by LEGITIMATE.

im•mi•gra•tion /ˌimə'grāsHən/ ▸ **n.** the action of coming to live permanently in a country of which one is not a native or citizen: *a barrier to control illegal immigration from Mexico.*
■ the place at an airport or country's border where government officials check the documents of people entering that country.

im•mov•a•ble /i(m)'mōōvəbəl/ ▸ **adj.** (of property) consisting of land, buildings, or other permanent items.
▸**n.** (**immovables**) immovable property: *most of the local notary's business dealt with sales of immovables in the surrounding parishes.*

im•pan•el /im'pænl/ (also **em•pan•el**) ▸ **v.** (**im•pan•eled, im•pan•el•ing**; Brit. **im•pan•elled, im•pan•el•ling**) [trans.] enlist or enroll (a jury): *the General Duty Judge is empowered to impanel one or more grand juries as the public interest requires.*
■ enroll (someone) on to a jury: *several of her friends have been impaneled.*
DERIVATIVES **im•pan•el•ment n.**
ORIGIN late Middle English (originally as *empanel*): from Anglo-Norman French *empaneller*, from *em-* 'in' + Old French *panel* 'panel.'

im•peach /im'pēCH/ ▸ v. [trans.] call into question the integrity or validity of (a judgment, etc.): *any deposition may be used for the purpose of impeaching the testimony of the deponent as a witness.*
■ charge (the holder of a public office) with misconduct: *the governor served only one year before being impeached and convicted for fiscal fraud.* ■ cast doubt on the credibility of (a witness).
DERIVATIVES **im•peach•a•ble adj.; im•peach•ment n.**
ORIGIN late Middle English (also in the sense 'hinder, prevent'; earlier as *empeche*): from Old French *empecher* 'impede,' from late Latin *impedicare* 'catch, entangle' (based on *pedica* 'a fetter,' from *pes, ped-* 'foot').

im•ped•i•ment /im'pedəmənt/ ▸ n. an obstruction to a legal right or power: *our current Building Code's complexity is often an impediment to new construction and drives up the cost of building.*
DERIVATIVES **im•ped•i•men•tal** /im,pedə'mentl/ **adj.**
ORIGIN late Middle English: from Latin *impedimentum*, from *impedire*.

im•pound /im'pownd/ ▸ v. [trans.] seize and take legal custody of (something, esp. a vehicle, goods, or documents) because of an infringement of a law or regulation: *vehicles parked where they cause an obstruction will be impounded.*
DERIVATIVES **im•pound•a•ble adj.; im•pound•er n.; im•pound•ment n.**

in•ad•mis•si•ble /,inəd'misəbəl/ ▸ adj. not able to be introduced in evidence (because prejudicial, irrelevant, etc.): *her written expression of sympathy for the victim was ruled inadmissible as evidence of liability.*
DERIVATIVES **in•ad•mis•si•bil•i•ty** /,inəd,misə'bilitē/ **n.; in•ad•mis•si•bly** /,inəd'misəblē/ **adv.**

in•al•ien•a•ble /in'ālēənəbəl/ ▸ adj. unable to be given away or transferred by the possessor: *the giant sequoias were granted to the State of California as an inalienable public trust.*
DERIVATIVES **in•al•ien•a•bil•i•ty** /in,ālēənə'bilitē/ **n.; in•al•ien•a•bly** /in'ālēənəblē/ **adv.**

in cam•er•a /in 'kæm(ə)rə/ ▸ phrase in private, in particular taking place in the private chambers of a judge, with the press and public excluded: *judges assess the merits of such claims in camera.*
ORIGIN late Latin, 'in the chamber.'

in•ca•pac•i•tate /,inkə'pæsi,tāt/ ▸ v. [trans.] deprive (someone) of their legal capacity.
DERIVATIVES **in•ca•pac•i•tant** /,inkə'pæsitnt/ **n.; in•ca•pac•i•ta•tion** /,inkə,pæsi'tāSHən/ **n.**

in•ca•pac•i•ty /,inkə'pæsitē/ ▸ n. (pl. **in•ca•pac•i•ties**) legal disqualification: *they are not subject to any legal incapacity.*

ORIGIN early 17th cent.: from French *incapacité* or late Latin *incapacitas*, from *in-* (expressing negation) + *capacitas* (see CAPACITY).

in•cest /ˈinˌsest/ ▸ n. sexual relations between people classed as being too closely related to marry each other.

■ the crime of having sexual intercourse with a parent, child, sibling, or grandchild.

ORIGIN Middle English: from Latin *incestus*, *incestum* 'unchastity, incest,' from *in-* 'not' + *castus* 'chaste.'

in•ces•tu•ous /inˈsesCHo͞oəs/ ▸ adj. involving or guilty of incest: *the child of an incestuous relationship.*

DERIVATIVES **in•ces•tu•ous•ly** adv.; **in•ces•tu•ous•ness** n.

ORIGIN early 16th cent.: from late Latin *incestuosus*, from Latin *incestus* (see INCEST).

in•cho•ate ▸ /inˈkō-it; -āt/ adj. (of an offense, such as incitement or conspiracy) anticipating a further criminal act: *the danger of inchoate crimes lies in the possibility that they will be carried to fruition.*

DERIVATIVES **in•cho•ate•ly** adv.; **in•cho•ate•ness** n.

ORIGIN mid 16th cent.: from Latin *inchoatus*, past participle of *inchoare*, variant of *incohare* 'begin.'

in•ci•dent /ˈinsidənt/ ▸ adj. attaching to: *the costs properly incident to a suit for foreclosure or redemption.*

ORIGIN late Middle English: via Old French from Latin *incident-* 'falling upon, happening to,' from the verb *incidere*, from *in-* 'upon' + *cadere* 'to fall.'

in•com•pe•tent /inˈkämpətənt; iNG-/ ▸ adj. not qualified to act in a particular capacity: *the patient is deemed legally incompetent.*

▸ n. an incompetent person.

DERIVATIVES **in•com•pe•tence** n.; **in•com•pe•ten•cy** n.; **in•com•pe•tent•ly** adv.

ORIGIN late 16th cent. (in the sense 'not legally competent'): from French, or from late Latin *incompetent-*, from *in-* 'not' + Latin *competent-* 'being fit or proper' (see COMPETENT).

in•cor•po•rate ▸ v. /inˈkôrpəˌrāt/ [trans.] (often **be incorporated**) constitute (a company, city, or other organization) as a legal corporation: *the Trust is incorporated as a national banking association.*

▸ adj. /inˈkôrp(ə)rit/ archaic another term for INCORPORATED.

DERIVATIVES **in•cor•po•ra•tion** /inˌkôrpəˈrāsHən/ n.; **in•cor•po•ra•tor** /inˈkôrpəˌrātər/ n.

ORIGIN late Middle English: from late Latin *incorporat-* 'embodied,' from the verb *incorporare*, from *in-* 'into' + Latin *corporare* 'form into a body' (from *corpus*, *corpor-* 'body').

in•cor•po•re•al /ˌinkôrˈpôrēəl/ ▸ adj. (often of a property interest) having no material existence: *there is no reason for the government to favor an incorporeal entity over a human developer.*

DERIVATIVES **in•cor•po•re•al•i•ty** /ˌinkôrˌpôrēˈælitē/ n.; **in•cor•po•re•al•ly** adv.; **in•cor•po•re•i•ty** /inˌkôrpəˈrēitē/ n.

ORIGIN late Middle English: from Latin *incorporeus*, from *in-* 'not' + *corporeus* (from *corpus*, *corpor-* 'body') + *-al*.

in•crim•i•nate /in'krimə‚nāt/ ▶ v. [trans.] make (someone) appear guilty of a crime or wrongdoing; strongly imply the guilt of (someone): *he refused to answer questions in order not to incriminate himself* | [as adj.] (**incriminating**) *incriminating evidence.*
DERIVATIVES **in•crim•i•na•tion** /in‚krimə'nāsHən/ n.; **in•crim•i•na•to•ry** /in'krimənə‚tôrē/ adj.
ORIGIN mid 18th cent.: from late Latin *incriminat-* 'accused,' from the verb *incriminare*, from *in-* 'into, toward' + Latin *crimen* 'crime.'

in•de•cen•cy /in'dēsənsē/ ▶ n. (pl. **in•de•cen•cies**) indecent behavior: *a law governing indecency on cable television.*
■ an indecent act, gesture, or expression.

in•de•cent as•sault /in'dēsənt ə'sôlt/ ▶ n. see SEXUAL ASSAULT.

in•de•cent ex•po•sure /in'dēsənt ik'spōzHər/ ▶ n. the crime of intentionally showing one's sexual organs in public.
■ the act of outraging public decency by being naked in a public place.

in•de•fea•si•ble /‚ində'fēzəbəl/ ▶ adj. Philosophy not able to be lost, annulled, or overturned: *an indefeasible right.*
DERIVATIVES **in•de•fea•si•bil•i•ty** /‚ində‚fēzə'bilitē/ n.; **in•de•fea•si•bly** /‚ində'fēzəblē/ adv.

in•dem•ni•fy /in'demnə‚fī/ ▶ v. (**in•dem•ni•fies**, **in•dem•ni•fied**) [trans.] compensate (someone) for harm or loss: *the insurance was inadequate to indemnify the owner.*
■ secure (someone) against such harm or loss: *are you sure that these arrangements will indemnify us?* ■ secure (someone) against legal responsibility for their actions: *the newspaper could not be forced to **indemnify** the city **for** personal-injury liability that might result from accidents involving newsstands.*
DERIVATIVES **in•dem•ni•fi•ca•tion** /in‚demnəfi'kāsHən/ n.; **in•dem•ni•fi•er** n.
ORIGIN early 17th cent.: from Latin *indemnis* 'unhurt, free from loss or damage,' from *in-* (expressing negation) + *damnum* 'loss, damage.'

in•dem•ni•ty /in'demnitē/ ▶ n. (pl. **in•dem•ni•ties**) security or protection against a loss or other financial burden: *no indemnity will be given for loss of cash.*
■ security against or exemption from legal responsibility for one's actions: *a deed of indemnity* | *even warranties and indemnities do not provide complete protection.* ■ a sum of money paid as compensation, esp. a sum exacted by a victor in war as one condition of peace.
ORIGIN late Middle English: from French *indemnite*, from late Latin *indemnitas*, from *indemnis* 'unhurt, free from loss.'

in•den•ture /in'denCHər/ ▶ n. a formal legal agreement, contract, or document, in particular:
■ an agreement binding an apprentice to a master: *the 30 apprentices*

received their indentures on completion of their training. ■ historical a deed of contract of which copies were made for the contracting parties with the edges indented for identification. ■ a formal list, certificate, or inventory. ■ historical a contract by which a person agreed to work for a set period for a landowner in a British colony in exchange for passage to the colony. ■ the fact of being bound to service by such an agreement: *men in their first year after* **indenture to** *the Company of Watermen and Lightermen.*

▸v. [trans.] (usu. **be indentured to**) chiefly historical bind (someone) by an indenture as an apprentice or laborer: [as adj.] (**indentured**) *landowners tried to get their estates cultivated by indentured laborers.*
DERIVATIVES **in•den•ture•ship** /in'denCHər,SHip/ n.

in•de•ter•mi•nate /,indi'tərmənit/ ▸ adj. 1 (of a judicial sentence) not fixed in length, typically so that the convicted person's conduct determines the date of release.
2 (of rules) not capable of mechanical application: *the initial pleading in this case was indeterminate as to removability.*
DERIVATIVES **in•de•ter•mi•na•cy** /,indi'tərmənəsē/ n.; **in•de•ter•mi•nate•ly** adv.; **in•de•ter•mi•nate•ness** n.
ORIGIN early 17th cent.: from late Latin *indeterminatus,* from *in-* 'not' + Latin *determinatus* 'limited, determined.'

in•dict /in'dīt/ ▸ v. [trans.] (usu. **be indicted**) formally, by a grand jury, accuse or charge (someone) with a crime: *his former manager was* **indicted for** *fraud.*
DERIVATIVES **in•dict•ee** /,indī'tē/ n.; **in•dict•er** n.
ORIGIN Middle English *endite, indite,* from Anglo-Norman French *enditer,* based on Latin *indicere* 'proclaim, appoint,' from *in-* 'toward' + *dicere* 'pronounce, utter.'

in•dict•a•ble /in'dītəbəl/ ▸ adj. (of an offense) rendering the person who commits it liable to be charged with a crime that warrants a trial by jury.
■ (of a person) liable to be charged with a crime.

in•dict•ment /in'dītmənt/ ▸ n. a formal charge or accusation, by a grand jury, of a crime: *an* **indictment for** *conspiracy.* See also **BILL OF INDICTMENT.**
■ the action of indicting or being indicted: *the indictment of twelve people who had imported cocaine.*
ORIGIN Middle English *enditement, inditement,* from Anglo-Norman French *enditement,* from *enditer* (see **INDICT**).

in•dis•pen•sa•ble /,indi'spensəbəl/ ▸ n. a person who must be made party to a legal action: *in a suit against a subordinate officer, the head of a department or other superior officer is an indispensable.*
ORIGIN mid 16th cent.: from medieval Latin *indispensabilis,* from *in-* 'not' + *dispensabilis* 'dispensable.'

in•duce•ment /in'd(y)o͞osmənt/ ▸ n. a thing that persuades or influences

someone to do something, especially enter into a contract: *companies were prepared to build only in return for massive inducements | there is no **inducement to** wait for payment.*
■ a bribe.

in•fa•mous /'infəməs/ ▶ adj. historical (of a person) deprived of all or some of a citizen's rights as a consequence of conviction for a serious crime.
■ (of a crime) leading to such deprivation.
DERIVATIVES **in•fa•mous•ly** adv.; **in•fa•my** /'infə,mē/ n. (pl. **in•fa•mies**) .
ORIGIN late Middle English: from medieval Latin *infamosus*, from Latin *infamis* (based on *fama* 'fame').

in•fan•cy /'infənsē/ ▶ n. the condition of being a minor; minority: *the disabilities of insanity or infancy.*
ORIGIN late Middle English: from Latin *infantia* 'childhood, inability to speak,' from *infans, infant-* (see INFANT).

in•fant /'infənt/ ▶ n. a person who has not attained legal majority: *the creditor was unaware that the debtor was an infant.*
ORIGIN late Middle English: from Old French *enfant*, from Latin *infant-* 'unable to speak,' from *in-* 'not' + *fant-* 'speaking' (from the verb *fari*).

in•fan•ti•cide /in'fænti,sīd/ ▶ n. **1** the crime of killing one's newborn or a very young child.
2 a person who kills an infant, esp. their own child.
DERIVATIVES **in•fan•ti•cid•al** /in,fænti'sīdl/ adj.
ORIGIN mid 17th cent.: via French from late Latin *infanticidium*, from Latin *infant-* (see INFANT) + *-cidium*, from *caedere* 'kill.'

in•fe•ri•or /in'firēər/ ▶ adj. (of a court or tribunal) subordinate to, and able to have its decisions overturned by, a higher court.
ORIGIN from Latin, comparative of *inferus* 'low.'

in fla•gran•te de•lic•to /,in flə'gräntā də'liktō; flə'græntē/ (also informal **in fla•gran•te**) ▶ adv. in the very act of wrongdoing, esp. in an act of sexual misconduct: *he had been **caught in flagrante** with the wife of the association's treasurer.*
ORIGIN late 18th cent.: Latin, literally 'in blazing crime.'

in•flu•ence /'inflo͞oəns/ ▶ n. see UNDER THE INFLUENCE.

in•form•ant /in'fômənt/ ▶ n. a person who informs on another person to the police or other authority: *an informant told the police that a large shipment of heroin would arrive in Rochester from New York City.*

in•for•ma•tion /,infər'māsHən/ ▶ n. a formal criminal charge lodged with a court or magistrate by a prosecutor without the aid of a grand jury: *the tenant may lay an information against his landlord.*
ORIGIN late Middle English (also in the sense 'formation of the mind, teaching'), via Old French from Latin *informatio(n-)*, from the verb *informare* 'shape, fashion, describe,' from *in-* 'into' + *forma* 'a form.'

in•form•er /in'fômər/ ▶ n. another term for INFORMANT.

in•frac•tion /in'fræksHən/ ▶ n. a violation or infringement of a law, an agreement, the rights of others, or a set of rules. An infraction typically is a minor offense: *traffic infractions.*
DERIVATIVES **in•frac•tor** /in'fræktər/ n.
ORIGIN late Middle English: from Latin *infractio(n-)*, from the verb *infringere* (see **INFRINGE**).

in•fringe /in'frinj/ ▶ v. [trans.] actively break the terms of (a law, agreement, etc.): *making an unauthorized copy would infringe copyright.*
■ act so as to limit or undermine (something); encroach on: *his legal rights were being infringed* | [intrans.] *I wouldn't infringe on his privacy.*
DERIVATIVES **in•fringe•ment** n.; **in•fring•er** n.
ORIGIN mid 16th cent.: from Latin *infringere*, from *in-* 'into' + *frangere* 'to break.'

in•here /in'hir/ ▶ v. [intrans.] (**inhere in/within**) (of rights, powers, etc.) be vested in a person or group or attached to the ownership of a property: *the rights inhering in the property they owned.*
ORIGIN mid 16th cent. (in the sense 'stick, cling to'): from Latin *inhaerere* 'stick to.'

in•her•ent /in'hirənt; -'her-/ ▶ adj. vested in (someone) as a right or privilege: *the president's inherent foreign affairs power.*
DERIVATIVES **in•her•ence** n.; **in•her•ent•ly** adv.
ORIGIN late 16th cent.: from Latin *inhaerent-* 'sticking to,' from the verb *inhaerere*, from *in-* 'in, toward' + *haerere* 'to stick.'

in•her•it /in'herit/ ▶ v. (**in•her•it•ed, in•her•it•ing**) [trans.] receive (money, property, or a title) as an heir, by will or operation of law, at the death of the previous holder: *she inherited a fortune from her father.*
DERIVATIVES **in•her•i•tor** /in'heritər/ n.
ORIGIN Middle English *enherite* 'receive as a right,' from Old French *enheriter*, from late Latin *inhereditare* 'appoint as heir,' from Latin *in-* 'in' + *heres, hered-* 'heir.'

in•her•it•a•ble /in'heritəbəl/ ▶ adj. capable of being inherited: *inheritable property.*
■ capable of inheriting.
DERIVATIVES **in•her•it•a•bil•i•ty** /in,heritə'bilitē/ n.
ORIGIN late Middle English (formerly also as *enheritable*): from Anglo-Norman French *enheritable* 'able to be made heir,' from Old French *enheriter* (see **INHERIT**).

in•her•it•ance /in'heritns/ ▶ n. a thing that is inherited: *he came into a comfortable inheritance.*
ORIGIN late Middle English (formerly also as *enheritance*): from Anglo-Norman French *enheritaunce* 'being admitted as heir,' from Old French *enheriter* (see **INHERIT**).

in•her•it•ance tax /in'heritns ,tæks/ ▶ n. a tax imposed on someone who inherits property or money. Also called **DEATH TAX**.

in•i•ti•a•tive /i'nisH(ē)ətiv/ ▶ n. (**the initiative**) (esp. in some US states and Switzerland) the right of citizens outside the legislature to originate legislation.

ORIGIN late 18th cent.: from French, from Latin *initiare*, from *initium* 'beginning.'

in•junc•tion /inˈjəNG(k)SHən/ ▸ n. a judicial order, equitable in origin and enforceable by contempt proceedings, that restrains a person from beginning or continuing an action threatening or invading the legal right of another, or that compels a person to carry out a certain act, e.g., to make restitution to an injured party: *an injunction prohibiting plutonium shipments.*

DERIVATIVES **in•junc•tive** /inˈjəNG(k)tiv/ **adj.**

ORIGIN late Middle English: from late Latin *injunctio(n-)*, from Latin *injungere* 'enjoin, impose.'

in•ju•ri•ous /inˈjo͝orēəs/ ▸ adj. causing or likely to cause damage or harm: *fish above the tolerance level are deemed to be **injurious to** people's health.*

■ (of language) maliciously insulting; libelous.

DERIVATIVES **in•ju•ri•ous•ly** adv.; **in•ju•ri•ous•ness** n.

ORIGIN late Middle English: from French *injurieux* or Latin *injuriosus*, from *injuria* 'a wrong' (see **INJURY**).

in•ju•ry /ˈinjərē/ ▸ n. (pl. **in•ju•ries**) an instance of being injured.

■ the fact of being injured; harm or damage: *awards are only available where injury is actually proved.* ■ wrong or harm done to another: *they held that exercise of the contract provisions inflicted injury.*

ORIGIN late Middle English: from Anglo-Norman French *injurie*, from Latin *injuria* 'a wrong,' from *in-* (expressing negation) + *jus, jur-* 'right.'

in•no•cent /ˈinəsənt/ ▸ adj. not guilty of a crime or offense: *the arbitrary execution of an innocent man* | *he was **innocent of** any fraud.*

ORIGIN Middle English: from Old French, or from Latin *innocent-* 'not harming,' from *in-* 'not' + *nocere* 'to hurt.'

USAGE: **Innocent** properly means 'harmless,' but it has long been extended in general language to mean 'not guilty.' The jury (or judge) in a criminal trial does not, strictly speaking, find a defendant 'innocent.' Rather, a defendant may be *guilty* or *not guilty* of the charges brought. In common use, however, owing perhaps to the concept of the *presumption of innocence*, which instructs a jury to consider a defendant free of wrongdoing until proven guilty on the basis of evidence, 'not guilty' and 'innocent' have come to be thought of as synonymous.

Inn of Court /ˈin əv ˈkôrt/ ▸ n. (pl. **Inns of Court**) (in the UK) each of the four legal societies having the exclusive right of admitting people to the English bar.

■ any of the sets of buildings in London occupied by these societies.

in•nu•en•do /ˌinyo͞oˈendō/ ▸ n. (pl. **in•nu•en•does** or **in•nu•en•dos**) the defamatory meaning of a libel: *we disagree with the assertion that the sexual references rely solely on innuendo.*

ORIGIN 17th cent.: Latin, 'by nodding at, by pointing to,' ablative gerund of *innuere,* from *in-* 'toward' + *nuere* 'to nod.'

in per•so•nam /ˌin pər'sōnəm/ ▸ **adj. & adv.** made or availing against or affecting a specific person only; imposing a personal duty or liability: [as postpositive adj.] *rights and duties in personam* | [as adv.] *the view that trusts operate in personam.* Compare with IN REM.

ORIGIN late 18th cent.: Latin, literally 'against a person.'

in•quest /'in,kwest; -'ING-/ ▸ **n.** a judicial inquiry to ascertain the facts relating to an incident, such as a death.

■ a body of people appointed to make such an inquiry.

ORIGIN Middle English: from Old French *enqueste,* based on Latin *inquirere* (see INQUIRE).

in•qui•si•tion /ˌinkwi'zisHən; ˌING-/ ▸ **n.** the verdict or finding of an official inquiry.

■ historical a judicial or official inquiry.

ORIGIN late Middle English (denoting a searching examination): via Old French from Latin *inquisitio(n-)* 'examination.'

in•quis•i•to•ri•al /in,kwizi'tôrēəl; iNG-/ ▸ **adj.** (of a trial or legal procedure) in which the judge has an examining or inquiring role: *administration is accompanied by a form of inquisitorial justice.* Compare with ACCUSATORIAL, ADVERSARIAL.

DERIVATIVES **in•quis•i•to•ri•al•ly adv.**

ORIGIN mid 18th cent.: from medieval Latin *inquisitorius* (from Latin *inquisitor,* from *inquirere* 'inquire') + *-al.*

in re /ˌin 'rā; 'rē/ ▸ **prep.** in the legal case of; with regard to: *in re Mancet's Estate.*

ORIGIN early 17th cent.: Latin, 'in the matter of.'

in rem /ˌin 'rem/ ▸ **adj.** [often postpositive] made or availing against or affecting a thing, and therefore other people generally; imposing a general duty or liability: *it confers a right in rem.* Compare with IN PERSONAM.

ORIGIN mid 18th cent.: Latin, 'against a thing.'

in•san•i•ty /in'sænitē/ ▸ **n.** the state of being seriously mentally ill; madness.

■ such a state when it makes one not liable or responsible for one's actions: [as complement] *he attempted to plead insanity.*

ORIGIN late 16th cent.: from Latin *insanitas,* from *insanus* (see INSANE).

in•sid•er trad•ing /'in,sīdər 'trādiNG/ (Brit. also **in•sid•er deal•ing** /'in ,sīdər 'dēliNG/) ▸ **n.** the illegal practice of trading on the stock exchange to one's own advantage through having access, because of personal or business relationship, to confidential information.

in•sti•tute /'insti,t(y)ōōt/ ▸ **v.** [trans.] **1** begin (legal proceedings) in a court: *before instituting any action under this section, the Secretary shall attempt to eliminate discriminatory practice.*

2 (often **be instituted**) appoint (someone) to a position, esp. as a cleric: *his sons were instituted to his benefice in 1986* | *McAndrews, the testator, has instituted his daughter heir.*

▶n. [usu. in names] (usu. **institutes**) archaic a commentary, treatise, or summary of principles, esp. concerning law.

ORIGIN Middle English (sense 2 of the **verb**): from Latin *institut-* 'established,' from the verb *instituere,* from *in-* 'in, toward' + *statuere* 'set up.' The noun is from Latin *institutum* 'something designed, precept.'

in•struct /in'strəkt/ ▶ v. [trans.] give a person direction, information, or authorization, in particular:

■ (of a judge) give information, esp. clarification of legal principles, to (a jury): *there were two minutes of testimony that the jury was instructed to disregard.*

ORIGIN from Latin *instruct-* 'constructed, equipped, taught,' from the verb *instruere,* from *in-* 'upon, toward' + *struere* 'pile up.'

in•struc•tions /in'strəksHənz/ ▶ plural noun directions to a jury.

ORIGIN late Middle English: via Old French from late Latin *instructio(n-),* from the verb *instruere* (see **INSTRUCT**).

in•stru•ment /'instrəmənt/ ▶ n. a formal document, esp. a legal one: *execution involves signature and unconditional delivery of the instrument.*

▶v. [trans.] equip (something) with measuring instruments.

ORIGIN Middle English: from Old French, or from Latin *instrumentum* 'equipment, implement,' from the verb *instruere* 'construct, equip.'

in•sur•ance pol•i•cy /in'sHŌŌrəns ˌpäləsē/ ▶ n. a document detailing the terms and conditions of a contract of insurance.

in•tel•lec•tu•al prop•er•ty /ˌintl'eksHŌŌəl 'präpərtē/ ▶ n. a work or invention that is the result of creativity, such as a manuscript or a design, to which one has rights and for which one may apply for a patent, copyright or trademark.

in•tent /in'tent/ ▶ n. intention or purpose.

PHRASES **with intent** with the intention of committing a specified wrongful act (tort) or crime: *he denied arson with intent to endanger life* | *charges of wounding with intent.*

ORIGIN Middle English: from Old French *entent, entente,* based on Latin *intendere* 'intend.'

in•ter•dict ▶ n. /'intərˌdikt/ an authoritative prohibition: *an interdict against marriage of those of close kin.*

▶v. /ˌintər'dikt/ [trans.] **1** prohibit or forbid (something).

■ (**interdict someone from**) prohibit someone from (doing something): *I have not been interdicted from consuming or holding alcoholic beverages.*

2 intercept and prevent the movement of (a prohibited commodity or person): *the police established roadblocks throughout the country for interdicting drugs.*

DERIVATIVES **in•ter•dic•tion** /ˌintər'diksHən/ n.

ORIGIN from Old French *entredit*, from Latin *interdictum*, past participle of *interdicere* 'interpose, forbid by decree,' from *inter-* 'between' + *dicere* 'say.'

in•ter•est /'int(ə)rist/ ▶ n. a legal concern, title, or right in property: *third parties having an interest in a building.*

ORIGIN late Middle English (originally as *interess*): from Anglo-Norman French *interesse*, from Latin *interesse* 'differ, be important,' from *inter-* 'between' + *esse* 'be.' The *-t* was added partly by association with Old French *interest* 'damage, loss,' apparently from Latin *interest* 'it is important.' The original sense was 'the possession of a share in or a right to something.'

in•ter•loc•u•to•ry /,intər'läkyə,tôrē/ ▶ adj. (of a decree or judgment) given provisionally during the course of a legal action; preliminary: *an interlocutory appeal.*

ORIGIN late 15th cent.: from medieval Latin *interlocutorius*, from Latin *interloqui* 'interrupt.'

In•ter•na•tion•al Court of Jus•tice /,intər'næsHənl 'kôrt əv 'jəstis/ a judicial court of the United Nations, formed in 1945, that meets at The Hague.

in•ter•na•tion•al law /,intər'næsHənl 'lô/ ▶ n. a body of rules established by custom or treaty and recognized by nations as binding in their relations with one another.

in•ter•plead•er /,intər'plēdər/ ▶ n. a suit pleaded between two parties to determine a matter of claim or right to property held by a third party: *an action in interpleader was filed to determine how the proceeds should be divided between the heirs.*

DERIVATIVES **in•ter•plead** /,intər'plēd/ v.

ORIGIN mid 16th cent.: from Anglo-Norman French *enterpleder*, from *enter-* 'between' + *pleder* 'to plead.'

in•ter•rog•a•to•ry /,intə'rägə,tôrē/ ▶ n. (pl. **in•ter•rog•a•to•ries**) a written question that is formally put to one party in a case by another party and that must be answered.

ORIGIN mid 16th cent.: the noun from medieval Latin *interrogatoria*, plural of *interrogatorium*; the adjective from late Latin *interrogatorius*, based on Latin *interrogare*, from *inter-* 'between' + *rogare* 'ask.'

in•ter•vene /,intər'vēn/ ▶ v. [intrans.] interpose in a lawsuit as a third party: *the university challenged NIH's action in court just days before the United States intervened in the case.*

DERIVATIVES **in•ter•ven•er** n.; **in•ter•ven•ient** /,intər'vēnyənt/ adj.; **in•ter•ve•nor** /,intər'vēnər/ n.

ORIGIN late 16th cent. (in the sense 'come in as an extraneous factor or thing'): from Latin *intervenire*, from *inter-* 'between' + *venire* 'come.'

in•tes•tate /in'testāt; -tit/ ▶ adj. [predic.] not having made a will before one dies: *he died intestate* | [postpositive] *in the event of his death intestate.*

■ [attrib.] of or relating to a person who dies without having made a will: *his brother's posthumous children are admissible as intestate heirs.*
▶n. a person who has died without having made a will.
DERIVATIVES **in•tes•ta•cy** /in'testəsē/ **n.**
ORIGIN late Middle English: from Latin *intestatus*, from *in-* 'not' + *testatus* 'testified, witness' (see TESTATE).

in•ure /i'n(y)ŏŏr/ (also **en•ure**) ▶ v. [intrans.] (**inure for/to**) come into operation; take effect: *a release given to one of two joint contractors inures to the benefit of both.*
DERIVATIVES **in•ure•ment n.**
ORIGIN late Middle English *inure, enure,* from an Anglo-Norman French phrase meaning 'in use or practice,' from *en* 'in' + Old French *euvre* 'work' (from Latin *opera*).

in•val•id /in'vælid/ ▶ adj. (esp. of an official document or procedure) not valid; void because contravening a regulation or law: *the vote was declared invalid due to a technicality.*
DERIVATIVES **in•val•id•ly adv.**
ORIGIN mid 16th cent. (earlier than *valid*): from Latin *invalidus,* from *in-* 'not' + *validus* 'strong.'

in•val•i•date /in'væli,dāt/ ▶ v. [trans.] deprive (an official document or procedure) of legal efficacy because of contravention of a regulation or law: *a technical flaw in her papers invalidated her nomination.*
DERIVATIVES **in•val•i•da•tion** /in,væli'dāsHən/ **n.; in•val•i•da•tor** /in'væli,dātər/ **n.**
ORIGIN mid 17th cent.: from medieval Latin *invalidat-* 'annulled,' from the verb *invalidare* (based on Latin *validus* 'strong').

is•sue /'isHŏŏ/ ▶ n. **1** a point of fact or law that is the subject of litigation and of the court's final determination. *most of her testimony did not involve the time periods **at issue** in this case* | *the state court had concurrent jurisdiction to decide the issue of the debtor's liability.*
2 children of one's own: *he died without male issue.*
DERIVATIVES **is•sue•less adj.**
ORIGIN Middle English (in the sense 'outflowing'): from Old French, based on Latin *exitus,* past participle of *exire* 'go out.'

J

J ▶ abbr. ▪ judge. ▪ justice.

JAG ▶ abbr. judge advocate general.

Jane Doe /ˈjān ˈdō/ ▶ n. an anonymous female party, typically the plaintiff, in a legal action. See also **JOHN DOE**.

JD ▶ abbr. juris doctor, the primary degree granted at most US law schools.

jeop•ard•y /ˈjepərdē/ ▶ n. danger (of conviction) arising from being on trial for a criminal offense: *pesticide retailers and end-users could also be subject to legal jeopardy.* See also **DOUBLE JEOPARDY**.

ORIGIN Middle English *iuparti,* from Old French *ieu parti* '(evenly) divided game.' The term was originally used in chess and other games to denote a problem, or a position in which the chances of winning or losing were evenly balanced, hence 'a dangerous situation.'

John Doe /ˈjän ˈdō/ ▶ n. an anonymous male party, typically the plaintiff, in a legal action. See also **JANE DOE**.

ORIGIN mid 18th cent.: originally in legal use as a name of a fictitious plaintiff, corresponding to *Richard Roe*, used to represent the defendant.

join•der /ˈjoindər/ ▶ n. the action of bringing parties (e.g., codefendants) or claims together in a legal action.

ORIGIN late Middle English: from Anglo-Norman French, from Old French *joindre* 'to join.'

joint /joint/ ▶ adj. [attrib.] shared, held, or made by both houses of a bicameral legislature: *a joint session of Congress | a joint congressional hearing.*

▪ applied, joined, or regarded together: *joint ownership.* Often contrasted with **SEVERAL**.

▶ n. informal (**the joint**) prison.

DERIVATIVES **joint•ly** adv.

ORIGIN Middle English: from Old French, past participle of *joindre* 'to join.'

joint and sev•er•al /ˈjoint ən(d) ˈsev(ə)rəl/ ▶ adj. (of a legal obligation) undertaken by two or more people, each individual having liability for the whole: *she was ordered to pay restitution, joint and several with her codefendants.*

joint ten•an•cy /'joint 'tenənsē/ ▶ n. the holding of an estate or property jointly by two or more parties, the share of each passing to the other or others on death.
DERIVATIVES **joint ten•ant** /'joint 'tenənt/ n.

JP ▶ abbr. justice of the peace.

judge /jəj/ ▶ n. a public official appointed or elected to decide cases in a court of law.
▶ v. [trans.] decide (a case) in a court of law: *other cases were judged by tribunal.*
■ [with complement] give a verdict on (someone) in a law court: *she was judged guilty of manslaughter.*
DERIVATIVES **judge•ship** /'jəj,SHip/ n.
ORIGIN Middle English: from Old French *juge* (noun), *juger* (verb), from Latin *judex*, *judic-*, from *jus* 'law' + *dicere* 'to say.'

judge ad•vo•cate /'jəj 'advəkit/ ▶ n. a lawyer who advises a court-martial on points of law and sums up the case.
■ a military lawyer.

judge ad•vo•cate gen•er•al /'jəj 'advəkit 'jen(ə)rəl/ (abbr.: **JAG**) ▶ n. the officer in supreme control of the courts-martial of one of the armed forces.

judge-made /'jəj 'mād/ ▶ adj. created by judicial decisions rather than legislation: *such an exemption from double patenting would contravene more than 100 years of judge-made law.*

judg•ment /'jəjmənt/ (also **judge•ment**) ▶ n. a decision of a court of law or a judge.
■ a monetary or other obligation awarded by a court: *it reversed a lower court decision upholding the $100,000 judgment.* ■ the document recording this obligation.
PHRASES **pass judgment** (of a court of law or a judge) give a decision concerning a defendant or legal matter: *he passed judgment on the accused.*
ORIGIN Middle English: from Old French *jugement*, from *juger* 'to judge.'

judg•ment in de•fault /'jəjmənt in di'fôlt/ ▶ chiefly Brit. another term for DEFAULT JUDGMENT.

ju•di•ca•ture /'jōōdikə,CHŏŏr; -,kāCHər/ ▶ n. the administration of justice.
■ (**the judicature**) judges collectively; the judiciary.
DERIVATIVES **ju•di•ca•to•ry** /'jōōdikə,tôrē/ adj.
ORIGIN mid 16th cent.: from medieval Latin *judicatura*, from Latin *judicare* 'to judge.'

ju•di•cial /jōō'disHəl/ ▶ adj. of, by, or appropriate to a court of law or a judge: *a judicial inquiry into the allegations* | *a judicial system.*
DERIVATIVES **ju•di•cial•ly** adv.
ORIGIN late Middle English: from Latin *judicialis*, from *judicium* 'judgment,' from *judex* (see JUDGE).

USAGE: **Judicial** means 'relating to judgment and the administration of justice': *the judicial system*; | *judicial robes*. Do not confuse it with **judicious**, which means 'prudent, reasonable': *getting off the highway the minute you felt tired was a judicious choice*. **Judiciary**, usually a noun and sometimes an adjective, refers to the judicial branch of government, the court system, or judges collectively.

ju•di•cial re•view /jōō'disHəl ri'vyōō/ ▸ n. (in the US) review by a court, especially the Supreme Court, of the constitutional validity of a legislative or administrative act or procedure.
■ (in the UK) a procedure by which a court can review an administrative action by a public body and (in England) secure a declaration, order, or award.

ju•di•cial sep•a•ra•tion /jōō'disHəl ˌsepə'rāsHən/ ▸ n. another term for LEGAL SEPARATION (sense 1).

ju•di•ci•ar•y /jōō'disHē,erē; -'disHərē/ ▸ n. (pl. **ju•di•ci•ar•ies**) (usu. **the judiciary**) the judicial authorities of a country; judges collectively.
ORIGIN early 19th cent.: from Latin *judiciarius*, from *judicium* 'judgment.'

USAGE: See usage at JUDICIAL.

ju•ral /'jŏŏrəl/ ▸ adj. formal of or relating to the law: *American jural heritage*.
ORIGIN mid 17th cent.: from Latin *jus, jur-* 'law, right' + *-al*.

ju•rat /'jŏŏræt/ ▸ n. **1** chiefly historical a person who has taken an oath or who performs a duty on oath, e.g., a juror.
2 a statement on an affidavit of when, where, and before whom it was sworn.
ORIGIN late Middle English: based on Latin *juratus* 'sworn,' past participle of *jurare* .

ju•rid•i•cal /jŏŏ'ridikəl/ ▸ adj. of or relating to judicial proceedings and the administration of the law: *the facts of the case did not involve any misuse of the juridicial process*.
DERIVATIVES **ju•rid•i•cal•ly** adv.
ORIGIN early 16th cent.: from Latin *juridicus* (from *jus, jur-* 'law' + *dicere* 'say') + *-al*.

ju•ris•dic•tion /ˌjŏŏris'diksHən/ ▸ n. the official power to make legal decisions and judgments: *federal courts had no **jurisdiction over** the case* | *the District of Columbia was placed under the **jurisdiction of** Congress*.
■ the extent of this power: *the claim will be **within the jurisdiction** of the Department of Transportation*. ■ a system of law courts; a judicature: *in some jurisdictions there is a mandatory death sentence for murder*. ■ the territory or sphere of activity over which the legal authority of a court or other institution extends: *several different tax jurisdictions*.

DERIVATIVES **ju•ris•dic•tion•al** /ˌjŏŏrisˈdiksHənl/ **adj.**

ORIGIN Middle English: from Old French *jurediction*, from Latin *jurisdictio(n-)*, from *jus, jur-* 'law' + *dictio* 'saying' (from *dicere* 'say').

ju•ris doc•tor /ˈjŏŏris ˈdäktər/ ▶ **n.** see **JD**.

ju•ris•pru•dence /ˌjŏŏrisˈprŏŏdns/ ▶ **n.** the theory or philosophy of law.
■ a legal system: *American jurisprudence.*

DERIVATIVES **ju•ris•pru•dent** adj. & n.; **ju•ris•pru•den•tial** /ˌjŏŏrisprŏŏˈdenCHəl/ **adj.**

ORIGIN early 17th cent.: from late Latin *jurisprudentia*, from Latin *jus, jur-* 'law' + *prudentia* 'knowledge.'

ju•rist /ˈjŏŏrist/ ▶ **n.** an expert in or writer on law.
■ a lawyer or a judge.

DERIVATIVES **ju•ris•tic** /jŏŏˈristik/ **adj.**

ORIGIN late 15th cent. (in the sense 'lawyer'): from French *juriste*, medieval Latin *jurista*, from *jus, jur-* 'law.'

ju•ror /ˈjŏŏrər; -ôr/ ▶ **n.** a member of a jury.

ORIGIN late Middle English: from Old French *jureor*, from Latin *jurator*, from *jurare* 'swear,' from *jus, jur-* 'law.'

ju•ry /ˈjŏŏrē/ ▶ **n.** (pl. **ju•ries**) a body of people (historically twelve in number) sworn to give a verdict in a legal case on the basis of evidence submitted to them in court. Also called **PETIT JURY, PETTY JURY**.

ORIGIN late Middle English: from Old French *juree* 'oath, inquiry,' from Latin *jurata*, feminine past participle of *jurare* 'swear' (see **JUROR**).

ju•ry box /ˈjŏŏrē ˌbäks/ ▶ **n.** a segregated area in which the jury sits in a court of law.

jus co•gens /ˈjəs ˈkōjənz/ ▶ **n.** the principles that form the norms of international law that cannot be set aside by treaty, etc.: [as adj.] *jus cogens norms.*

ORIGIN Latin, literally 'compelling law.'

jus gen•ti•um /ˈjəs ˈjensHēəm/ ▶ **n.** international law.

ORIGIN Latin, literally 'law of nations.'

jus•tice /ˈjəstis/ ▶ **n. 1** just behavior or treatment.
■ the administration of the law or authority in maintaining this: *a tragic miscarriage of justice.* ■ (**Justice**) the personification of justice, usually a blindfolded woman holding scales and a sword.
2 a judge or magistrate, in particular a judge of the supreme court of a country or state.

PHRASES **bring someone to justice** arrest someone for a crime and ensure that they are tried in court.

DERIVATIVES **jus•tice•ship** /ˈjəstisˌsHip/ **n.** (in sense 2).

ORIGIN late Old English *iustise* 'administration of the law,' via Old French from Latin *justitia*, from *justus*, from *jus* 'law, right.'

jus•tice of the peace /ˈjəstis əv THə ˈpēs/ ▶ **n.** a magistrate appointed to hear minor cases, perform marriages, grant licenses, etc., in a town, county, or other local district.

jus•ti•ci•a•ble /jəˈstisH(ē)əbəl/ ▶ **adj.** subject to trial in a court of law;

capable of being tried: *defendant maintains that plaintiff's claim is not justiciable.*

ORIGIN late Middle English: from Old French, from *justicier* 'bring to trial,' from medieval Latin *justitiare*, from Latin *justitia* 'equity,' from *justus* (see **JUSTICE**).

jus•ti•fi•a•ble hom•i•cide /ˌjəstə'fīəbəl 'hämə͵sīd/ ▶ n. the killing of a person in circumstances (especially self-defense) that allow the act to be regarded in law as without criminal guilt.

ju•ve•nile /'jo͞ovə͵nīl; -vənl/ ▶ n. a person below the age at which adult criminal prosecution is possible (18 in most countries).

ORIGIN early 17th cent.: from Latin *juvenilis*, from *juvenis* 'young, a young person.'

ju•ve•nile court /'jo͞ovə͵nīl 'kôrt; 'jo͞ovənl/ ▶ n. a court of law responsible for the trial or legal supervision of children under a specified age (18 in most countries).

ju•ve•nile de•lin•quen•cy /'jo͞ovə͵nīl də'liNGkwənsē; 'jo͞ovənl/ ▶ n. the committing of criminal acts or offenses by a young person, esp. one below the age at which ordinary criminal prosecution is possible.

DERIVATIVES **ju•ve•nile de•lin•quent** n.

ju•ve•nile of•fend•er /'jo͞ovə͵nīl ə'fendər; 'jo͞ovənl/ ▶ n. a person below a specific age (18 in most countries) who has committed a crime.

K

kan•ga•roo court /ˌkæNGgəˈroo ˌkôrt/ ▶ n. an improperly constituted court with no legal standing, which ignores procedures guaranteeing fair trials.

KC ▶ abbr. (in the UK) King's Counsel.

King's Bench /ˈkiNGz ˈbenCH/ ▶ n. (in the UK) in the reign of a king, the term for QUEEN'S BENCH.

King's Coun•sel /ˈkiNGz ˈkownsəl/ (abbr.: **KC**) ▶ n. (in the UK) in the reign of a king, the term for QUEEN'S COUNSEL.

WHAT IS A POWER OF ATTORNEY?

A *power of attorney* is a document designating an agent. If you sign a power of attorney, you are authorizing someone to act in your place in financial or other important matters, with the same legal effect as if you had taken the action personally. The person who executes a power of attorney is called the *principal.* The authority conferred upon the agent by the principal, like the document itself, is called *power of attorney.*

In a general sense, *attorney* refers to anyone authorized to act on another's behalf. Although we usually think of the word as short for *attorney-at-law*—an individual who represents others in legal proceedings—the agent named in a power of attorney is an *attorney-in-fact.* This need not be a lawyer; you can name as your attorney-in-fact any competent adult, or two or more individuals, or even an institution such as a bank. If you name two or more attorneys-in-fact, they can be authorized to act only *jointly* (all must agree) or also *severally* (any one can act). You can name an alternate attorney-in-fact to serve if the first-named agent becomes unable to do so, and have different attorneys-in-fact for different purposes. And if you change your mind later, you can revoke the power of attorney—although you will still be legally liable for anything that was done pursuant to the power of attorney while it was in effect.

A power of attorney may be *general* or *special.* A special (sometimes called *limited* or *specific*) power of attorney designates an attorney-in-fact for a particular purpose, such as voting the principal's shares in a corporate election, signing a contract, or bidding at an auction. A general power of attorney grants the attorney-in-fact general power to handle a range of matters—for example, paying bills or handling investments.

With a general power of attorney, a friend or relative can handle your financial affairs at home during your extended travel or military service. Such an application of power of attorney is a matter of convenience, but having someone else handle your affairs is crucial if you become incapable of doing it yourself through illness or mental incapacity. Unfortunately, the very circumstance that makes it impossible to sign one's own checks or make legally binding decisions also makes it impossible to execute a legally effective power of attorney. It has to be done before the need arises.

Until recently, however, even that was not good enough. The British common law, adopted almost everywhere in the United States, held that since an attorney-in-fact is merely a stand-in for the principal, the agent's authority ceased upon incapacity of the principal. Just when the need for the services of the attorney-in-fact became critical, the power of attorney became ineffective. In the United States, only Louisiana, whose legal system was heavily influenced by the French, was spared this perverse common law rule.

Beginning in the 1960s, the idea of permitting exceptions to this rule gradually caught on, and now all states have statutes permitting what is called a *durable* power of attorney—one that will remain in effect even if the principal becomes legally incapacitated. In most states, a power of attorney is still presumed to be *non*durable; to make it durable you have to include specific language, typically something like: "This power of attorney shall not be affected by subsequent disability or incapacity of the principal."

Some people are not comfortable with a durable power of attorney because it authorizes the attorney-in-fact to act before the need arises, while the principal is still capable of handling his or her own affairs. Some states therefore authorize a *standby* or *springing* power of attorney—one that lies dormant until the principal becomes incapacitated and then springs into effect. This requires language like: "This power of attorney shall become effective upon the disability or incapacity of the principal." The durable power of attorney is usually preferable because it avoids the complex issue of exactly when the principal becomes sufficiently incapacitated for the springing power of attorney to take effect. Besides, if you do not trust your attorney-in-fact to let you handle your own affairs so long as you want to and are able to, then you probably would not want that person in control of your affairs when you really need the help.

Although a power of attorney can be tailored to any individual situation, to be legally effective it must meet the requirements of your state law and be executed in the proper way—usually before a notary public. Some institutions, such as banks, will recognize the authority of an attorney-in-fact only if their own printed form is used for the power of attorney. For other purposes, a printed form using standard language set forth in a state statute, perhaps containing check boxes for inclusion or exclusion of various standard provisions (sometimes called a *statutory* or *short-form* power of attorney), can usually be obtained from stationery or office-supply stores, or over the Internet. You do not need a lawyer to prepare a power of attorney, but a lawyer can inform both the principal and the attorney-in-fact of the serious legal consequences of the instrument, make sure that a power of attorney is the best device for the intended purposes, and make sure that it is in proper form. For this reason, general powers of attorney are often prepared with legal counsel in connection with the making of a will and other estate and health planning.

A final kind of power of attorney is one that extends beyond the traditional subject matter of financial and business affairs to the realm of health care. For more on that, see *Making a Living Will*, p. 87.

L

lach•es /'læCHiz/ ▸ n. unreasonable delay in making an assertion or claim, such as asserting a right, claiming a privilege, or making an application for redress, which may result in refusal: *the court did not reach the issue of compliance because it found plaintiffs' claim to be barred by the doctrine of laches.*

ORIGIN late Middle English (in the sense 'slackness, negligence'): from Old French *laschesse*, from *lasche* 'loose, lax,' based on Latin *laxus* . The current sense dates from the late 16th cent.

lapse /læps/ ▸ n. the termination of a right or privilege through disuse or failure to follow appropriate procedures: *statutory exceptions had prevented a lapse of the water rights in question.*

▸ v. [intrans.] (of a right, privilege, or agreement) become invalid because it is not used, claimed, or renewed; expire: *the time for an appeal has not yet lapsed.*

ORIGIN late Middle English: from Latin *lapsus*, from *labi* 'to glide, slip, or fall'; the verb reinforced by Latin *lapsare* 'to slip or stumble.'

lar•ce•ny /'lärs(ə)nē/ ▸ n. (pl. **lar•ce•nies**) theft of personal property. See also **GRAND LARCENY, PETTY LARCENY.**

DERIVATIVES **lar•ce•ner** /'lärs(ə)nər/ n. (archaic); **lar•ce•nist** /'lärs(ə)nist/ n.; **lar•ce•nous** /'lärs(ə)nəs/ adj.

ORIGIN late 15th cent.: from Old French *larcin*, from Latin *latrocinium*, from *latro(n-)* 'robber,' earlier 'mercenary soldier,' from Greek *latreus*.

law /lô/ ▸ n. (often **the law**) the system of rules that a particular country or community recognizes as regulating the actions of its members and may enforce by the imposition of penalties, award of damages, and injunction: *they were taken to court for **breaking the law** | a license is required **by law** |* [as adj.] *law enforcement.*

■ an individual rule as part of such a system: *an initiative to tighten up the laws on pornography.* ■ such systems as a subject of study or as the basis of the legal profession: *he was still practicing law |* [as adj.] *a law firm.* Compare with **JURISPRUDENCE.** ■ **(the law)** informal the police: *he'd never been in trouble with the law in his life.* ■ statutory law and the common law. Compare with **EQUITY.**

PHRASES **at** (or **in**) **law** according to or concerned with the laws of a country: *an agreement enforceable at law* | *an attorney-at-law.* **go to law** resort to legal action in order to settle a matter. **law and order** a situation characterized by respect for and obedience to the rules of a society. **take someone to law** initiate legal proceedings against someone. ORIGIN Old English *lagu*, from Old Norse *lag* 'something laid down or fixed,' of Germanic origin and related to the verb *lay*.

law•break•er /'lô͵brākər/ ▶ n. a person who violates the law. DERIVATIVES **law•break•ing** n. & adj.

law court /'lô ͵kôrt/ ▶ n. a court of law.

law•ful /'lôfəl/ ▶ adj. conforming to, permitted by, or recognized by law or rules: *it is an offense to carry a weapon in public without lawful authority.* DERIVATIVES **law•ful•ly** adv.; **law•ful•ness** n.

law•giv•er /'lô͵givər/ ▶ n. a person who draws up and enacts laws.

law•mak•er /'lô͵mākər/ ▶ n. a legislator. DERIVATIVES **law•mak•ing** /'lô͵mākiNG/ adj. & n.

law•man /'lômən; -͵mæn/ ▶ n. (pl. **-men**) a law-enforcement officer, esp. a sheriff.

law of•fice /'lô ͵ôfis; ͵äfis/ ▶ n. a lawyer's office.

law of na•tions /'lô əv 'nāsHənz/ ▶ n. international law.

law of suc•ces•sion /'lô əv sək'sesHən/ ▶ n. the law regulating the inheritance of property.
■ the law regulating the appointment of a new monarch or head of state.

law•suit /'lô͵so͞ot/ ▶ n. a claim or dispute brought to a court of law for adjudication: *his lawyer filed a lawsuit against Los Angeles County.*

law•yer /'loi-ər; 'lôyər/ ▶ n. a person who practices or studies law; an attorney or a counselor.
▶ v. [intrans.] practice law; work as a lawyer: [as n.] (**lawyering**) *lawyering is a craft that takes a long time to become proficient at.*
■ [trans.] (of a lawyer) work on the legal aspects of (a contract, lawsuit, etc.): *there is always a danger that the deal will be lawyered to death.* DERIVATIVES **law•yer•ly** adj.

lease /lēs/ ▶ n. a contract by which one party conveys land, property, services, etc., to another for a specified time, usually in return for a periodic payment: *the company occupies 89 acres at Port Newark under a lease that expires in 2006.*
▶ v. [trans.] grant (property) on lease; let: *she leased the site to a local company.*
■ take (property) on lease; rent: *land was leased from the city.* DERIVATIVES **leas•a•ble** adj. ORIGIN late Middle English: from Old French *lais, leis,* from *lesser, laissier* 'let, leave,' from Latin *laxare* 'make loose,' from *laxus* 'loose, lax.'

lease•back /'lēs͵bæk/ ▶ n. [often as adj.] the leasing of a property back to its seller: *leaseback agreements.*

lease•hold /ˈlēs͵hōld/ ▶ n. the holding of property by lease: *a form of leasehold* | [as adj.] *leasehold premises.* Often contrasted with FREE-HOLD.
■ a property held by lease.
DERIVATIVES **lease•hold•er** n.
ORIGIN early 18th cent.: from LEASE, on the pattern of *freehold.*

leg•a•cy /ˈlegəsē/ ▶ n. (pl. **leg•a•cies**) an amount of money or property left to someone in a will: *the bonds were redeemed to satisfy a specific dollar amount legacy.*
■ a thing handed down by a predecessor.
ORIGIN late Middle English (also denoting the function or office of a deputy, esp. a papal legate): from Old French *legacie,* from medieval Latin *legatia* 'legateship,' from *legatus* 'person delegated.'

le•gal /ˈlēgəl/ ▶ adj. **1** [attrib.] of, based on, or concerned with the law: *the American legal system.*
■ appointed or required by the law: *a legal requirement.* ■ recognized by common or statutory law, as distinct from equity.
2 permitted by law: *he claimed that it had all been legal.*
DERIVATIVES **le•gal•ly** adv. [sentence adverb] *legally, we're still very much married.*
ORIGIN late Middle English (in the sense 'to do with Mosaic law'): from French, or from Latin *legalis,* from *lex, leg-* 'law.'

le•gal aid /ˈlēgəl ˈād/ ▶ n. payment from public funds allowed, in cases of need, to help pay for legal advice or proceedings.
■ (**Legal Aid**) an organization that provides free legal services to the indigent.

le•gal ca•pac•i•ty /ˈlēgəl kəˈpæsitē/ ▶ n. a person's authority under law to engage in a particular undertaking or maintain a particular status.

le•gal ea•gle /ˈlēgəl ˈēgəl/ (also **le•gal bea•gle** /ˈlēgəl ˈbēgəl/) ▶ n. informal a lawyer, esp. one who is keen and astute.

le•gal•ese /͵lēgəˈlēz; -ˈlēs/ ▶ n. informal, derogatory the formal and technical language of legal documents.

le•gal fic•tion /ˈlēgəl ˈfiksHən/ ▶ n. an assertion accepted as true, though probably fictitious, to achieve a useful purpose in legal matters: *an unqualified claim of "Made in USA" for products that are partly foreign is a legal fiction.*

le•gal•i•ty /liˈgælitē/ ▶ n. (pl. **le•gal•i•ties**) the quality or state of being in accordance with the law: *documentation testifying to the legality of the arms sale.*
■ (**legalities**) obligations imposed by law; legal procedures.
ORIGIN late Middle English: from French *légalité* or medieval Latin *legalitas* 'relating to the law,' from Latin *legalis* (see LEGAL).

le•gal•ize /ˈlēgə͵līz/ ▶ v. [trans.] make (something that was previously illegal) permissible by law: *a measure legalizing gambling in Deadwood.*
DERIVATIVES **le•gal•i•za•tion** /͵lēgələˈzāsHən; -͵līˈzā-/ n.

le•gal per•son /'lēgəl 'pərsən/ ▶ n. an individual or incorporated entity that has legal rights and is subject to obligations.

le•gal sep•a•ra•tion /'lēgəl ˌsepə'rāsHən/ ▶ n. **1** an arrangement by which a husband or wife remain married but live apart, following a court order. Also called JUDICIAL SEPARATION.
2 an arrangement by which a child lives apart from a natural parent and with the other natural parent or a foster parent, following a court order.

le•gal ten•der /'lēgəl tendər/ ▶ n. coins or banknotes that must be accepted if offered in payment of a debt: *only the federal government can mint coins that are legal tender.*

leg•a•tee /ˌlegə'tē/ ▶ n. a person who receives a legacy.
ORIGIN late 17th cent.: from 15th-cent. *legate* 'bequeath' (from Latin *legare* 'delegate, bequeath') + *-ee*.

le•ga•tor /li'gātər/ ▶ n. rare a testator, esp. one who leaves a legacy.
ORIGIN mid 17th cent.: from Latin, from *legat-* 'deputed, delegated, bequeathed,' from the verb *legare*.

leg•is•late /'leji,slāt/ ▶ v. [intrans.] make or enact laws: *he didn't want to name anyone to the Court who would legislate from the bench.*
■ [trans.] cover, affect, or create by making or enacting laws: *Congress must legislate strong new laws.*
ORIGIN early 18th cent.: back-formation from LEGISLATION.

leg•is•la•tion /ˌleji'slāsHən/ ▶ n. the action of making or enacting laws: *the framework for the market should be developed through legislation, not dictation.*
■ laws enacted by a legislature, considered collectively: *tax legislation.*
ORIGIN mid 17th cent. (denoting the enactment of laws): from late Latin *legis latio(n-)*, literally 'proposing of a law,' from *lex* 'law' and *latus* 'raised' (past participle of *tollere*).

leg•is•la•tive /'leji,slātiv/ ▶ adj. having the power to make laws: *the country's supreme legislative body.*
■ of or relating to laws or the making of them: *legislative proposals.* Often contrasted with EXECUTIVE. ■ of or relating to a legislature: *legislative elections.*
DERIVATIVES **leg•is•la•tive•ly** adv.

leg•is•la•tor /'leji,slātər/ ▶ n. a person who makes laws; a member of a legislative body.
ORIGIN late 15th cent.: from Latin *legis lator*, literally 'proposer of a law,' from *lex* 'law' and *lator* 'proposer, mover' (see also LEGISLATION).

leg•is•la•ture /'leji,slācHər/ ▶ n. the legislative body of a country or state.
ORIGIN late 17th cent.: from LEGISLATION, on the pattern of *judicature*.

le•git•i•mate ▶ adj. /li'jiṯəmit/ conforming to the law or to rules: *his claims to legitimate authority.*
■ (of a child) born of parents lawfully married to each other.

▶v. /li'jitə,māt/ [trans.] make legitimate; justify or make lawful: *the regime was not legitimated by popular support.*
DERIVATIVES **le•git•i•ma•cy** /li'jitəməsē/ n.; **le•git•i•mate•ly** /li'jitəmitlē/ **adv.**; **le•git•i•ma•tion** /li,jitə'māsHən/ n.; **le•git•i•ma•tize** /li'jitəmə,tīz/ **v.**
ORIGIN late Middle English (in the sense 'born of parents lawfully married to each other'): from medieval Latin *legitimatus* 'made legal,' from the verb *legitimare*, from Latin *legitimus* 'lawful,' from *lex, leg-* 'law.'
le•git•i•mize /li'jitə,mīz/ ▶ v. [trans.] make legitimate: *voters legitimize the government through the election of public officials.*
DERIVATIVES **le•git•i•mi•za•tion** /li,jitəmə'zāsHən/ n.
les•see /le'sē/ ▶ n. a person who holds the lease of a property; a tenant.
DERIVATIVES **les•see•ship** /le'sē,sHip/ n.
ORIGIN late 15th cent.: from Old French *lesse*, past participle of *lesser* 'to let, leave,' + *-ee*.
les•sor /'lesôr; le'sôr/ ▶ n. a person who leases or lets a property to another; a landlord.
ORIGIN late Middle English: from Anglo-Norman French, from Old French *lesser* 'let, leave.'
let•ters of ad•min•is•tra•tion /'letərz əv əd,minə'strāsHən/ ▶ plural n. authority to administer the estate of someone who has died without making a will.
let•ters pat•ent /'letərz 'pætnt/ ▶ plural n. a public document issued by a government or monarch conferring a patent or other right.
ORIGIN late Middle English: from medieval Latin *litterae patentes*, literally 'letters lying open.'
let•ters rog•a•to•ry /'letərz 'rōgə,tôrē; 'rägə,tôrē/ ▶ plural n. documents making a request through a foreign court for the obtaining of information or evidence from a specified person within the jurisdiction of that court.
ORIGIN mid 19th cent.: *rogatory* from medieval Latin *rogatorius* 'interrogatory.'
le•vy /'levē/ ▶ v. (**lev•ies, lev•ied**) [intrans.] (**levy on/upon**) seize (property) to satisfy a legal judgment: *there were no goods to levy upon.*
▶n. (pl. **lev•ies**) an item or set of items of property seized to satisfy a legal judgment.
ORIGIN Middle English (as a noun): from Old French *levee*, feminine past participle of *lever* 'raise,' from Latin *levare*, from *levis* 'light.'
lex fo•ri /'leks 'fôr,ī; 'fôr,ē/ ▶ n. the law of the state or country in which an action is brought.
ORIGIN Latin, 'law of the court.'
lex lo•ci /'leks 'lōsī; 'lōsē; 'lōkē; 'lōkī/ ▶ n. the law of the state or country in which a contract is made, a transaction is performed, a tort is committed, or a property is situated.
ORIGIN Latin, 'law of the place.'

lex ta•li•o•nis /ˈleks ˌtälēˈōnis; ˌtælēˈōnis/ ▶ n. the (supposed) law of retaliation, whereby a punishment resembles the offense committed in kind and degree.

ORIGIN Latin, from *lex* 'law' and *talio(n-)* 'retaliation' (from *talis* 'such').

li•a•ble /ˈlī(ə)bəl/ ▶ adj. responsible by law; legally answerable, especially when required to pay damages: *the supplier of goods or services can become **liable for** breach of contract in a variety of ways.*

ORIGIN late Middle English: perhaps from Anglo-Norman French, from French *lier* 'to bind,' from Latin *ligare.*

li•bel /ˈlībəl/ ▶ n. **1** a published false statement that is damaging to a person's reputation; a written defamation. Compare with SLANDER.

■ the action or crime of publishing such a statement: *a teacher who sued two newspapers for libel* | [as adj.] *a libel action.* ■ a false and malicious statement about a person. ■ a thing or circumstance that brings undeserved discredit on a person by misrepresentation.

2 (in admiralty, civil, and ecclesiastical law) a plaintiff's written declaration.

▶v. (**li•beled, li•bel•ing**; Brit. **li•belled, li•bel•ling**) [trans.] **1** defame (someone) by publishing a libel: *she alleged the magazine had libeled her.*

■ make a false and malicious statement about.

2 (in admiralty, civil, and ecclesiastical law) bring a suit against (someone).

DERIVATIVES **li•bel•er** n.

ORIGIN Middle English (in the general sense 'a document, a written statement'): via Old French from Latin *libellus,* diminutive of *liber* 'book.'

li•bel•ous /ˈlībələs/ (Brit. **li•bel•lous**) ▶ adj. containing or constituting a libel: *a libelous newspaper story.*

DERIVATIVES **li•bel•ous•ly** adv.

lib•er•ty /ˈlibərtē/ ▶ n. (pl. **-ies**) the state of being free within society from oppressive restrictions imposed by authority on one's way of life, behavior, or political views: *compulsory retirement would interfere with individual liberty.*

■ (usu. **liberties**) an instance of this; a right or privilege, esp. a statutory one: *the Bill of Rights was intended to secure basic civil liberties.* ■ the state of not being imprisoned or enslaved: *people who have lost property or liberty without due process.*

PHRASES **at liberty** not imprisoned: *he was at liberty for three months before he was recaptured.*

ORIGIN late Middle English: from Old French *liberte,* from Latin *libertas,* from *liber* 'free.'

li•cense /ˈlīsəns/ ▶ n. (Brit. **li•cence**) a permit from an authority to own or use something, do a particular thing, or carry on a trade (esp. in alcoholic beverages): *a gun license* | [as adj.] *vehicle license fees.*

■ formal or official permission to do something: *logging is permitted under license from the Forest Service.*

▶v. (Brit. also li•cence) [trans.] (often be licensed) grant a license to (someone or something) to permit the use of something or to allow an activity to take place: *brokers must be licensed to sell health-related insurance* | [with obj. and infinitive] *he ought not to have been licensed to fly a plane* | [as adj.] (licensing) *a licensing authority.*

■ authorize the use, performance, or release of (something): *the drug is already licensed for human use* | *firearms importers must be federally licensed.*

DERIVATIVES li•cens•a•ble adj.; li•cens•er n.; li•cen•sor /'līsənsər; ˌlīsən'sôr/ n.

ORIGIN late Middle English: via Old French from Latin *licentia* 'freedom, licentiousness' (in medieval Latin 'authority, permission'), from *licere* 'be lawful or permitted.'

li•censed /'līsənst/ ▶ adj. having an official license: *a licensed taxi operator.*

li•cen•see /ˌlīsən'sē/ ▶ n. the holder of a license.

lie /lī/ ▶ v. (lied /līd/, ly•ing /'lī-iNG/; past lay /lā/; past part. lain /lān/) [intrans.] (of an action, charge, or claim) be admissible or sustainable: *judicial review of such a declaratory ruling would have lain in the court of appeals.*

ORIGIN Old English *licgan*, of Germanic origin; related to Dutch *liggen* and German *liegen*, from an Indo-European root shared by Greek *lektron, lekhos* and Latin *lectus* 'bed.'

lie de•tec•tor /'lī di,tektər/ ▶ n. an instrument for determining whether a person is telling the truth by testing for physiological changes considered to be associated with lying.Compare with POLYGRAPH.

lien /'lē(ə)n/ ▶ n. a right to take or keep possession of property belonging to another person until a debt owed by that person is discharged: *creditor holds a judicial lien against the property in the amount of $2,472.01.*

ORIGIN mid 16th cent.: from French, via Old French *loien* from Latin *ligamen* 'bond,' from *ligare* 'to bind.'

life in•ter•est /'līf 'int(ə)rist/ ▶ n. a right to property that a person holds for life but cannot dispose of further.

life sen•tence /'līf 'sentns/ ▶ n. a criminal punishment of imprisonment for life.

lim•i•ta•tion /ˌlimi'tāSHən/ ▶ n. 1 the action of limiting something: *the limitation of local authorities' powers.*

2 (also limitation period) a legally specified period beyond which an action may be defeated or a property right is not to continue. See also STATUTE OF LIMITATIONS.

ORIGIN late Middle English: from Latin *limitatio(n-)*, from the verb *limitare*, from *limes* 'boundary, frontier.'

liq•ui•date /'likwi,dāt/ ▶ v. [trans.] close the affairs of (a company or firm) by ascertaining liabilities and apportioning assets: *no concluding inventory is necessary until the fiduciary liquidates the business.* ■ [intrans.] (of a company) undergo such a process. ■ convert (assets) into cash: *the plan allows them to liquidate $10,000,000 worth of property over seven years.* ■ pay off (a debt): *this system allows us to wait until recording the expense to liquidate the obligation.*

DERIVATIVES **liq•ui•da•tion** /ˌlikwi'dāsHən/ n.

ORIGIN mid 16th cent. (in the sense 'set out (accounts) clearly'): from medieval Latin *liquidat-* 'made clear,' from the verb *liquidare*, from Latin *liquidus*, from *liquere* 'be liquid.'

lis pen•dens /'lis 'pendenz/ ▶ n. a pending legal action: *there is now a lis pendens against the Jones's home.*

■ a formal notice of this.

ORIGIN Latin.

lit•er•ar•y ex•ec•u•tor /'litə,rerē ig,zekyətər/ ▶ n. a person entrusted with a dead writer's papers and copyrighted and unpublished works.

lit•i•gant /'litəgənt/ ▶ n. a person involved in a lawsuit.

▶adj. [postpositive] archaic involved in a lawsuit: *the parties litigant.*

ORIGIN mid 17th cent.: from French, from Latin *litigant-* 'carrying on a lawsuit,' from the verb *litigare* (see LITIGATE).

lit•i•gate /'litə,gāt/ ▶ v. [intrans.] go to law; be a party to or subject of a lawsuit: *that issue has been fully litigated.*

■ be counsel to a party to a lawsuit. ■ [trans.] take (a claim or a dispute) to a court of law: *once a taxpayer has litigated a particular year, no other litigation of that year is permitted.*

DERIVATIVES **lit•i•ga•tion** /ˌlitə'gāsHən/ n.; **lit•i•ga•tive** /'litə,gātiv/ adj.; **lit•i•ga•tor** /'litə,gātər/ n.

ORIGIN early 17th cent.: from Latin *litigat-* 'disputed in a lawsuit,' from the verb *litigare*, from *lis, lit-* 'lawsuit.'

li•ti•gious /lə'tijəs/ ▶ adj. concerned with lawsuits or litigation: *defense nuclear facilities are increasingly vulnerable to litigious proceedings.*

■ unreasonably prone to go to law to settle disputes. ■ suitable to become the subject of a lawsuit.

DERIVATIVES **li•ti•gious•ly** adv.; **li•ti•gious•ness** n.

ORIGIN late Middle English: from Old French *litigieux* or Latin *litigiosus*, from *litigium* 'litigation,' from *lis, lit-* 'lawsuit.'

liv•ing will /'liviNG 'wil/ ▶ n. a written statement detailing a person's desires regarding their medical treatment in circumstances in which they are no longer able to express informed consent, esp. an advance directive.

LLB ▶ abbr. Bachelor of Laws, formerly the first degree in law.

ORIGIN from Latin *legum baccalaureus.*

LLD ▶ abbr. Doctor of Laws, typically an honorary degree.

ORIGIN from Latin *legum doctor.*

LLM ▶ abbr. Master of Laws.

ORIGIN from Latin *legum magister.*

lo•cus /'lōkəs/ ▶ n. (pl. **lo•ci** /'lō,sī; -,sē; -,kī; -,kē/) the place where a particular event, especially a trespass, occurred: *a suspected locus of marijuana dealing.*
ORIGIN early 18th cent.: from Latin, 'place.'

lodge /läj/ ▶ v. [trans.] present (a complaint, appeal, claim, etc.) formally to the proper authorities: *he has 28 days in which to lodge an appeal.*

loi•ter /'loitər/ ▶ v. [intrans.] stand or wait around idly or without apparent purpose: *report suspicious activity or persons loitering around bike racks to the police.*
DERIVATIVES **loi•ter•er** n.
ORIGIN late Middle English: perhaps from Middle Dutch *loteren* 'wag around.'

loss of con•sor•ti•um /'lôs əv kən'sôrsHəm/ ▶ see CONSORTIUM.

low•er court /'lōər 'kôrt/ ▶ n. a court whose decisions may be overruled by another court on appeal.

lynch /linCH/ ▶ v. [trans.] (of a mob) kill (someone), esp. by hanging, for an alleged offense without legal authority: *four of eight suspected thieves were lynched when a mob broke into the Nyaburara subcounty jail.*
DERIVATIVES **lynch•er** n.
ORIGIN mid 19th cent.: from *Lynch's law*, early form of *lynch law* 'the practice of killing an alleged criminal by lynching,' named after Capt. William *Lynch*, head of a self-constituted judicial tribunal in Virginia *c.*1780.

M

mag•is•trate /ˈmæjəˌstrāt/ ▶ n. a civil officer or lay judge who administers the law, esp. one who conducts a court that deals with minor offenses and holds preliminary hearings for more serious ones.
■ in federal courts, a lower judicial officer.
DERIVATIVES **mag•is•tra•ture** /ˈmæjisˌstrāCHər; -strəˌCHo͞o(ə)r/ n.
ORIGIN late Middle English: from Latin *magistratus* 'administrator,' from *magister* 'master.'

main•te•nance /ˈmān̲t̲(ə)nəns/ ▶ n. the provision of financial support for a person's living expenses, or the support so provided.
■ alimony or child support: *spousal maintenance.*
ORIGIN Middle English (in the sense 'aiding a party in a legal action without lawful cause'): from Old French, from *maintenir,* from Latin *manu tenere* 'hold in the hand.'

ma•jor•i•ty /məˈjôrət̲ē; -ˈjär-/ ▶ n. (pl. **ma•jor•i•ties**) the age when a person is legally considered an adult, in most contexts either 18 or 21: *a minor claimant may wait until her majority to file a claim on her own behalf.*
ORIGIN mid 16th cent. (denoting superiority): from French *majorité,* from medieval Latin *majoritas,* from Latin *major,* comparative of *magnus* 'great.'

mal•fea•sance /mælˈfēzəns/ ▶ n. wrongdoing, esp. misconduct in the performance of duty by a public official: *corporate malfeasance.*
DERIVATIVES **mal•fea•sant** /mælˈfēzənt/ n. & adj.
ORIGIN late 17th cent.: from Anglo-Norman French *malfaisance,* from *mal-* 'evil' + Old French *faisance* 'activity.' Compare with **MIS-FEASANCE**.

mal•ice /ˈmælis/ ▶ n. wrongful or harmful intention, esp. as increasing the guilt of certain offenses: *petitioner's papers continuously assert that respondent **acted with malice** and in bad faith.*
ORIGIN Middle English: via Old French from Latin *malitia,* from *malus* 'bad.'

mal•ice a•fore•thought /ˈmælis əˈfôrˌTHôt/ ▶ n. a special form of the intention to kill or harm, which is held to distinguish manslaughter from murder.

ma•li•cious /məˈlishəs/ ▶ adj. characterized by malice, especially malice

aforethought; intending or intended to do harm: *malicious destruction of property.*
DERIVATIVES **ma•li•cious•ly** adv.; **ma•li•cious•ness** n.
ORIGIN Middle English (also in the sense 'wicked'): from Old French *malicios*, from Latin *malitiosus*, from *malitia* (see **MALICE**).

mal•prac•tice /mæl'præktis/ ▸ n. improper, illegal, or negligent professional treatment or activity, esp. by a medical practitioner, lawyer, or public official: *victims of medical malpractice | investigations into malpractices and abuses of power.*

man•da•mus /mæn'dāməs/ ▸ n. a judicial writ issued as a command to an inferior court or ordering a person or agency to perform a public or statutory duty: *a writ of mandamus.*
ORIGIN mid 16th cent.: from Latin, literally 'we command.'

man•date /'mæn,dāt/ ▸ n. an official order or commission to do something: *a mandate to seek the release of political prisoners.*
■ a commission by which a party is entrusted to perform a service, esp. without payment and with indemnity against loss by that party. ■ an order from an appellate court to a lower court to take a specific action. ■ a written authority enabling someone to carry out transactions on another's bank account.
▸v. [trans.] require (something) to be done; make mandatory: *the government began mandating better car safety.*
ORIGIN early 16th cent.: from Latin *mandatum* 'something commanded,' neuter past participle of *mandare*, from *manus* 'hand' + *dare* 'give.'

man•da•to•ry /'mændə,tôrē/ ▸ adj. required by law or rules; compulsory: *wearing helmets was made mandatory for cyclists.*
DERIVATIVES **man•da•to•ri•ly** /'mændə,tôrəlē/ adv.
ORIGIN late 15th cent.: from late Latin *mandatorius*, from Latin *mandatum* 'something commanded.'

man•slaugh•ter /'mæn,slôtər/ ▸ n. the crime of killing a human being without malice aforethought, or otherwise in circumstances not amounting to murder: *the defendant was convicted of manslaughter.*

ma•re clau•sum /,märä 'klowsəm; 'klôzəm/ ▸ n. (pl. **ma•ri•a clau•sa** /,mä-rēə 'klowsə; 'klôzə/) a sea or body of navigable water under the jurisdiction of a particular country.
ORIGIN Latin, 'closed sea.'

ma•re li•be•rum /,märä 'lēbə,rŏŏm; 'lībərəm/ ▸ n. (pl. **ma•ri•a li•be•ra** /,märēə 'lēbərə; 'lībərə/) a sea open to all nations.
ORIGIN Latin, literally 'free sea.'

mar•riage /'mærij; 'mer-/ ▸ n. the formal union of a man and a woman, typically recognized by law, by which they become husband and wife.
■ a relationship between married people or the period for which it lasts: *the children from his first marriage.*
PHRASES **by marriage** as a result of a marriage: *a distant cousin by*

marriage. **marriage of convenience** a marriage concluded to achieve a practical purpose.

ORIGIN Middle English: from Old French *mariage,* from *marier* 'marry.'

mar•riage li•cense /'mærij ˌlīsəns; 'merij/ ▸ n. a document giving official permission, as from a county, to marry.

■ a copy of the record of a legal marriage, with details of names, date, etc.

mar•ry[1] /'mærē; 'merē/ ▸ v. (**mar•ries, mar•ried**) [trans.] join in marriage: *I was married in church | the priest who married us*

■ take (someone) as one's wife or husband in marriage: *Eric asked me to marry him.* ■ [intrans.] enter into marriage: *they had no plans to marry.* ■ [intrans.] (**marry into**) become a member of (a family) by marriage. ■ (of a parent or guardian) give (a son or daughter) in marriage, esp. for reasons of expediency: *her parents married her to a wealthy landowner.*

ORIGIN Middle English: from Old French *marier,* from Latin *maritare,* from *maritus,* literally 'married,' (as a noun) 'husband.'

mar•shal /'märsHəl/ ▸ n. a federal or municipal law officer, typically with specified duties relating to court functions.

■ the head of a police department. ■ the head of a fire department.

DERIVATIVES **mar•shal•ship** /'märsHəlˌsHip/ n.

ORIGIN Middle English (denoting a high-ranking officer of state): from Old French *mareschal* 'blacksmith, commander,' from late Latin *mariscalcus,* from Germanic elements meaning 'horse' and 'servant.'

mar•tial law /'märsHəl 'lô/ ▸ n. military government involving the suspension of ordinary law.

mas•ter /'mæstər/ ▸ n. an officer appointed to assist the judge in a court case, as by making special findings.

ORIGIN Old English *mæg(i)ster* (later reinforced by Old French *maistre*), from Latin *magister;* probably related to *magis* 'more' (i.e., 'more important').

ma•te•ri•al /mə'tirēəl/ ▸ adj. (of evidence or a fact) significant or influential, esp. to the extent of determining a cause or affecting a judgment: *information that could be material to a murder inquiry.*

ORIGIN late Middle English (in the sense 'relating to matter'): from late Latin *materialis,* adjective from Latin *materia* 'matter.'

ma•te•ri•al•i•ty /mə,tirē'ælətē/ ▸ n. (pl. **ma•te•ri•al•i•ties**) the quality of being significant or influential: *the applicant must establish materiality on the balance of probabilities.*

mat•ter /'mætər/ ▸ n. something that is to be tried or proved in court; a case: *the Supreme Court granted certiorari in the matter of the second WorldCom order.*

PHRASES **a matter of record** see RECORD.

ORIGIN Middle English: via Old French from Latin *materia* 'timber, substance,' also 'subject of discourse,' from *mater* 'mother.'

may•hem /'māhem/ ▸ n. chiefly historical the crime of maliciously injuring or maiming someone, originally so as to render the victim defenseless.

ORIGIN early 16th cent.: from Old French *mahaignier*, from which *maim* is derived.

meas•ure /'mezHər/ ▸ n. a legislative bill: *the Senate passed the measure by a 48–30 vote.*

ORIGIN Middle English (as a noun in the senses 'moderation,' 'instrument for measuring,' 'unit of capacity'): from Old French *mesure*, from Latin *mensura*, from *mens-* 'measured,' from the verb *metiri*.

med•i•cal ju•ris•pru•dence /'medikəl ˌjo͞ori'spro͞odns/ ▸ n. forensic medicine.

mens re•a /menz 'rēə/ ▸ n. the intention or knowledge of wrongdoing that constitutes part of a crime, as opposed to the action or conduct of the accused. Compare with ACTUS REUS.

ORIGIN mid 19th cent.: Latin, literally 'guilty mind.'

men•tal cru•el•ty /'mentl 'kro͞oəltē/ ▸ n. conduct that makes another person, especially one's spouse, suffer but does not involve physical assault: *a divorce on the grounds of mental cruelty.*

merge /mərj/ ▸ v. combine or cause to combine to form a single entity, esp. a commercial organization: [intrans.] *the utility companies are cutting costs and **merging with** other companies* | [trans.] *the company plans to **merge** its US oil production operations **with** those of a London-based organization.*

ORIGIN mid 17th cent. (in the sense 'immerse (oneself)'): from Latin *mergere* 'to dip, plunge.' The use in legal contexts is from Anglo-Norman French *merger*.

merg•er /'mərjər/ ▸ n. a combination of two things, esp. companies, into one: *a **merger between** two supermarket chains* | *local companies ripe for merger or acquisition.*

■ the incorporation of one right, estate, claim, etc., into another.

ORIGIN early 18th cent.: from Anglo-Norman French *merger* (verb used as a noun): see MERGE.

mer•ger clause /'mərjər ˌklôz/ ▸ n. in a contract, provision stating that the written agreement constitutes the entire agreement between the parties.

mer•i•to•ri•ous /'meri ˌtôrēəs/ ▸ adj. (of an action or claim) likely to succeed on the merits of the case: *defendant failed to raise even a hint of a defense that the court considered meritorious.*

DERIVATIVES **mer•i•to•ri•ous•ly** adv.; **mer•i•to•ri•ous•ness** n.

ORIGIN late Middle English (in the sense 'entitling a person to reward'): from late Latin *meritorius* (from *merit-* 'earned,' from the verb *mereri*) + *-ous.*

mer•its /'merits/ ▸ n. the intrinsic rights and wrongs of a case, outside of any other considerations, such as jurisdiction: *a plaintiff who has a good arguable case **on the merits**.*

ORIGIN Middle English (originally in the sense 'deserved reward or punishment'): via Old French from Latin *meritum* 'due reward,' from *mereri* 'earn, deserve.'

mesne /mēn/ ▸ **adj.** in the midst of an action; intermediate: *the Escrow Account is not subject to lien, garnishment, attachment, or any other similar process, mesne or final, on the part of the bank.*

ORIGIN late Middle English (as adverb and noun): from legal French, variant of Anglo-Norman French *meen* 'middle.'

mesne prof•its /ˈmēn ˌpräfits/ ▸ **plural n.** the profits of an estate received by a tenant in wrongful possession and recoverable by the landlord.

mes•suage /ˈmeswij/ ▸ **n.** a dwelling house with outbuildings and land assigned to its use.

ORIGIN late Middle English: from Anglo-Norman French, based on Latin *manere* 'dwell.'

mil•i•tar•y law /ˈmiliˌterē ˌlô/ ▸ **n.** the law governing the armed forces.

min•i•mum wage /ˈminəməm ˈwāj/ ▸ **n.** the lowest wage permitted by law or by a special agreement (such as one with a labor union).

min•is•te•ri•al /ˌminəˈstirēəl/ ▸ **adj.** of or relating to the duties of a government official: *ministerial acts.*

DERIVATIVES **min•is•te•ri•al•ly adv.**

ORIGIN mid 16th cent.: from French *ministériel* or late Latin *ministerialis*, from Latin *ministerium* 'ministry.'

Mi•ran•da /məˈrændə/ ▸ **adj.** denoting or relating to the duty of the police to inform a person taken into custody of their right to legal counsel and the right to remain silent under questioning: *the patrolman read Lee his Miranda rights.*

ORIGIN mid 20th cent.: from *Miranda* v. Arizona (1966), the case that led to this ruling by the US Supreme Court.

mis•car•riage of jus•tice /misˈkærij əv ˈjəstis/ ▸ **n.** a failure of a court or judicial system to attain the ends of justice, esp. one that results in the conviction of an innocent person.

mis•chief /ˈmisCHif/ ▸ **n.** harm or trouble caused by someone or something: *criminal mischief.*

ORIGIN late Middle English (denoting misfortune or distress): from Old French *meschief*, from the verb *meschever*, from *mes-* 'adversely' + *chever* 'come to an end' (from *chef* 'head').

mis•de•mean•ant /ˌmisdəˈmēnənt/ ▸ **n.** formal a person convicted of a misdemeanor.

■ a person guilty of misconduct.

ORIGIN early 19th cent.: from archaic *misdemean* 'misbehave' + *-ant.*

mis•de•mean•or /ˈmisdiˌmēnər/ (Brit. **mis•de•mean•our**) ▸ **n.** a crime regarded in the US (and formerly in the UK) as less serious than a felony.

mis•fea•sance /misˈfēzəns/ ▸ **n.** a transgression, esp. the wrongful exercise of lawful authority.

ORIGIN early 17th cent.: from Old French *mesfaisance*, from *mesfaire*, from *mes-* 'wrongly' + *faire* 'do' (from Latin *facere*). Compare with **MALFEASANCE, NONFEASANCE.**

mis•pri•sion /mis'priZHən/ (also **mis•pri•sion of trea•son** or **fel•o•ny**) ▶ n. chiefly historical the deliberate concealment of one's knowledge of a treasonable act or a felony.
ORIGIN late Middle English: from Old French *mesprision* 'error,' from *mesprendre*, from *mes-* 'wrongly' + *prendre* 'to take.'

mis•rep•re•sen•ta•tion /mis,reprəzən'tāSHən/ ▶ n. a false or misleading statement: *persons who suffer from a realtor's misrepresentation may be able to recover their losses.*
■ the legal action to provide a remedy for a false or misleading statement.

mis•tri•al /'mis,trī(ə)l/ ▶ n. a trial rendered invalid through an error in the proceedings: *the juvenile court judge disqualified himself because of concerns about his impartiality and declared a mistrial.*
■ an inconclusive trial, such as one in which the jury cannot agree on a verdict.

mit•i•ga•tion /,miti'gāSHən/ ▶ n. the action of reducing the severity, seriousness, or painfulness of something.
PHRASES **in mitigation** so as to make something, esp. a crime, appear less serious and thus be punished more leniently: *in mitigation she said her client had been deeply depressed.*
DERIVATIVES **mit•i•gate** /'miti,gāt/ v.; **mit•i•gat•ing as adj.**: *mitigating circumstances.*
ORIGIN late Middle English: from Old French, or from Latin *mitigatio(n-)*, from the verb *mitigare* 'alleviate.'

moi•e•ty /'moi-itē/ ▶ n. (pl. **moi•e•ties**) formal technical each of two parts into which a thing is or can be divided, especially a joint tenancy.
■ a part or portion, esp. a lesser share.
ORIGIN late Middle English: from Old French *moite*, from Latin *medietas* 'middle,' from *medius* 'mid, middle.'

moot /mo͞ot/ ▶ adj. subject to debate, dispute, or uncertainty, and typically not admitting of a final decision.
▶n. a mock trial set up to examine a hypothetical case as an academic exercise.
ORIGIN Old English *mōt* 'assembly or meeting' and *mōtian* 'to converse,' of Germanic origin; related to *meet*. The adjective (originally an attributive noun use: see **MOOT COURT**) dates from the mid 16th cent.

moot court ▶ n. a mock court at which law students argue imaginary cases for practice.

mor•a•to•ri•um /,môrə'tôrēəm; ,mär-/ ▶ n. (pl. **mor•a•to•ri•ums** or **mor•a•to•ri•a** /,môrə'tôrēə; ,mär-/) a legal authorization to debtors to postpone payment.
■ the period of this postponement.
ORIGIN late 19th cent.: modern Latin, neuter (used as a noun) of late Latin *moratorius* 'delaying,' from Latin *morat-* 'delayed,' from the verb *morari*, from *mora* 'delay.'

mort•gage /'môrgij/ ▶ n. the conveyance of real (or personal) property by a debtor to a creditor as security for a debt (esp. one incurred by the debtor in the purchase of the property), on the condition that it shall be returned on payment of the debt within a certain period. ■ a deed effecting such a transaction. ■ a loan obtained through the conveyance of property as security: *I put down a hundred thousand in cash and took out a mortgage for the rest.*

▸v. [trans.] (often **be mortgaged**) convey (a property) to a creditor as security on a loan: *the estate was mortgaged up to the hilt.*

DERIVATIVES **mort•gage•a•ble** adj.

ORIGIN late Middle English: from Old French, literally 'dead pledge,' from *mort* (from Latin *mortuus* 'dead') + *gage* 'pledge.'

mort•ga•gee /ˌmôrgəˈjē/ ▸n. the lender in a mortgage, typically a bank.

mort•ga•gor /ˌmôrgiˈjôr; ˈmôrgijər/ ▸n. the borrower in a mortgage, typically a homeowner.

mo•tion /ˈmōsHən/ ▸n. an application for a rule or order of court: *the agency's motion to block the acquisition was denied.*

ORIGIN late Middle English: via Old French from Latin *motio(n-)*, from *movere* 'to move.'

mouth•piece /ˈmowTHˌpēs/ ▸n. informal a lawyer.

mov•a•ble /ˈmo͞ovəbəl/ (also **move•a•ble**) ▸adj. (of property) of the nature of a chattel, as distinct from land or buildings; personal.

▸n. (usu. **movables**) property or possessions not including land or buildings: *we have not appraised the movables as part of the real estate.* ■ an article of furniture that may be removed from a house, as distinct from a fixture.

ORIGIN late Middle English: from Old French, from *moveir* 'to move.'

mov•ant /ˈmo͞ovənt/ ▸n. a person who applies to or petitions a court or judge for a ruling in his or her favor.

ORIGIN late 19th cent.: from *move* + *-ant.*

move /mo͞ov/ ▸v. [trans.] make a formal request or application to (a court or assembly) for something: *his family moved the court for adequate "maintenance expenses" to run the household.*

ORIGIN Middle English: from Old French *moveir*, from Latin *movere.*

mur•der /ˈmərdər/ ▸n. the unlawful premeditated killing of one human being by another. Compare with MANSLAUGHTER.

▸v. [trans.] kill (someone) unlawfully and with premeditation.

PHRASES **murder one** (or **two**) informal first-degree (or second-degree) murder.

DERIVATIVES **mur•der•er** n.; **mur•der•ess** /ˈmərdərəs/ n.

ORIGIN Old English *morthor*, of Germanic origin; related to Dutch *moord* and German *Mord*, from an Indo-European root shared by Sanskrit *mará* 'death' and Latin *mors*; reinforced in Middle English by Old French *murdre.*

THINKING ABOUT
LAW SCHOOL

Why go to law school?

L aw school is said to be good preparation for just about any career. However, while it can't hurt to have a legal education, you should think twice before subjecting yourself to the time and expense unless you envision yourself with a career in law.

If you are not sure whether law school is for you, note that there is much more to law than the trial work misleadingly portrayed on television. (See *Watching Lawyer Shows*, p. 205.) Most practicing lawyers never set foot in a courtroom unless they are summoned for jury duty. Lawyers work in areas as diverse as personal injury, immigration, real estate, trusts and estates, intellectual property (trademark, patent, and copyright), taxation, civil rights, labor, entertainment, environmental law, family law, elder law, international law, and business law of every kind—from helping a new enterprise get on its feet to helping multinational corporations with securities, antitrust, international trade, and countless other matters.

In addition to practicing in law firms, many lawyers do legal work in corporations, banks, the military, nonprofit organizations such as charities and universities, or civil rights and international human rights organizations. Thousands upon thousands of lawyers work at every level of government, in fields as wide-ranging as the scope of government itself. Lawyers often go into politics. Some lawyers become law school professors.

Choosing a school

In one important respect, choosing a law school—or rather, a set of law schools to apply to—is easier than it used to be. Every law school has a Web site filled with information about its program, campus, costs, financial aid, student body, alumni, faculty, library, career counseling, and so on. To help organize this information and focus on the schools most likely to be of interest to you, books that compile basic information about all law schools in standardized form are invaluable.

The factors to be considered include:

Accreditation.

Most states require lawyers to have a degree from a law school accredited by the American Bar Association (ABA). California recognizes degrees from unaccredited schools, but only if the students pass a special state examination.

Location.

If you are certain where you want to settle with your law degree, there may be some advantage to choosing a law school in that area or state. A degree and network of contacts from the local university might advance your career more than one from a widely renowned institution far away.

Prestige.

On the other hand, a degree from a well-known, prestigious school can certainly help you get a foot in the door in many places, especially the major national law firms. In assessing quality, though, do not give too much weight to publications that purport to "rank" law schools in detail.

Specialties.

You are not expected to be sure what kind of law will most interest you before you start law school, and you are not required to specialize once you get there. But if you are going to law school to pursue your dream of working in a particular area, you will certainly want to consider law schools that have special programs or expertise in that area.

Part-time programs.

For those who have to keep working, some law schools offer the option of attending at night. This takes four grueling years instead of three, but if you have the stamina, go for it. Once you have the degree, it counts the same as any other degree from that school; in fact, a potential employer may respect you all the more for the dedication and capacity for hard and sustained work that your degree represents.

Scores.

No school evaluates candidates solely on the basis of scores, but scores are important. Be aware of the odds that a person with your college grades and your scores on the Law School Admissions Test (LSAT) will be accepted at a particular school. As a rule of thumb, you want to apply to several schools, from one or two where you are almost certain to be accepted to one or two that you would like to attend but where your odds of acceptance are lower.

Cost.

Most people leave law school with a mountain of debt. Tuition, living costs, books, computers, and forgoing working for three years make law school expensive. Public universities, especially in your home state, are usually less costly than private law schools, but be sure to aggressively explore the possibilities for financial aid at any school that interests you.

Party schools.

Forget it; there aren't any. Law school is not college. The student body is older, the atmosphere can be competitive, the work is often a grind—good practice for life as a new lawyer! Most lawyers remember law school as challenging, stimulating, and even a happy time; fewer would say that it was fun.

How to prepare

Many books can help with getting into law school—preparing for the LSAT, writing the personal essay, and so on. It is best to start this process at least a year and a half before you plan to start law school. But preparation for law school itself is a broader process—one of education and experience.

A broad college education is useful for law school, but your particular undergraduate major is irrelevant. For law schools, the purpose of college is to develop maturity, expand horizons, acquire a general intellectual background, and above all gain experience with rigorous thinking and cogent writing. If you are still in a position to choose courses, include some that will force you to think analytically and write precisely. If you have work or other experience after college, most law schools would say so much the better; they recognize that a diversity of interests, experiences, and backgrounds is essential to the intellectual richness of the law school experience.

neg•li•gence /'neglijəns/ ▶ n. failure to use reasonable care, resulting in damage or injury to another: *manslaughter by negligence.*

neg•li•gent /'neglijənt/ ▶ adj. failing to take proper or reasonable care in doing something: *directors have been negligent in the performance of their duties.*

DERIVATIVES **neg•li•gent•ly** adv.

ORIGIN late Middle English: from Old French, or from Latin *negligent-* 'disregarding,' from the verb *negligere* (variant of *neglegere* 'disregard, slight.'

ne•go•ti•a•ble /nə'gōsн(ē)əbəl/ ▶ adj. open to discussion or modification: *the price was not negotiable.*

■ (of a document) able to be transferred or assigned to the legal ownership of another person: *negotiable securities.*

DERIVATIVES **ne•go•ti•a•bil•i•ty** /nə,gōsн(ē)ə'bilitē/ n.

ni•si /'nīsī/ ▶ adj. [postpositive] (of a decree, order, or rule) taking effect or having validity only after a specified period of time, as long as certain changes of condition have not occurred: *a decree nisi.*

ORIGIN mid 19th cent.: from Latin, literally 'unless.'

no-fault /'nō 'fôlt/ ▶ adj. [attrib.] not assigning fault or blame, in particular:

■ denoting an insurance policy that is valid regardless of whether the policyholder was at fault: *no-fault automobile insurance.* ■ denoting an insurance or compensation plan (esp. one covering medical or industrial accidents) whereby a claimant need not legally prove negligence against any party. ■ of or denoting a form of divorce granted without requiring one party to prove that the other is to blame for the breakdown of the marriage.

no-knock /'nō 'näk/ ▶ adj. denoting or relating to a search or raid by the police made without warning or identification: *a no-knock raid.*

nol•le pros /,nälē 'präs/ (also **nol-pros** /,nôl 'präs/) (abbr.: **nol. pros.**) ▶ v. (**prossed, pros•sing**) [trans.] abandon or dismiss (a suit) by issuing a nolle prosequi: *all of the bills are marked "fugitive" and were nolle prossed in 1952.*

nol•le pros•e•qui /,nälē 'präsi,kwī/ ▶ n. a formal notice of abandonment by a plaintiff or prosecutor of all or part of a suit or action.

■ the entry of this in a court record.

ORIGIN late 17th cent.: Latin, literally 'be unwilling to pursue.'

no•lo con•ten•de•re /ˌnōlō kənˈtendərē/ ▸ n. (also **no•lo**) a plea by which a criminal defendant accepts conviction as though a guilty plea had been entered but does not admit guilt: *he pleaded nolo contendere in Providence County Superior Court to a charge of possession of heroin.*

ORIGIN Latin, literally 'I do not wish to contend.'

non•ap•pear•ance /ˌnänəˈpirəns/ ▸ n. failure to appear or be present in a court of law, esp. as a witness, defendant, or plaintiff.

non•cap•i•tal /nänˈkæpitl/ ▸ adj. (of an offense) not punishable by death.

non•de•liv•er•y /ˌnändiˈlivərē/ ▸ n. failure to deliver property: *nondelivery of merchandise ordered on the Internet.*

non•fea•sance /nänˈfēzəns/ ▸ n. failure to perform an act that one should perform: *the injury is directly traceable to the Commission's alleged nonfeasance.*

non•ju•ry /nänˈjo͝orē/ ▸ adj. denoting a trial or legal action not involving or requiring a jury.

non•suit /nänˈso͞ot/ ▸ v. [trans.] (of a judge or court) subject (a plaintiff) to the stoppage of a suit on the grounds of failure to make a legal case or bring sufficient evidence. *the judge at the circuit nonsuited the plaintiff, then fifth district affirmed.*

▸ n. the stoppage of a suit on such grounds: *a motion for nonsuit.*

ORIGIN late Middle English (as a noun): from Anglo-Norman French, literally 'not pursuing.'

no•ta•rize /ˈnōtəˌrīz/ ▸ v. [trans.] have (a document) legalized by a notary.

■ (of a notary) legalize a document by certifying its authenticity.

no•ta•ry /ˈnōtərē/ (in full **no•ta•ry pub•lic**) ▸ n. (pl. **no•ta•ries**) a person authorized to perform certain legal formalities, esp. to certify contracts, deeds, and other documents.

DERIVATIVES **no•tar•i•al** /nōˈterēəl/ adj.

ORIGIN Middle English (in the sense 'clerk or secretary'): from Latin *notarius* 'secretary,' from *nota* 'mark.'

no•va•tion /nōˈvāsHən/ ▸ n. the substitution of a new contract (especially with a substitute debtor) in place of an old one.

DERIVATIVES **no•vate** /ˈnōvāt; nōˈvāt/ v.

ORIGIN early 16th cent.: from late Latin *novatio(n-)*, from the verb *novare* 'make new.'

nui•sance /ˈn(y)o͞osəns/ ▸ n. a person, thing, or circumstance causing inconvenience or annoyance.

■ (also **private nuisance**) an unlawful interference with the use and enjoyment of a person's property. ■ see **PUBLIC NUISANCE**.

ORIGIN late Middle English (in the sense 'injury, hurt'): from Old French, 'hurt,' from the verb *nuire*, from Latin *nocere* 'to harm.'

null /nəl/ ▸ adj. having no legal or binding force; invalid: *the establishment of a new interim government was declared null and void.*

ORIGIN late Middle English: from French *nul*, *nulle*, from Latin *nullus* 'none,' from *ne* 'not' + *ullus* 'any.'

nul•li•ty /'nəlitē/ ▶ n. (pl. **nul•li•ties**) an act or thing that is legally void: *the decision is not a nullity simply because it has been appealed.*

■ the state of being legally void; invalidity, esp. of a marriage.

ORIGIN mid 16th cent.: from French *nullité*, from medieval Latin *nullitas*, from Latin *nullus* 'none.'

nun•cu•pa•tive /'nəNGkyə,pātiv/ ▶ adj. (of a will or testament) declared orally as opposed to in writing, often by a mortally wounded person: *nuncupative wills are valid only in a minority of states.*

ORIGIN mid 16th cent.: from late Latin *nuncupativus*, from Latin *nuncupat-* 'named, declared,' from the verb *nuncupare*.

O

oath /ōTH/ ▸ n. (pl. **oaths** /ōTHs; ōT͟Hz/) a sworn declaration that one will tell the truth, esp. in a court of law.

PHRASES **under oath** having sworn to tell the truth, esp. in a court of law.

ORIGIN Old English *āth*, of Germanic origin; related to Dutch *eed* and German *Eid*.

ob•i•ter dic•tum /'ōbiţər 'diktəm/ ▸ n. (pl. **ob•i•ter dic•ta** /'ōbiţər 'diktə/) a judge's incidental expression of opinion, not essential to the decision of a case and not establishing precedent.

ORIGIN Latin *obiter* 'in passing' + *dictum* 'something that is said.'

ob•li•ga•tion /ˌäbli'gāSHən/ ▸ n. the condition of being morally or legally bound to do something: *a juvenile* **under obligation** *to pay restitution may petition the court for modification of the restitution order.*

■ a binding agreement committing a person to a payment or other action. ■ a document containing a binding agreement; a written contract or bond.

DERIVATIVES **ob•li•ga•tion•al** /ˌäbli'gāSHənl/ adj.

ORIGIN Middle English (in the sense 'formal promise'): via Old French from Latin *obligatio(n-)*, from the verb *obligare*, *ob-* 'toward' + *ligare* ' to bind.'

ob•li•gee /ˌäbli'jē/ ▸ n. a person to whom another is bound by contract or other legal procedure. Compare with OBLIGOR.

ob•li•gor /ˌäbli'gôr/ ▸ n. a person who is bound to another by contract or other legal procedure. Compare with OBLIGEE.

ob•scene /əb'sēn/ ▸ adj. (of the portrayal or description of sexual matters) offensive or disgusting by accepted standards of morality and decency: *obscene literature.*

DERIVATIVES **ob•scene•ly** adv.

ORIGIN late 16th cent.: from French *obscène* or Latin *obscaenus* 'ill-omened or abominable.'

ob•scen•i•ty /əb'seniţē/ ▸ n. (pl. **ob•scen•i•ties**) the state or quality of being obscene; obscene behavior, language, or images: *the book was banned for obscenity.*

■ an extremely offensive word or expression: *they muttered obscenities.*

ORIGIN late 16th cent.: from French *obscénité* or Latin *obscaenitas*, from *obscaenus* (see OBSCENE).

ob•struct /əb'strəkt; äb-/ ▶ v. [trans.] commit the offense of intentionally hindering (a legal process): *the defendant knowingly obstructed a federal grand jury investigation.*
DERIVATIVES **ob•struc•tion** /əb'strəksHən; äb-/ n.; **ob•struc•tor** /əb 'strəktər; äb-/ n.
ORIGIN late 16th cent.: from Latin *obstruct-* 'blocked up,' from the verb *obstruere*, from *ob-* 'against' + *struere* 'build, pile up.'

oc•cu•pan•cy /'äkyəpənsē/ ▶ n. the action or fact of occupying a place: *the right of private occupancy of a room* .

oc•cu•pant /'äkyəpənt/ ▶ n. a person holding property, esp. land, in actual possession.
ORIGIN late 16th cent. (in the legal sense 'person who establishes a title'): from French, or from Latin *occupant-* 'seizing,' from the verb *occupare.*

of•fense /ə'fens/ (Brit. **of•fence**) ▶ n. a breach of a law or rule; an illegal act: *neither offense violates any federal law.*
ORIGIN late Middle English: from Old French *offens* 'misdeed,' from Latin *offensus* 'annoyance,' reinforced by French *offense*, from Latin *offensa* 'a striking against, a hurt, or displeasure'; based on Latin *offendere* 'strike against.'

of•fi•cer /'ôfisər; 'äf-/ ▶ n. a bailiff.
ORIGIN Middle English: via Anglo-Norman French from medieval Latin *officiarius*, from Latin *officium* 'performance of a task.'

Old Bai•ley /ˌōld 'bālē/ the central criminal court in London, England.

o•mis•sion /ō'misHən/ ▶ n. a failure to do something, esp. something that one has a moral or legal obligation to do: *they were fined for a wrongful omission of material information.*
DERIVATIVES **o•mis•sive** /ō'misiv/ adj.
ORIGIN late Middle English: from late Latin *omissio(n-)*, from the verb *omittere*, from *ob-* 'down' + *mittere* 'let go.'

o•pen•ing /'ōp(ə)niNG/ ▶ n. an attorney's preliminary statement of a case in a court of law: [as adj.] *the defense's opening statement.*

o•pin•ion /ə'pinyən/ ▶ n. a formal statement of reasons for a judgment given: *a five-justice majority opinion.*
■ a lawyer's or official's advice on the merits of a case or legalities of an issue.
ORIGIN Middle English: via Old French from Latin *opinio(n-)*, from the stem of *opinari* 'think, believe.'

or•deal /ôr'dēl/ ▶ n. historical an ancient test of guilt or innocence by subjection of the accused to severe pain, survival of which was taken as divine proof of innocence.
ORIGIN Old English *ordāl*, *ordēl*, of Germanic origin; related to German *urteilen* 'give judgment,' from a base meaning 'share out.' The word is not found in Middle English (except once in

Chaucer's *Troylus*); modern use of this sense began in the late 16th cent.

or•der /ˈôrdər/ ▸ **n. 1** the prescribed or established procedure followed by a meeting, legislative assembly, debate, or court of law: *the meeting was **called to order**.*
2 a written direction of a court or judge: *a judge's order forbidding the reporting of evidence.*
■ a written direction to pay money or deliver property: *a spousal maintenance order.*
▸ **v.** [reporting verb] give an authoritative direction or instruction to do something: [with clause] *the court ordered that the case should be heard at the end of August* | [trans.] *the judge ordered a retrial.*
PHRASES **by order of** according to directions given by the proper authority: *he was released from prison by order of the court.* **in order** in accordance with the rules of procedure at a meeting, legislative assembly, etc. **Order!** a call for silence or the observance of prescribed procedures by someone in charge of a trial, legislative assembly, etc. **out of order** not according to the rules of a meeting, legislative assembly, etc.
ORIGIN Middle English: from Old French *ordre*, from Latin *ordo*, *ordin-* 'row, series, rank.'

or•di•nance /ˈôrdn-əns/ ▸ **n. 1** a piece of legislation enacted by a municipal authority: *a city ordinance banned smoking in nearly all types of restaurants.*
2 an authoritative order; a decree.
ORIGIN Middle English (also in the sense 'arrangement in ranks'): from Old French *ordenance*, from medieval Latin *ordinantia*, from Latin *ordinare* 'put in order.'

or•di•nar•y /ˈôrdn,erē/ ▸ **adj.** (esp. of a judge) exercising authority by virtue of office and not by delegation.
▸ **n.** (pl. **or•di•nar•ies**) Brit. a person, esp. a judge, exercising authority by virtue of office and not by delegation.
■ in some US states, a judge of probate.
ORIGIN late Middle English: the noun partly via Old French; the adjective from Latin *ordinarius* 'orderly' (reinforced by French *ordinaire*), from *ordo*, *ordin-* 'order.'

o•rig•i•nal jur•is•dic•tion /əˈrijənl ˌjo͝orisˈdikSHən/ ▸ **n.** the authority of a court to hear and decide a matter prior to any other court's review of the matter: *the Supreme Court shall have original jurisdiction of all controversies between two or more states.*

oust /owst/ ▸ **v.** [trans.] deprive (someone) of or exclude (someone) from possession of something: *Roberts was in serious jeopardy of being ousted from his apartment.*
ORIGIN late Middle English (as a legal term): from Anglo-Norman French *ouster* 'take away,' from Latin *obstare* 'oppose, hinder.'

oust•er /ˈowstər/ ▸ **n.** ejection from a freehold or other possession; deprivation of an inheritance.

out /owt/ ▸ **adv. 1** no longer detained in custody or in jail: *they would be out on bail in no time.*
2 (of a jury) considering its verdict in secrecy: *they settled on a confidential basis with one of the defendants while the jury was out.*
ORIGIN Old English *ūt* (adverb), *ūtian* (verb), of Germanic origin; related to Dutch *uit* and German *aus.*

out•law /'owt‚lô/ ▸ **n.** a person who has broken the law, esp. one who remains at large or is a fugitive.
■ a person or group regarded as acting outside accepted norms of behavior: [as adj.] *outlaw nations.* ■ historical a person deprived of the benefit and protection of the law.
▸**v.** [trans.] ban; make illegal: *Maryland outlawed cheap small-caliber pistols* | [as adj.] (**outlawed**) *the outlawed terrorist group.*
■ historical deprive (someone) of the benefit and protection of the law.
DERIVATIVES **out•law•ry** /'owt‚lôrē/ **n.**
ORIGIN late Old English *ūtlaga* (noun), *ūtlagian* (verb), from Old Norse *útlagi,* noun from *útlagr* 'outlawed or banished.'

out-of-court /'owt əv 'kôrt/ ▸ **adj.** [attrib.] (of a settlement) made or done without a court decision.

WHAT IS LEGAL ETHICS?

Lawyers are not just hired guns. They must serve not only the people who hire them, but also the legal system itself. An ethical lawyer is faithful to both.

Every state has a code of legal ethics and a disciplinary system to enforce it. This discourages willful misconduct by lawyers who might be so inclined. But the vast majority of lawyers want to do the right thing; for them, the importance of the rules is that they provide guidance and support in the sometimes difficult task of satisfying their dual loyalty to the client and to the law.

Origins

Ethics codes drafted by the American Bar Association (ABA) have been generally accepted throughout the United States ever since the first one was adopted in 1908. But the subject suddenly gained widespread attention in the Watergate scandal of the mid-1970s, in which dozens of lawyers were implicated and a considerable number, including a former attorney general and the White House counsel to the president, landed in prison. This wound to the profession led to a comprehensive reexamination of ethics rules, mandatory courses on professional responsibility in law schools, and the supplementing of traditional bar examinations with a nationwide test on professional ethics as a requirement for legal licensing.

In 1983, after six years of work, the ABA adopted a completely restructured set of ethics rules, the *Model Rules of Professional Conduct*. These have been accepted in almost every state—although always with some local modifications, leaving no two states with exactly the same rules. The ABA has updated the Model Rules several times, most notably in a comprehensive series of amendments in 2002 that left few rules untouched. The rules can be viewed on the ABA Web site at http://www.abanet.org/cpr/mrpc/mrpc_home.html; a corresponding code for judges (the *Model Code of Judicial Conduct*) is at http://www.abanet.org/cpr/mcjc/mcjc_home.html.

Core concepts

Although individual rules can be somewhat technical, the basic principles of contemporary American legal ethics cut across all of them. Among the most important principles are these:

Independent judgment and undivided loyalty.

Legal advice and strategy must not be clouded by conflicting interests or subject to pressure from anyone other than the client. In many situations, a client, if fully informed of a potential conflict, can agree that it is not serious and allow the lawyer to proceed. But some conflicts are too serious for that; for example, lawyers from the same law firm can never represent opposing parties in the same case.

Client control.

Key decisions—such as whether to settle or go to trial, whether to testify, or for that matter whether to keep or fire the lawyer—belong to the client. If there is a fundamental disagreement, the lawyer may resign (unless the court directs otherwise) but cannot overrule the client. If the client insists upon a course of conduct that would be illegal or unethical, the lawyer *must* resign.

Informed consent.

As a corollary to the principle of client control, the lawyer must keep the client informed. Some actions are specifically forbidden unless the client consents after a full explanation of the options.

Confidentiality.

As a general rule, confidential information from a client or prospective client must be kept confidential forever. But lawyers are allowed to use such information in their own defense if they are later sued by the client. And the Model Rules allow a lawyer to disclose client information if necessary "to prevent reasonably certain death or substantial bodily harm."

Honesty and fairness . . . up to a point.
Lawyers may not knowingly offer false evidence, and if a lawyer learns later in a proceeding that evidence he or she introduced was false, that lawyer must set the matter straight. But absolute knowledge is a rare thing. If a lawyer reasonably believes that certain evidence is false but does not know for sure, the lawyer is free to introduce it or not, depending upon his or her own conscience—or strategy. Moreover, if a lawyer discovers that some inadvertently helpful evidence presented by the *other* side was false, the lawyer need not correct it. That's the adversary's problem!

Although the rules apply to all aspects of law, not just trial work, the intensely adversarial nature of American law underlies the entire system of legal ethics. Even though trial by jury replaced trial by battle many centuries ago, the judicial system is still based upon the assumption that the best outcome will be achieved through a battle royal between well-represented adversaries. (For an alternative approach, see *The Common Law and the Civil Law*, p. 77.) This is reflected in ethical principles like those just outlined, imposing an extremely high duty of loyalty to the client and only minimal duties of honesty to the court and concern for the public at large. The rules of ethics are to law what the Marquess of Queensberry Rules are to boxing: they prevent the adversaries from hitting below the belt, but they do not change the fundamental nature of the contest.

Enforcement
Lawyer misconduct can be reported to the appropriate disciplinary agency (complete list at http://www.abanet.org/cpr/disciplinary.html), which can lead to a warning, reprimand, probation, suspension, or even disbarment. In cases involving misappropriation of client funds, the lawyer can also be ordered to refund the money.

This protects the public at large, but, except in misappropriation cases, it does nothing to compensate the client or other person injured by the lawyer's misconduct. It would therefore be reasonable to expect that a violation of the rules of ethics could be used as the basis for a lawsuit against the lawyer to recover for any resulting loss. As originally adopted in 1983, however, the Model Rules specifically stated that they should not be used for any such purpose. Some courts went along with this, but most regarded it as foolishness and allowed malpractice plaintiffs to point out to the jury that the conduct they were complaining about was in fact a violation of the ethical standards of the profession.

In 2002, the ABA compromised somewhat and added language conceding that a lawyer's violation of the Model Rules could be relevant in a case against the lawyer. Although clients are now normally permitted to use the rules, nonclients—for example, adversaries in court or purchasers of stock in a company represented by the lawyer—are still generally barred from basing a claim against a lawyer upon ethical misconduct adversely affecting them.

The future of ethics

For lawyers, an issue sure to be debated in decades to come concerns the desire of some to create "multijurisdictional" and "multidisciplinary" firms that could offer a package of business services—not just legal services—nationwide. Under current rules, practice is largely limited to states where one is admitted to the bar, and partnerships with nonlawyers are forbidden.

For the public at large, a major cause of concern is the traditional ethical ban on divulging information about a client even when the information might prevent harm to others. Many states have already gone beyond the Model Rules, allowing lawyers to reveal the intention of a client to engage in conduct that would cause substantial financial or property damage, or even to commit a crime of any kind. This much is certain: as the demands of society change, the law will change—and legal ethics with it.

P

pack /pæk/ ▶ v. [trans.] fill (a jury, committee, etc.) with people likely to support a particular decision or tendency: *his efforts to **pack** the Supreme Court **with** men who shared his ideology are being cricitized.*
ORIGIN early 16th cent. (in the sense 'enter into a private agreement'): probably from the obsolete verb *pact* 'enter into an agreement with,' the final *-t* being interpreted as an inflection of the past tense.

pan•el /'pænl/ ▶ n. a list of available jurors or a jury.
■ a group of judges drawn from a larger body to hear a particular matter: *the case went to a three-judge panel.*

par•a•le•gal /ˌpærə'lēgəl/ ▶ n. a person trained in subsidiary legal matters but not fully qualified as a lawyer, who typically works as an assistant to a lawyer.
▶ adj. of or relating to auxiliary aspects of the law.

par•don /'pärdn/ ▶ n. a remission of the legal consequences of an offense or conviction: *he offered a full pardon to five convicted men.*
▶ v. [trans.] release (an offender) from the legal consequences of an offense or conviction, and often implicitly from blame: *he was pardoned for his treason.*
DERIVATIVES **par•don•a•ble** adj.
ORIGIN Middle English: from Old French *pardun* (noun), *pardoner* (verb), from medieval Latin *perdonare* 'concede, remit,' from *per-* 'completely' + *donare* 'give.'

pa•rens pa•tri•ae /ˌperənz 'pætri-ē/ ▶ n. the government, or any other authority, regarded as the legal protector of citizens unable to protect themselves.
■ the principle that political authority carries with it the responsibility for such protection.
ORIGIN modern Latin, literally 'parent of the country.'

pa•rol /pə'rōl; 'pærəl/ ▶ adj. given or expressed orally: *the parol evidence.*
■ (of a document) agreed orally, or in writing but not under seal: *there was a parol agreement.*
PHRASES **by parol** by oral declaration.
ORIGIN late 15th cent. (as a noun): from Old French *parole* 'word' (see PAROLE).

pa•role /pəˈrōl/ ▶ n. the release of a prisoner temporarily (for a special purpose) or permanently before the completion of a sentence, on the promise of good behavior and under continuing supervision: *he committed a burglary while* **on parole.**

■ historical a promise or undertaking given by a prisoner of war not to escape or, if released, to return to custody under stated conditions.

▶v. [trans.] (usu. **be paroled**) release (a prisoner) on parole: *he was paroled after serving nine months of a two-year sentence.*

DERIVATIVES **pa•rol•ee** /pəˌrōˈlē/ n.

ORIGIN late 15th cent.: from Old French, literally 'word,' also 'formal promise,' from ecclesiastical Latin *parabola* 'speech'; compare with **PAROL.**

par•ri•cide /ˈperəˌsīd; ˈpærə-/ ▶ n. the killing of a parent or other near relative.

■ a person who commits parricide.

DERIVATIVES **par•ri•cid•al** /ˌperəˈsīdl; ˌpærə-/ adj.

ORIGIN late 16th cent.: from French, from Latin *parricidium* 'murder of a parent,' with first element of unknown origin, but long associated with Latin *pater* 'father' and *parens* 'parent.'

pass /pæs/ ▶ v. **1** [intrans.] be transferred from one person or place to another, esp. by inheritance: *if Ann remarried the estate would* **pass to** *her new husband.*

2 [trans.] (of a legislative or other official body) approve or put into effect (a proposal or law) by voting on it: *the bill was passed despite fierce opposition.*

■ (of a proposal or law) be examined and approved by (a legislative body or process): *bills that passed committees last year.* ■ [intrans.] (of a proposal) be approved: *the bill passed by 164 votes to 107.*

3 [trans.] pronounce (a judgment or judicial sentence): *don't shrink from* **passing** *judgment* **on** *this crucial issue* | *it is now my duty to* **pass** *sentence* **upon** *you.*

■ [intrans.] (**pass on/upon**) archaic adjudicate or give a judgment on: *a jury could not be trusted to pass upon the question of Endicott's good faith.*

ORIGIN Middle English: from Old French *passer*, based on Latin *passus* 'pace.'

Pat. ▶ abbr. Patent.

pat•ent /ˈpætnt/ ▶ n. /ˈpætnt/ a government authority to an individual or organization conferring a right or title, esp. the sole right to make, use, or sell some invention: *he* **took out** *a patent for an improved steam hammer.* [ORIGIN: Compare with **LETTERS PATENT.**]

▶v. [trans.] obtain a patent for (an invention): *an invention is not your own until it is patented.*

DERIVATIVES **pat•ent•a•ble** adj.

ORIGIN late Middle English: from Old French, from Latin *patent-* 'lying open,' from the verb *patere.*

pat•ent•ee /ˌpætn'tē/ ▸ n. a person or organization that obtains or holds a patent for something.

pat•ent of•fice /'pætnt ˌôfis; ˌäfis/ ▸ n. an office from which patents are issued.

pa•ter•ni•ty /pə'tərniţē/ ▸ n. the state of being someone's father: *he refused to admit paternity of the child.*
ORIGIN late Middle English: from Old French *paternité*, from late Latin *paternitas*, from *paternus* 'relating to a father.'

pa•ter•ni•ty suit /pə'tərniţē ˌsōōt/ ▸ n. a legal action to establish formally the identity of a child's father, typically in order to require him to support the child financially.

pat•ri•cide /'pætriˌsīd/ ▸ n. the killing of one's father.
■ a person who kills their father.
DERIVATIVES **pat•ri•cid•al** /ˌpætri'sīdl/ **adj.**
ORIGIN early 17th cent.: from late Latin *patricidium*, alteration of Latin *parricidium* (see **PARRICIDE**).

peace of•fi•cer /'pēs ˌôfisər; ˌäf-/ ▸ n. a civil officer appointed to preserve law and order, such as a sheriff or police officer.

pe•nal /'pēnl/ ▸ adj. of, relating to, or prescribing the punishment of offenders under the legal system: *she is a champion of penal reform | under the Penal Code, this bill would permit certain exempt organizations to conduct raffles.*
■ used or designated as a place of punishment: *a former penal colony.*
■ (of an act or offense) punishable by law.
DERIVATIVES **pe•nal•ly adv.**
ORIGIN late Middle English: from Old French *penal*, from Latin *poenalis*, from *poena* 'pain, penalty.'

pe•nal•ize /'pēnlˌīz; 'pen-/ ▸ v. [trans.] (often **be penalized**) make or declare (an act or offense) legally punishable: *section twenty penalizes possession of a firearm when trespassing.*
DERIVATIVES **pe•nal•i•za•tion** /ˌpēnəli'zāsHən; ˌpen-/ **n.**

pen•den•te li•te /pen'dentē 'līţē/ ▸ adv. during litigation: *a judge may award interim fees pendente lite where the complainant has prevailed on an important allegation.*
ORIGIN Latin, literally 'with the lawsuit pending.'

per cu•ri•am /pər 'kyōōrēəm/ ▸ adv. by decision of a court in unanimous agreement: *the court dismissed, per curiam, union petitions for review of two Authority decisions.*
▸ n. such a decision: *in only a few cases did the panel publish a per curiam.*
■ an opinion signed by a court as a whole, rather than by an individual judge.
ORIGIN Latin, literally 'by the court.'

per•emp•to•ry /pə'remptərē/ ▸ adj. not open to appeal or challenge; final: *there has been no disobedience of a peremptory order of the court.*
DERIVATIVES **per•emp•to•ri•ly** /pə'remptərəlē/ **adv.**; **per•emp•to•ri•ness n.**

ORIGIN late Middle English (as a legal term): via Anglo-Norman French from Latin *peremptorius* 'deadly, decisive,' from *perempt*- 'destroyed, cut off,' from the verb *perimere*, from *per*- 'completely' + *emere* 'take, buy.'

per•emp•to•ry chal•lenge /pəˈremptərē CHælinj/ ▶ n. a defendant's or lawyer's objection to a proposed juror, made without needing to give a reason.

per•fect /pərˈfekt/ ▶ v. [trans.] satisfy the necessary conditions or requirements for the transfer of (a gift, title, etc.): *equity will not perfect an imperfect gift.*

ORIGIN Middle English: from Old French *perfet*, from Latin *perfectus* 'completed,' from the verb *perficere*, from *per*- 'through, completely' + *facere* 'do.'

per•jure /ˈpərjər/ ▶ v. (**perjure oneself**) willfully tell an untruth when giving evidence to a court; commit perjury: *when a defendant perjures himself on the stand, the court is warranted in enhancing the defendant's offense level.*

DERIVATIVES **per•jur•er** n.

ORIGIN late Middle English (as *perjured* in the sense 'guilty of perjury'): from Old French *parjurer*, from Latin *perjurare* 'swear falsely,' from *per*- 'to ill effect' + *jurare* 'swear.'

per•jured /ˈpərjərd/ ▶ adj. (of evidence) involving willfully told untruths. ■ (of a person) guilty of perjury: *a perjured witness.*

per•ju•ry /ˈpərjərē/ ▶ n. (pl. **per•ju•ries**) the offense of willfully telling an untruth, especially in a court, after having taken an oath or made an affirmation.

DERIVATIVES **per•ju•ri•ous** /pərˈjoŏrēəs/ adj.

ORIGIN late Middle English: from Anglo-Norman French *perjurie*, from Latin *perjurium* 'false oath,' from the verb *perjurare* (see PER-JURE).

per•mis•sive /pərˈmisiv/ ▶ adj. allowed or optional, but not obligatory: *the Hague Convention was permissive, not mandatory.*

ORIGIN late 15th cent. (in the sense 'tolerated, allowed'): from Old French, or from medieval Latin *permissivus*, from *permiss*- 'allowed,' from the verb *permittere*, from *per*- 'through' + *mittere* 'send, let go.'

per•pe•tu•i•ty /ˌpərpiˈt(y)oŏitē/ ▶ n. (pl. **per•pe•tu•i•ties**) a thing that lasts forever or for an indefinite period, in particular:
■ a restriction making an estate inalienable perpetually or for a period beyond certain limits fixed by law: *the property must be used and maintained as a park or recreation area* **in perpetuity**. ■ an estate so restricted.

ORIGIN late Middle English: from Old French *perpetuite*, from Latin *perpetuitas*, from *perpetuus* 'continuing throughout.'

per•son•al in•ju•ry /ˈpərs(ə)nl ˈinjərē/ ▶ n. injury inflicted on a person's body or mind, as opposed to damage to property or reputation: [as adj.] *personal injury lawyers.*

per•son•al pro•per•ty /'pərs(ə)nl 'präpərtē/ ▶ n. all of someone's property except land and those interests in land that pass to their heirs. Compare with REAL PROPERTY.

per•son•al•ty /'pərsənəltē/ ▶ n. a person's personal property. The opposite of REALTY.

ORIGIN mid 16th cent. (in the legal phrase *in the personalty* 'for damages'): from Anglo-Norman French *personaltie,* from medieval Latin *personalitas,* from Latin *personalis* 'of a person.'

per•tain /pər'tān/ ▶ v. [intrans.] belong to something as a part, appendage, or accessory: *the premises, stock, and all assets **pertaining to** the business.*

ORIGIN late Middle English: from Old French *partenir,* from Latin *pertinere* 'extend to, have reference to,' from *per-* 'through' + *tenere* 'to hold.'

pet•it /'petē/ ▶ adj. (of a crime) petty: *petit larceny.*

ORIGIN late Middle English (in the sense 'small or insignificant'): from Old French, 'small'; the same word as PETTY, with retention of the French spelling.

pe•ti•tion /pi'tisHən/ ▶ n. an application to a court for a writ, judicial action in a suit, etc.: *a divorce petition.*

▶ v. [trans.] make or present a formal request to (an authority) with respect to a particular cause: *Americans who moved west **petitioned** Congress for admission to the Union as states* | [with obj. and infinitive] *leaders petitioned the government to hold free elections soon.*

■ make a formal application to (a court) for a writ, judicial action in a suit, etc.: *the custodial parent **petitioned** the court for payment of the arrears* | [intrans.] *the process allows both spouses to jointly **petition** for divorce.*

DERIVATIVES **pe•ti•tion•ar•y** /pitisHə,nerē/ adj.; **pe•ti•tion•er** n.

ORIGIN Middle English: from Latin *petitio(n-),* from *petit-* 'aimed at, sought, laid claim to,' from the verb *petere.*

pet•it ju•ry /'petē 'jo͝orē/ ▶ n. see JURY.

pet•ty /'petē/ ▶ adj. (**pet•ti•er, pet•ti•est**) (of a crime) of lesser importance: *petty theft.* Compare with GRAND).

ORIGIN late Middle English (in the sense 'small in size'): from a phonetic spelling of the pronunciation of French *petit* 'small.' Compare with PETIT.

pet•ty ju•ry /'petē ˌjo͝orē/ ▶ n. see JURY.

pet•ty lar•ce•ny /'petē lärsənē/ ▶ n. theft of personal property having a value less than a legally specified amount.

pi•ra•cy /'pīrəsē/ ▶ n. the practice of attacking and robbing ships at sea.

■ a similar practice in other contexts, esp. hijacking: *air piracy.*

■ the unauthorized use or reproduction of another's work: *software piracy.*

ORIGIN mid 16th cent.: via medieval Latin from Greek *pirateia,* from *peiratēs,* from *peirein* 'to attempt, attack.'

plain•tiff /'plāntif/ ▶ n. a person who brings a case against another in a court of law. Compare with **DEFENDANT**.
ORIGIN late Middle English: from Old French *plaintif* 'plaintive' (used as a noun). The *-f* ending has come down through Law French; the word was originally the same as *plaintive*.

plea /plē/ ▶ n. a formal statement by or on behalf of a defendant or prisoner, stating guilt or innocence in response to a charge, offering an allegation of fact, or claiming that a point of law should apply: *he changed his plea to not guilty.*
ORIGIN Middle English (in the sense 'lawsuit'): from Old French *plait, plaid* 'agreement, discussion,' from Latin *placitum* 'a decree,' neuter past participle of *placere* 'to please.'

plea bar•gain•ing /'plē ˌbärgəniNG/ ▶ n. an arrangement between a prosecutor and a criminal defendant whereby the defendant pleads guilty to a lesser charge in the expectation of leniency from the court.
DERIVATIVES **plea-bar•gain** v.: *he plea-bargained his way out of stealing $20,000 from a client.*; **plea bar•gain** n.

plead /plēd/ ▶ v. (past and past part. **plead•ed** or **pled** /pled/) [trans.] present and argue for (a position), esp. in court or in another public context: *she's famous for using cheap melodrama to plead her clients' causes.*
■ [intrans.] address a court as an advocate on behalf of a party: *the State Council pleaded on behalf of the Commander for an adjournment.*
■ [no obj., with complement] state formally in court whether one is guilty or not guilty of the offense with which one is charged: *he pleaded guilty to the drug charge.* ■ invoke (a reason or a point of law) as an accusation or defense: *on trial for attempted murder, she pleaded self-defense.*
DERIVATIVES **plead•er** n.
ORIGIN Middle English (in the sense 'to wrangle'): from Old French *plaidier* 'resort to legal action,' from *plaid* 'discussion' (see **PLEA**).

USAGE: In a court of law, a person can **plead guilty** or **plead not guilty**. The phrase **plead innocent**, although commonly found in general use, is not a technical legal term. Note that one *pleads guilty to* (not *of*) a charge, and may be *found guilty of* an offense.

plead•ing /'plēdiNG/ ▶ n. (usu. **pleadings**) a formal statement of the cause of an action or defense.

pledge /plej/ ▶ n. a thing that is given as security for the fulfillment of a contract or the payment of a debt and is liable to forfeiture in the event of failure: *the Administrator may accept other forms of security, such as a pledge of revenues.*
▶ v. [trans.] give as security on a loan: *the creditor to whom the land is pledged.*
DERIVATIVES **pledg•or** /'plejər/ n.

ORIGIN Middle English (denoting a person acting as surety for another): from Old French *plege*, from medieval Latin *plebium*, perhaps related to the Germanic base of *plight*.

pol•i•cy /'pälisē/ ▶ n. (pl. **pol•i•cies**) a contract of insurance: *they took out a joint policy.*

ORIGIN mid 16th cent.: from French *police* 'bill of lading, contract of insurance,' from Provençal *poliss(i)a*, probably from medieval Latin *apodissa*, *apodixa*, based on Greek *apodeixis* 'evidence, proof,' from *apodeiknunai* 'demonstrate, show.'

pol•y•graph /'päli‚græf/ ▶ n. a machine designed to detect and record changes in physiological characteristics, such as a person's pulse and breathing rates, used esp. as a lie detector: *Rhinehart contends that the polygraph is too easily manipulated by both the examiner and the examinee.*

■ a lie-detector test carried out with a machine of this type: *should the polygraph be admissible as evidence?*

DERIVATIVES **pol•y•graph•ic** /‚päli'græfik/ **adj.**

pos•se /'päsē/ ▶ n. historical a body of men, typically armed, summoned by a sheriff to enforce the law.

■ (also **pos•se co•mi•ta•tus** /'päsē ‚kämi'tātəs/) historical the body of men in a county whom the sheriff could summon to enforce the law. [ORIGIN: **comitatus** from medieval Latin, 'of the county.'] ■ informal a gang of youths involved in (usually drug-related) crime.

ORIGIN mid 17th cent.: from medieval Latin, literally 'power,' from Latin *posse* 'be able.'

Pos•se Com•i•ta•tus Act /'päsē ‚kämi'tātəs ‚ækt/ ▶ a federal statute prohibiting use of the military in civilian law enforcement.

ORIGIN Latin *posse comitatus* 'power of the county.'

pos•sess /pə'zes/ ▶ v. [trans.] have possession of as distinct from ownership: *a two-year suspended sentence for possessing cocaine.*

ORIGIN late Middle English: from Old French *possesser*, from Latin *possess-* 'occupied, held,' from the verb *possidere*, from *potis* 'able, capable' + *sedere* 'sit.'

pos•ses•sion /pə'zesHən/ ▶ n. 1 visible power or control over something, as distinct from lawful ownership; holding or occupancy: *they were imprisoned for possession of explosives.*

■ informal the state of possessing an illegal drug: *they're charged with possession.*

2 (usu. **possessions**) an item of property; something belonging to one: *his will did not specifically dispose of any possessions.*

ORIGIN Middle English: from Old French, from Latin *possessio(n-)*, from the verb *possidere* (see POSSESS).

pos•ses•sor /pə'zesər/ ▶ n. a person who takes, occupies, or holds something without necessarily having ownership, or as distinguished from the owner.

DERIVATIVES **pos•ses•so•ry** /pə'zes(ə)rē/ **adj.**

power of ap•point•ment /ˈpow(-ə)r əv əˈpointmənt/ ▶ n. phrase power to decide the disposal of property, in exercise of a right conferred by the owner.

pow•er of at•tor•ney /ˈpow(-ə)r əv əˈtərnē/ ▶ n. the authority to act for another person in specified or all legal or financial matters.
  ▪ a legal document giving such authority to someone: *the debtor has signed a power of attorney giving the attorney authority to issue consents.*

prac•tice /ˈpræktis/ ▶ n. the carrying out or exercise of a profession, especially that of a lawyer or doctor: *her interest in the legal practice began in high school.*
  ▪ the business or premises of a lawyer or doctor: *the practice of Perry and Erikson has moved to Linwood Park.* ▪ an established method of legal procedure.
▶ v. [trans.] (Brit. **practise**) actively pursue or be engaged in (a particular profession, especially law or medicine): *he began to practice law* | [intrans.] *he practiced as an attorney*
  ORIGIN late Middle English: the verb from Old French *practiser* or medieval Latin *practizare*, alteration of *practicare* 'perform, carry out,' from *practica* 'practice,' from Greek *praktikē*, feminine (used as a noun) of *praktikos* 'concerned with action'; the noun from the verb in the earlier spelling *practise*, on the pattern of pairs such as *advise, advice.*

prae•ci•pe /ˈprēsə,pē; ˈpres-/ ▶ n. an order requesting a writ or other legal document: *court clerks provide forms for making the request, or a praecipe can be filed.*
  ▪ historical a writ demanding action or an explanation of nonaction: *a praecipe for discontinuance.*
  ORIGIN Latin (the first word of the writ), imperative of *praecipere* 'enjoin, command.'

pre•am•ble /ˈprē,æmbəl/ ▶ n. the introductory part of a statute, deed, or other similar document, stating its purpose, aims, and justification.
  DERIVATIVES **pre•am•bu•lar** /prēˈæmbyələr/ adj. (formal).
  ORIGIN late Middle English: from Old French *preambule*, from medieval Latin *praeambulum*, from late Latin *praeambulus* 'going before.'

prec•a•to•ry /ˈprekə,tôrē/ ▶ adj. (in a will) expressing a wish or intention of the testator that is advisory but not binding: *a trust can be left in precatory words.*
  ORIGIN mid 17th cent.: from late Latin *precatorius*, from *precat-* 'prayed,' from the verb *precari.*

prec•e•dent ▶ n. /ˈpresid(ə)nt/ a previous case or legal decision that may be or (**binding precedent**) must be followed in subsequent similar cases: *the decision set a precedent for others to be sent to trial in the United States.*
▶ adj. /priˈsēd(ə)nt; ˈpresid(ə)nt/ preceding in time, order, or importance: *a precedent case.*
  ORIGIN late Middle English: from Old French, literally 'preceding.'

pre•cept /'prē‚sept/ ▸ n. a writ or warrant: *the Commissioner issued precepts requiring the companies to provide information.*
ORIGIN late Middle English: from Latin *praeceptum*, neuter past participle of *praecipere* 'warn, instruct,' from *prae* 'before' + *capere* 'take.'

pre•empt /prē'empt/ ▸ v. [trans.] **1** (of a superior authority) take action to prevent an inferior authority from acting: *Congress has preempted the regulation of cigarette advertising.*
2 take (something, esp. public land) for oneself so as to have the right of preemption.
DERIVATIVES **pre•emp•tor** /prē'emptôr; -tər/ n.
ORIGIN mid 19th cent.: back-formation from **PREEMPTION**.

pre•emp•tion /prē'empsHən/ ▸ n. **1** action by a superior authority that prevents an inferior authority from acting.
2 the purchase of goods or shares by one person or party before the opportunity is offered to others: *the commission had the right of preemption.*
■ historical the right to purchase public land in this way.
ORIGIN early 17th cent.: from medieval Latin *praeemptio(n-)*, from the verb *praeemere*, from *prae* 'in advance' + *emere* 'buy.'

pre•fer /pri'fər/ ▸ v. (**pre•ferred, pre•fer•ring**) [trans.] submit (a charge or a piece of information) for consideration: *the police will prefer charges.*
ORIGIN late Middle English: from Old French *preferer*, from Latin *praeferre*, from *prae* 'before' + *ferre* 'to bear, carry.'

pref•er•ence /'pref(ə)rəns/ ▸ n. a prior right or precedence, esp. in connection with the payment of debts: *debts owed to the community should be accorded a preference.*
ORIGIN late Middle English (in the sense 'promotion'): from Old French, from medieval Latin *praeferentia*, from Latin *praeferre* 'carry in front' (see **PREFER**).

prej•u•dice /'prejədis/ ▸ n. harm or injury that results or may result from some action or judgment: *prejudice resulting from delay in the institution of the proceedings.*
▸ v. [trans.] **1** give rise to prejudice in (someone); make biased: *the statement might prejudice the jury.*
2 cause harm to (a state of affairs): *delay is likely to prejudice the child's welfare.*
PHRASES **with prejudice** (of a judgment) with binding effect: *the case is dismissed with prejudice.* **without prejudice** without detriment to any existing right or claim: *the payment was made **without** any **prejudice to** her rights.*
ORIGIN Middle English: from Old French, from Latin *praejudicium*, from *prae* 'in advance' + *judicium* 'judgment.'

prej•u•di•cial /‚prejə'disHəl/ ▸ adj. harmful to someone or something; detrimental: *the behavior is **prejudicial to** good order and discipline.*

■ (of evidence) tending to lead to an incorrect decision (and therefore excludable); likely to cause prejudice: *the district court sustained Jones's objection to admission of this evidence as prejudicial.*
DERIVATIVES **prej•u•di•cial•ly** adv.
ORIGIN late Middle English: from Old French *prejudiciel*, from *prejudice* (see **PREJUDICE**).

pre•med•i•tate /prē'medi͵tāt/ ▶ v. [trans.] [usu. as adj.] (**premeditated**) think out or plan (an action, esp. a crime) beforehand: *premeditated murder.*
DERIVATIVES **pre•med•i•ta•tion** /prē͵medə'tāsHən/ n.
ORIGIN mid 16th cent.: from Latin *praemeditat-* 'thought out before,' from the verb *praemeditari*, from *prae* 'before' + *meditari* 'meditate.'

prem•is•es /'premisiz/ ▶ plural n. a house or building, together with its land and outbuildings, occupied by a business or considered in an official context: *business premises* | *supplying alcoholic liquor for consumption on the premises.*

pre•nup•tial a•gree•ment /prē'nəpsHəl ə'grēmənt; prē'nəpCHəl/ ▶ n. an agreement made by a couple before they marry concerning the ownership of their respective assets should the marriage fail.

pre•rog•a•tive /p(r)i'rägətiv/ ▶ n. a right or privilege exclusive to a particular individual, institution, or class: *the case affirmed the right of the state to overrule a parental prerogative for the welfare of the child.*
■ (also **royal prerogative**) the right of the sovereign, which in British law is theoretically subject to no restriction.
▶ adj. [attrib.] Brit. arising from the prerogative of the Crown (usually delegated to the government or the judiciary) and based in common law rather than statutory law: *the monarch retained the formal prerogative power to appoint the Prime Minister.*
ORIGIN late Middle English: via Old French from Latin *praerogativa* '(the verdict of) the political division that was chosen to vote first in the assembly,' feminine (used as noun) of *praerogativus* 'asked first,' from *prae* 'before' + *rogare* 'ask.'

pre•rog•a•tive writ /pri'rägətiv 'rit/ ▶ n. an order in exercise of a court's discretionary power: *nine men applied for a prerogative writ of habeas corpus after being in detention since 1994 on aggravated robbery and/or murder charges.*

pre•scrip•tion /pri'skripsHən/ ▶ n. (also **positive prescription**) the establishment of a claim founded on the basis of a long or indefinite period of uninterrupted use or of long-standing custom. *Alvey had a 16.5-foot easement by prescription on the western portion of Lot 32.*
ORIGIN late Middle English (as a legal term): via Old French from Latin *praescriptio(n-)*, from the verb *praescribere* 'direct in writing,' from *prae* 'before' + *scribere* 'write.'

pre•scrip•tive /pri'skriptiv/ ▶ adj. (of a right, title, or institution) having become legally established or accepted by long usage or the passage of time: *a prescriptive right of way.*

DERIVATIVES **pre•scrip•tive•ly** adv.; **pre•scrip•tive•ness** n.

ORIGIN mid 18th cent.: from late Latin *praescriptivus* 'relating to a legal exception,' from *praescript-* 'directed in writing,' from the verb *praescribere* (see **PRESCRIPTION**).

pre•sent•ment /pri'zentmənt/ ▶ n. chiefly historical a formal presentation of information to a court, esp. by a grand jury regarding an offense or other matter not contained in a bill of indictment it has considered.

ORIGIN Middle English: from Old French *presentement*, from *presenter* 'place before.'

pre•sump•tion /pri'zəmpSHən/ ▶ n. an attitude adopted in law or as a matter of policy toward an action or proposal in the absence of acceptable reasons or proof to the contrary: *the **presumption of** guilt has changed to a presumption of innocence.*

ORIGIN Middle English: from Old French *presumpcion*, from Latin *praesumptio(n)* 'anticipation,' from the verb *praesumere* 'anticipate' (in Late Latin 'take for granted'), from *prae* 'before' + *sumere* 'take.'

pre•sump•tive /pri'zəmptiv/ ▶ adj. giving grounds for the inference of a fact or of the appropriate interpretation of the law: *the document sets out rules for a finding of presumptive disability or presumptive blindness.*

DERIVATIVES **pre•sump•tive•ly** adv.

ORIGIN late Middle English: from French *présomptif, -ive*, from late Latin *praesumptivus*, from *praesumpt-* 'taken before,' from the verb *praesumere* (see **PRESUMPTION**).

pre•ven•tive de•ten•tion /pri'ventiv di'tenCHən/ ▶ n. the imprisonment of a person prior to conviction, with the aim of preventing them from committing further offenses or of maintaining public order.

pri•ma fa•ci•e /prīmə 'fāSHē(ˌē)/ ▶ adj. & adv. based on the first impression; accepted as correct until proved otherwise: [as adj.] *a prima facie case of professional misconduct* | [as adv.] *the original lessee prima facie remains liable for the payment of the rent.*

ORIGIN Latin, from *primus* 'first' + *facies* 'face.'

prin•ci•pal /'prinsəpəl/ ▶ n. a person directly responsible for a crime, by committing, instigating, or assisting in it. Compare with **ACCESSORY**.

ORIGIN Middle English: via Old French from Latin *principalis* 'first, original,' from *princeps, princip-* 'first, chief.'

pris•on /'prizən/ ▶ n. a building or place to which people are legally committed, typically as a punishment for crimes they have committed: *he died **in prison** | both men were **sent to prison**.*

■ confinement in such a building: *prison saves one man and hardens another.*

ORIGIN late Old English: from Old French *prisun*, from Latin *prensio(n-)*, variant of *prehensio(n-)* 'laying hold of,' from the verb *prehendere*.

pris•on•er /'priz(ə)nər/ ▶ n. a person legally committed to prison as a punishment for crimes they have committed.

■ a person held otherwise by the law, as in jail while awaiting trial. ■ a person captured and kept confined by an enemy, opponent, or criminal: *American citizens were being* **held prisoner** *in Iran* | *200 rebels were* **taken prisoner**.
ORIGIN late Middle English: from Old French *prisonier*, from *prison* (see PRISON).

pri•vate law /ˈprīvit ˈlô/ ▶ n. a branch of the law (such as contract, tort, or property law) that deals with the relations between individuals or institutions, rather than relations between these and the government.

pri•vate prac•tice /ˈprīvit ˈpræktis/ ▶ n. the work of a professional practitioner, such as a lawyer or doctor, who is self-employed or employed by a firm or group rather than by the government: *there was a preference for judicial nominees who had substantial experience* **in private practice**.
DERIVATIVES **pri•vate prac•ti•tion•er** /ˈprīvit prækˈtisHənər/ n.

priv•i•lege /ˈpriv(ə)lij/ ▶ n. (also **absolute privilege**) (in a parliamentary context) the right to say or write something without the risk of incurring punishment or legal action for defamation.
■ the right of a person, especially a lawyer or official, to refuse to divulge confidential information, especially at trial.
▶ v. [trans.] formal grant a privilege or privileges to: *English inheritance law privileged the eldest son*.
■ (usu. **be privileged from**) exempt (someone) from a liability or obligation to which others are subject: *some officers are privileged from obeying any subpoena to testify*.
ORIGIN Middle English: via Old French from Latin *privilegium* 'bill or law affecting an individual,' from *privus* 'private' + *lex, leg-* 'law.'

priv•i•leged /ˈpriv(ə)lijd/ ▶ adj. (of information) legally protected from being revealed in the legal process or made public: *the intelligence reports are privileged*.

priv•i•ty /ˈprivitē/ ▶ n. (pl. **priv•i•ties**) a relation between two parties that is recognized by law, particularly by contract or property interest: *the parties no longer have privity with each other*.
ORIGIN Middle English (in the sense 'secrecy, intimacy'): from Old French *privete*, from medieval Latin *privitas*, from Latin *privus* 'private.'

prob•a•ble cause /ˈpräbəbəl ˈkôz/ ▶ n. reasonable grounds (for making a search, pressing a charge, etc.): *the government still has to* **show probable cause** *that the target of the surveillance is a public threat*.

pro•bate /ˈprō,bāt/ ▶ n. the official proving of a will: *the will was in probate* | [as adj.] *a probate court*.
■ a verified copy of a will with a certificate as handed to the executors.
■ the processing of the estate of a decedent.
▶ v. [trans.] establish the validity of (a will): *there is no set time frame in which a will must be probated*.

ORIGIN late Middle English: from Latin *probatum* 'something proved,' neuter past participle of *probare* 'to test, prove.'

pro•ba•tion /prō'bāsHən/ ▸ n. the release of an offender from detention, subject to a period of good behavior under supervision: *I went to court and was put on probation.*

DERIVATIVES **pro•ba•tion•ar•y** /prō'bāsHə,nerē/ adj.

ORIGIN late Middle English (denoting testing, investigation, or examination): from Old French *probacion*, from Latin *probatio(n-)*, from *probare* 'to test, prove' (see PROVE). The legal use dates from the late 19th cent.

pro•ba•tion•er /prō'bāsHənər/ ▸ n. a person who is serving a probationary or trial period in a job or position to which they are newly appointed.

■ an offender on probation.

pro•ba•tion of•fi•cer /prō'bāsHən ,ôfisər; ,äfisər/ ▸ n. a person appointed to supervise offenders who are on probation.

pro•ba•tive /'prōbət̲iv/ ▸ adj. having the quality or function of proving or demonstrating something; affording proof or evidence: *it places the probative burden on the defendant.*

ORIGIN late Middle English (describing something that serves as a test): from Latin *probativus*, from *probat-* 'proved,' from the verb *probare* (see PROVE).

pro•ceed /prə'sēd; prō-/ ▸ v. [intrans.] start a lawsuit against someone: *he may still be able to proceed against the contractor under the common law negligence rules.*

ORIGIN late Middle English: from Old French *proceder*, from Latin *procedere*, from *pro-* 'forward' + *cedere* 'go.'

pro•ceed•ings /prə'sēdiNGz; prō-/ ▸ plural n. action taken in a court to enforce a law or settle a dispute: *criminal proceedings were brought against him.*

proc•ess /'präses; -səs; 'prō-/ ▸ n. a summons or writ requiring a person to appear in court.

ORIGIN Middle English: from Old French *proces*, from Latin *processus* 'progression, course,' from the verb *procedere*, from *pro-* 'forward' + *cedere* 'go.'

proc•ess serv•er /'präses ,sərvər; 'präsəs; 'prō-/ ▸ n. a person, esp. a sheriff or deputy, who serves writs, warrants, subpoenas, etc.

proc•tor /'präktər/ ▸ n. an attorney in an admiralty court.

DERIVATIVES **proc•to•ri•al** /präk'tôrēəl/ adj.; **proc•tor•ship** /'präktər ,sHip/ n.

ORIGIN late Middle English: contraction of PROCURATOR.

proc•u•ra•tor /'präkyə,rāt̲ər/ ▸ n. an agent representing others in a court of law in countries retaining Roman civil law.

DERIVATIVES **proc•u•ra•to•ri•al** /,präkyərə'tôrēəl/ adj.; **proc•u•ra•tor•ship** /'präkyə,rāt̲ər,sHip/ n.

ORIGIN Middle English (denoting a steward): from Old French *procu-*

ratour or Latin *procurator* 'administrator, agent,' from *procurat-* 'taken care of,' from the verb *procurare* 'take care of, manage,' from *pro-* 'on behalf of' + *curare* 'see to.'

pro•hi•bi•tion /ˌprō(h)ə'bisHən/ ▶ n. 1 the action of forbidding something, esp. by law: *they argue that prohibition of drugs will always fail.*

■ a law or regulation forbidding something: *prohibitions on insider trading.*

2 (Pro•hi•bi•tion) the prevention by law of the manufacture and sale of alcoholic beverages, esp. in the US between 1920 and 1933.

DERIVATIVES **pro•hi•bi•tion•ar•y** /ˌprō(h)ə'bisHəˌnerē/ adj.; **Pro•hi•bi•tion•ist** /ˌprō(h)ə'bisHənist/ n.

ORIGIN late Middle English: from Old French, from Latin *prohibitio(n-)*, from *prohibere* 'keep in check.'

prom•is•ee /ˌprämə'sē/ ▶ n. a person to whom a promise is made.

prom•i•sor /'präməsər; -ˌsôr/ ▶ n. a person who makes a promise.

prom•is•so•ry /'präməˌsôrē/ ▶ adj. conveying or implying a promise: *statements that are promissory in nature | promissory words.*

ORIGIN late Middle English: from medieval Latin *promissorius*, from *promiss-* 'promised.'

prom•is•so•ry note /'präməˌsôrē 'nōt/ ▶ n. a signed document containing a written promise to pay a stated sum to a specified person or the bearer at a specified date or on demand.

pro•nounce /prə'nowns/ ▶ v. [trans.] declare or announce, typically formally or solemnly: *the legislature tried a second time to craft a congressional plan, but the court pronounced it unconstitutional.*

■ [intrans.] (**pronounce on**) pass judgment or make a decision on: *the secretary of state will shortly pronounce on alternative measures.*

DERIVATIVES **pro•nounce•ment** n.

ORIGIN late Middle English: from Old French *pronuncier*, from Latin *pronuntiare*, from *pro-* 'out, forth' + *nuntiare* 'announce' (from *nuntius* 'messenger').

proof /prōof/ ▶ n. the evidence in a trial.

■ the action or process of establishing the truth of a statement: *it shifts the onus of proof in convictions from the police to the public.*

ORIGIN Middle English *preve*, from Old French *proeve*, from late Latin *proba*, from Latin *probare* 'to test, prove.' The change of vowel in late Middle English was due to the influence of PROVE.

prop•er•ty /'präpərtē/ ▶ n. (pl. **prop•er•ties**) a thing or things belonging to someone; possessions collectively: *she wanted Oliver and his property out of her house | the stolen property was not recovered.*

■ short for REAL PROPERTY. ■ short for PERSONAL PROPERTY. ■ the right to the possession, use, or disposal of something; ownership: *rights of property.*

ORIGIN Middle English: from an Anglo-Norman French variant of Old French *propriete*, from Latin *proprietas*, from *proprius* 'one's own, particular.'

pros•e•cute /ˈpräsiˌkyo͞ot/ ▶ v. [trans.] institute legal, especially criminal, proceedings against (a person or organization): *they were prosecuted for obstructing the highway.*
■ institute legal proceedings in respect of (a claim or offense): *the state's attorney's office seemed to decide that this was a case worth prosecuting* | [intrans.] *the company didn't prosecute because of his age.* ■ [intrans.] (of a lawyer) conduct the case against the party being accused or sued in a lawsuit: *Mr. Ryan will be prosecuting this morning.*
DERIVATIVES **pros•e•cut•a•ble** adj.
ORIGIN late Middle English: from Latin *prosecut-* 'pursued, accompanied,' from the verb *prosequi,* from *pro-* 'onward' + *sequi* 'follow.'
pros•e•cu•tion /ˌpräsiˈkyo͞osHən/ ▶ n. the institution and conducting of legal proceedings against someone in respect of a criminal charge: *Olesky faces prosecution on charges he spied for Russian intelligence.*
■ **(the prosecution)** [treated as sing. or pl.] the party (specifically, the government) instituting or conducting criminal proceedings against someone: *the main witness for the prosecution.*
ORIGIN mid 16th cent.: from Old French, or from late Latin *prosecutio(n-),* from *prosequi* 'pursue, accompany' (see **PROSECUTE**).
pros•e•cu•tor /ˈpräsiˌkyo͞otər/ ▶ n. a public official who institutes legal proceedings against someone.
■ a lawyer who conducts the case against a defendant in a criminal court. Also called **prosecuting attorney**.
DERIVATIVES **pros•e•cu•to•ri•al** /ˌpräsikyəˈtôrēəl/ adj.
pro•test ▶ n. /ˈprōˌtest/ a written declaration that a bill has been presented and payment or acceptance refused: *you have 30 days from the date the notice was mailed to file a protest.*
▶ v. /prəˈtest; prōˈtest; ˈprōˌtest/ [trans.] write or obtain a protest in regard to (a bill).
DERIVATIVES **pro•tes•tor** /ˈprōˌtestər; prəˈtes-/ n.
ORIGIN late Middle English (as a verb in the sense 'make a solemn declaration'): from Old French *protester,* from Latin *protestari,* from *pro-* 'forth, publicly' + *testari* 'assert' (from *testis* 'witness').
pro•tho•no•ta•ry /ˌprōtəˈnōtərē; prōˈtänəˌterē/ (also **pro•to•no•ta•ry**) ▶ n. (pl. **pro•tho•no•ta•ries**) chiefly historical a chief clerk in some courts of law.
ORIGIN late Middle English: via medieval Latin from late Greek *prōtonotarios,* from *prōtos* 'first' + *notarios* 'notary.'
pro•to•col /ˈprōtəˌkôl; -ˌkäl/ ▶ n. 1 the official procedure or system of rules governing affairs of state or diplomatic occasions: *protocol forbids the prince from making any public statement in his defense.*
2 the original draft of a diplomatic document, esp. of the terms of a treaty agreed to in conference and signed by the parties.
■ an amendment or addition to a treaty or convention: *a protocol to the treaty allowed for this Danish referendum.*

ORIGIN late Middle English (denoting the original record of an agreement, forming the legal authority for future dealings relating to it): from Old French *prothocole*, via medieval Latin from Greek *prōtokollon* 'first page, flyleaf,' from *prōtos* 'first' + *kolla* 'glue.' Sense 1 derives from French *protocole*, the collection of set forms of etiquette to be observed by the French head of state, and the name of the government department responsible for this (in the 19th cent.).

prove /prōōv/ ▸ v. (past part. **proved** or **prov•en** /ˈprōōvən/) [trans.] demonstrate the truth or existence of (something) by evidence or argument: *the concept is difficult to prove.*
■ demonstrate by evidence or argument (someone or something) to be: *innocent until proven guilty.* ■ establish the genuineness and validity of (a will).
DERIVATIVES **prov•a•bil•i•ty** /ˌprōōvəˈbilitē/ n.; **prov•a•ble** adj.
ORIGIN Middle English: from Old French *prover*, from Latin *probare* 'test, approve, demonstrate,' from *probus* 'good.'

prov•o•ca•tion /ˌprävəˈkāsHən/ ▸ n. action or speech held to be likely to prompt physical retaliation: *the assault had taken place under provocation.*
ORIGIN late Middle English: from Old French, from Latin *provocatio(n-)*, from the verb *provocare* 'challenge,' from *pro-* 'forth' + *vocare* 'to call.'

pub•lic act /ˈpəblik ˈækt/ ▸ n. an act of legislation affecting the public as a whole; public law: *as a state legislator she authored over 50 public acts.*

pub•lic de•fend•er /ˈpəblik diˈfendər/ ▸ n. a lawyer employed at public expense in a criminal trial to represent a defendant who is unable to afford legal assistance.

pub•lic do•main /ˈpəblik dōˈmān/ ▸ n. the state of belonging or being available to the public as a whole.
■ not subject to copyright: *the photograph had been in the public domain for 15 years* | [as adj.] *public-domain software.* ■ public land: *a grazing permit on public domain.*

pub•lic law /ˈpəblik ˈlô/ ▸ n. 1 the law of relationships between individuals and the government, such as constitutional, criminal, and administrative law.
2 another term for PUBLIC ACT.

pub•lic nui•sance /ˈpəblik ˈn(y)ōōsəns/ ▸ n. an act, condition, or thing that is illegal because it interferes with the rights of the public generally.
■ informal an obnoxious or dangerous person or group of people.

pub•lic pros•e•cu•tor /ˈpəblik ˈpräsəˌkyōōtər/ ▸ n. a law officer who conducts criminal proceedings on behalf of the government or in the public interest.

pub•lish /ˈpəblisH/ ▸ v. [trans.] communicate (a defamatory statement) to a third party or to the public: *Nelson alleges that the defendants caused these false and malicious statements to be published.*

ORIGIN Middle English (in the sense 'make generally known'): from the stem of Old French *puplier*, from Latin *publicare* 'make public.'

pu•ni•tive damages /'pyo͞onitiv 'dæmijiz/ ▶ **plural n.** damages exceeding simple compensation and awarded to punish the defendant; exemplary damages.

pur•chase /'pərCHəs/ ▶ v. [trans.] acquire (something) by paying for it; buy: *all items purchased must be removed the day of the auction.*

▶ **n.** the acquisition of property by means other than inheritance.

DERIVATIVES **pur•chas•er n.**

ORIGIN Middle English: from Old French *pourchacier* 'seek to obtain or bring about,' the earliest sense also in English, which soon gave rise to the senses 'gain' (hence, in nautical use, the notion of "gaining" one portion of rope after another) and 'buy.'

purge /pərj/ ▶ v. [trans.] atone for or wipe out (contempt of court).

ORIGIN Middle English (in the legal sense 'clear oneself of a charge'): from Old French *purgier*, from Latin *purgare* 'purify,' from *purus* 'pure.'

Q

QC ▸ **abbr.** Queen's Counsel.

qual•i•fi•ca•tion /ˌkwäləfiˈkāsHən/ ▸ **n.** a condition that must be fulfilled before a right can be acquired; an official requirement: *there is a five-year residency qualification for presidential candidates.*
  ORIGIN mid 16th cent.: from medieval Latin *qualificatio(n-)*, from the verb *qualificare*, from Latin *qualis* 'of what kind, of such a kind.'

quan•tum me•ru•it /ˌkwäntəm ˈmero͞oit/ ▸ **n.** [usu. as adj.] a reasonable sum of money to be paid for services rendered or work done when the amount due is not stipulated in a legally enforceable contract: *plaintiff was entitled to be paid for its contract efforts on an quantum meruit basis.*
  ORIGIN Latin, literally 'as much as he has deserved.'

quash /kwôsH; kwäsH/ ▸ **v.** [trans.] reject as invalid, esp. by legal procedure: *his conviction was quashed on appeal.*
  O'RIGIN Middle English: from Old French *quasser* 'annul,' from late Latin *cassare* (medieval Latin also *quassare*), from *cassus* 'null, void.'

qua•si con•tract /ˈkwäzī ˈkänträkt; ˈkwäzē/ (also **quasi-contract**) ▸ **n.** an obligation of one party to another imposed by law independently of a formal agreement between the parties: *an express contract precludes the existence of a contract implied by law or a quasi contract.*
  DERIVATIVES **qua•si-con•trac•tu•al** /ˈkwäzī kəntrækCHo͞oəl; ˈkwäzē/ **adj.**

Queen's Bench /ˈkwēnz ˈbenCH/ (in full **Queen's Bench Division**) ▸ **n.** (in the UK) a division of the High Court of Justice.

Queen's Coun•sel /ˈkwēnz ˈkownsəl/ (abbr.: **QC**) ▸ **n.** a senior barrister appointed on the recommendation of the Lord Chancellor.

ques•tion of fact /ˈkwesCHən əv ˈfækt/ ▸ **n. phrase** an issue of factual circumstances, decided at trial, usually by a jury, and not appealable: *whether a physician-patient relationship is created is a question of fact.*

ques•tion of law /ˈkwesCHən əv ˈlô/ ▸ **n. phrase** an issue of the law's application, decided by a judge and appealable: *the military judge properly decided the issue of lawfulness as a question of law in this case.*

qui•et /ˈkwīət/ ▸ **adj.** not interfered with, as by an adverse claim: *quiet enjoyment of land.*

▸**v.** [trans.] settle or establish the fact of ownership of (a title, etc.): *the court will not quiet title in favor of a foreclosure purchaser.*

quit•claim /ˈkwitˌklām/ ▸ **n.** a formal renunciation or relinquishing of a claim.

▸**v.** [trans.] renounce or relinquish a claim: *Aikins quitclaimed his interest in the three parcels of real estate.*

▸**adj.** (of a deed) relinquishing all of the grantor's claim to land: *the club executed a quitclaim deed conveying the five lots to the decedant's immediate heirs.*

quo war•ran•to /ˌkwō wəˈræntō/ ▸ **n.** [usu. as adj.] a writ or legal action requiring a person to show by what warrant an office or franchise is held, claimed, or exercised: *the DA argues that he is not subject to a quo warranto proceeding because the plaintiffs have an adequate remedy at law.*

ORIGIN Law Latin, literally 'by what warrant.'

R

r ▸ **abbr.** ■ rule: *under r 7.4 (6) the court may hear an application imme-diately.*

rape /rāp/ ▸ n. the crime, committed by a man, of forcing another person to have sexual intercourse with him without their consent and against their will, esp. by the threat or use of violence against them: *he denied two charges of attempted rape* | *he had committed at least two rapes.* Compare with **STAUTORY RAPE.**

▸ v. [trans.] (of a man) force (another person) to have sexual intercourse with him without their consent and against their will, esp. by the threat or use of violence against them: *the woman was raped at knifepoint.*
ORIGIN late Middle English (originally denoting violent seizure of property, later carrying off a woman by force): from Anglo-Norman French *rap* (noun), *raper* (verb), from Latin *rapere* 'seize.'

rap•ist /'rāpist/ ▸ n. a man who commits rape.

ra•ti•o de•ci•den•di /'rätē,ō ,desi'dendē; 'ræte,ō/ ▸ n. (pl. **ra•ti•o•nes de•ci•den•di** /,rätē'ōnēz ,desi'dendē; ,ræte'ōnēz/) the rule of law on which a judicial decision is based: *the ratio decidendi of the judgment creates a precedent for the future.*
ORIGIN Latin, literally 'reason for deciding.'

re•al es•tate /'rē(ə)l i,stāt/ ▸ n. another term for **REAL PROPERTY.**

realm /relm/ ▸ n. a kingdom: *the defense of the realm.*
ORIGIN Middle English *rewme*, from Old French *reaume*, from Latin *regimen* 'government.' The spelling with *-l-* (standard from *c.*1600) was influenced by Old French *reiel* 'royal.'

re•al prop•er•ty /'rē(ə)l 'präpərtē/ ▸ n. property consisting of land, build-ings, and other related immovables (e.g., the rights to resources in or on the land). Compare with **PERSONAL PROPERTY.**

re•al•ty /'rē(ə)ltē/ ▸ n. a person's real property. The opposite of **PERSON-ALTY.**

re•but•tal /ri'bətl/ ▸ n. a refutation or contradiction: *his rebuttal claimed that the health of the defendant was indeed a precipitating factor.*
■ the presenting of one's refutation or contradiction: *normally the court will not grant additional time for rebuttal.* ■ evidence offered in contradiction: *yes, Judge, I've got some rebuttal.*

re•ceiv•er•ship /ri'sēvər,SHip/ ▸ n. the state of being dealt with by a court-appointed receiver: *the company went into receivership last week.*

re•cit•al /ri'sītl/ ▸ n. (usu. **recitals**) the part of a legal document, such as a deed, that explains its purpose and gives factual information: *he trustee's deed may contain recitals of compliance with the following requirements.*

re•cog•ni•zance /ri'kä(g)nəzəns/ ▸ n. a bond by which a person undertakes before a court or magistrate to observe some condition, esp. to appear when summoned: *he was released on his own recognizance.*
ORIGIN Middle English: from Old French *reconnissance*, from *reconnaistre* 'recognize.'

re•com•mit /,rēkə'mit/ ▸ v. (**re•com•mit•ted, re•com•mit•ting**) [trans.] commit again.
▪ return (a motion, proposal, or legislative bill) to a committee for further consideration: *the entire bill has been recommitted* | [intrans.] *a motion to recommit.*
DERIVATIVES **re•com•mit•ment** n.; **re•com•mit•tal** /,rēkə'mitl/ n.

rec•ord ▸ n. /'rekərd/ **1** (also **court record**) an official report of the proceedings and judgment in a court.
2 short for CRIMINAL RECORD.
▸ v. /ri'kôrd/ [trans.] set down in writing or some other permanent form for later reference, esp. officially: *they were asked to keep a diary and record everything they observed* | [as adj.] (**recorded**) *levels of recorded crime.*
▪ state or express publicly or officially; make an official record of: *the coroner recorded a verdict of accidental death.*
PHRASES **a matter of record** a thing that is established as a fact through being officially recorded: *the circumstances of his death are now a matter of record.* **off the record** not made as an official or attributable statement: *anything I may tell you is strictly off the record.* **on record** (also **on the record**) used in reference to the making of an official or public statement: *Ives was unwilling to go on record when the discussion turned to gun control.* **set** (or **put**) **the record straight** give the true version of events that have been reported incorrectly; correct a misapprehension.
DERIVATIVES **re•cord•a•ble** /ri'kôrdəbəl; rē-/ adj.
ORIGIN Middle English: from Old French *record* 'remembrance,' from *recorder* 'bring to remembrance,' from Latin *recordari* 'remember,' based on *cor, cord-* 'heart.' The noun was earliest used in law to denote the fact of being written down as evidence. The verb originally meant 'narrate orally or in writing,' also 'repeat so as to commit to memory.'

re•cov•er /ri'kəvər/ ▸ v. [trans.] find or regain possession of (something stolen or lost): *police recovered a stolen video.*
▪ regain or secure (compensation) by means of a legal process or sub-

sequent profits: *many companies recovered their costs within six months.*

ORIGIN Middle English (originally with reference to health): from Anglo-Norman French *recoverer,* from Latin *recuperare* 'get again.'

re•cov•er•y /ri'kəv(ə)rē/ ▸ n. (pl. **re•cov•er•ies**) the action or process of regaining possession or control of something stolen or lost.

■ the action of regaining or securing compensation or money lost or spent by means of a legal process or subsequent profits: *debt recovery.*

■ an object or amount of money recovered: *the recoveries included gold jewelry.*

ORIGIN late Middle English (denoting a means of restoration): from Anglo-Norman French *recoverie,* from *recovrer* 'get back.'

re•cuse /ri'kyo͞oz/ ▸ v. [trans.] (**recuse oneself**) (of a judge) excuse oneself from a case because of a possible conflict of interest or lack of impartiality: *the Justice Department demanded that he recuse himself from the case.*

DERIVATIVES **re•cus•al** /ri'kyo͞ozəl/ n.

ORIGIN late Middle English: from Latin *recusare* 'to refuse,' from *re-* (expressing opposition) + *causa* 'a cause.' The sense 'excuse (oneself from a case)' dates from the early 19th cent.

re•dress /ri'dres; 'rē,dres/ ▸ v. [trans.] remedy or set right (an undesirable or unfair situation): *the power to redress the grievances of our citizens.*

▸n. remedy or compensation for a wrong or grievance: *those seeking redress for an infringement of public law rights.*

ORIGIN Middle English: the verb from Old French *redresser;* the noun via Anglo-Norman French *redresse.*

re•en•act /,rēə'nækt/ ▸ v. [trans.] bring (a law) into effect again when the original statute has been repealed: *chapter forty-eight of said code shall be amended and reenacted.*

DERIVATIVES **re•en•act•ment n.**

re•en•try /rē'entrē/ ▸ n. (pl. **re•en•tries**) the action of retaking or repossession of property that had been let or granted: *reentry may be allowed if the buyer defaults.*

re•ex•am•ine /,rē-ig'zæmin/ ▸ v. [trans.] examine again or further: *I will have the body reexamined.*

■ examine (a witness) again, after cross-examination by the opposing counsel; submit a witness to redirect examination: *the prosecuting lawyer may reexamine the witness.*

DERIVATIVES **re•ex•am•i•na•tion** /,rēig,zæmə'nāsHən/ n.

Re•gi•na /rə'jīnə/ ▸ n. (in the UK) the reigning queen (used following a name or in the titles of lawsuits, e.g., *Regina v. Jones,* the Crown versus Jones).

ORIGIN Latin, literally 'queen.'

reg•is•trar /'reji,strär/ ▸ n. an official responsible for keeping a register or official records: *the registrar of births and deaths.*

ORIGIN late 17th cent.: from medieval Latin *registrarius*, from *registrum*, singular of Late Latin *regesta* 'things recorded,' from *regerere* 'enter, record.'

re•hear /rēˈhir/ ▸ v. (past and past part. **re•heard** /rēˈhərd/) [trans.] hear (a case or plaintiff) in a court again: [as n.] (**rehearing**) *the parents produced fresh evidence and won a rehearing.*

re•la•tor /riˈlātər/ ▸ n. a person who brings a public lawsuit, typically in the name of the attorney general, regarding the abuse of an office or franchise: *if the government declines to intervene, the relator may go forward with the lawsuit.*

re•lease /riˈlēs/ ▸ v. [trans.] **1** allow or enable to escape from confinement; set free: *the government announced that the prisoners would be released.*

2 remit or discharge (a debt): *releasing a debt is merely dealing with symptoms.*

■ surrender (a right): *the New York Power Authority released rights to land at Hyde Park Golf Course.* ■ make over (property or money) to another: *the sum of $8,000 has been released to the nephew's account.*

▸n. **1** the action or process of releasing or being released: *upon her release, Wanda returned to the streets.*

2 the action of releasing property, money, or a right to another: *the father consented to the release of his parental rights.*

■ a document effecting this: *signing this release allows Dayco the commercial use of your poem* | [as adj.] *a release form.*

DERIVATIVES **re•leas•ee** /riˌlēˈsē/ n.; **re•leas•or** /riˈlēsôr/ n.

ORIGIN Middle English: from Old French *reles* (noun), *relesser* (verb), from Latin *relaxare* 'stretch out again, slacken.'

rel•e•vant /ˈreləvənt/ ▸ adj. (of evidence or a fact) pertinent; closely connected or appropriate to the matter at hand, especially to the extent of proving or disproving the matter: *evidence which is not relevant is not admissible.*

DERIVATIVES **rel•e•vance** n.; **rel•e•van•cy** /-vənsē/ n.

ORIGIN early 16th cent. (as a Scots legal term meaning 'legally pertinent'): from medieval Latin *relevant-* 'raising up,' from Latin *relevare.*

re•lief /riˈlēf/ ▸ n. the redress of a hardship or grievance: *debt relief.*

ORIGIN late Middle English: from Old French, from *relever* 'raise up, relieve,' from Latin *relevare* 'raise again, alleviate.'

re•main•der /riˈmāndər/ ▸ n. an interest in an estate that becomes effective in possession only when a prior interest (devised at the same time) ends: *after all other bequests and expenses of the estate are met, the remainder is your charitable gift.*

ORIGIN late Middle English: from Anglo-Norman French, from Latin *remanere*, from *re-* (expressing intensive force) + *manere* 'to stay.'

re•mand /riˈmænd/ ▸ v. [trans.] place (a defendant) on bail or in custody, esp. when a trial is adjourned: *I had a seventeen-year-old son remanded to a drug-addiction program.*

■ return (a case) to a lower court for reconsideration: *the Supreme Court summarily vacated the opinion and remanded the matter back to the California Court of Appeal.*

▶n. a committal to custody.

ORIGIN late Middle English (as a verb in the sense 'send back again'): from late Latin *remandare*, from *re-* 'back' + *mandare* 'commit.' The noun dates from the late 18th cent.

rem•e•dy /ˈremədē/ ▶n. (pl. **rem•e•dies**) a means of legal reparation: *the doctrine took away their only remedy against merchants who refused to honor their contracts.*

ORIGIN Middle English: from Anglo-Norman French *remedie*, from Latin *remedium*, from *re-* 'back' (also expressing intensive force) + *mederi* 'heal.'

re•mis•sion /riˈmisHən/ ▶n. the cancellation of a debt, charge, or penalty: *the plan allows for the partial remission of tuition fees.*

ORIGIN Middle English: from Old French, or from Latin *remissio(n-)*, from *remittere* 'send back, restore' (see **REMIT**).

re•mit ▶v. /riˈmit/ (**re•mit•ted, re•mit•ting**) [trans.] **1** cancel or refrain from exacting or inflicting (a debt or punishment): *the excess of the sentence over 12 months was remitted.*

2 send back (a case) to a lower court: *the case should be remitted back to the Commissioners for further findings of fact.*

■ send (someone) from one tribunal to another for a trial or hearing.

▶n. /riˈmit; ˈrēˌmit/ **1** the task or area of activity officially assigned to an individual or organization: *the committee was becoming caught up in issues that did not fall within its remit.*

2 an item referred to someone for consideration.

DERIVATIVES **re•mit•ta•ble adj.; re•mit•tal** /riˈmitl/ **n.; re•mit•ter n.**

ORIGIN late Middle English: from Latin *remittere* 'send back, restore,' from *re-* 'back' + *mittere* 'send.' The noun dates from the early 20th cent.

re•nounce /riˈnowns/ ▶v. [trans.] formally declare one's abandonment of (a claim, right, or possession): *we renounce our right to Israeli citizenship.*

■ [intrans.] refuse or resign a right or position, esp. one as an heir or trustee: *there will be forms enabling the allottee to renounce.*

DERIVATIVES **re•nounce•a•ble adj.; re•nounce•ment n.; re•nounc•er n.**

ORIGIN late Middle English: from Old French *renoncer*, from Latin *renuntiare* 'protest against,' from *re-* (expressing reversal) + *nuntiare* 'announce.'

re•nun•ci•a•tion /riˌnənsēˈāsHən/ ▶n. the formal rejection of something, typically a belief, claim, or course of action: *the heirs have ten years to retract their renunciation of the succession.*

■ a document expressing renunciation.

DERIVATIVES **re•nun•ci•ant** /ri'nənsēənt/ **n. & adj.**

ORIGIN late Middle English: from late Latin *renuntiatio(n-)*, from Latin *renuntiare* 'protest against' (see RENOUNCE).

re•peal /ri'pēl/ ▶ v. [trans.] revoke or annul (a law or congressional act): *the legislation was repealed five months later.*

▶n. the action of revoking or annulling a law or congressional act: *the House voted in favor of repeal.*

DERIVATIVES **re•peal•a•ble adj.**

ORIGIN late Middle English: from Anglo-Norman French *repeler*, from Old French *re-* (expressing reversal) + *apeler* 'to call, appeal.'

re•plev•in /ri'plevən/ ▶ n. a procedure whereby goods wrongfully taken or detained may be provisionally restored to their owner pending the outcome of an action to determine the rights of the parties concerned: *an attorney filed a complaint for replevin on his own behalf* | [as adj.] *the creditor may seek a determination of ownership rights as a part of a replevin action.*

■ an action arising from such a process.

ORIGIN late Middle English: from Anglo-Norman French, from Old French *replevir* 'recover' (see REPLEVY).

re•plev•y /ri'plevē/ ▶ v. (**re•plev•ies, re•plev•ied**) [trans.] recover (goods taken or detained) by replevin: *a defendant who replevies the property is not required to account for the revenue of the property* | [as adj.] *all of the replevied cattle were sold at Bassett or Burwell.*

ORIGIN mid 16th cent.: from Old French *replevir* 'recover'; apparently related to PLEDGE.

re•ply /ri'plī/ ▶ n. (pl. **re•plies**) a plaintiff's response to the defendant's plea.

DERIVATIVES **re•pli•er n.**

ORIGIN late Middle English (as a verb): from Old French *replier*, from Latin *replicare* 'repeat,' later 'make a reply.'

re•port /ri'pôrt/ ▶ v. [trans.] (of a legislative committee) formally announce that the committee has dealt with (a bill): *the chairman shall report the bill to the House.*

▶n. a detailed formal account of a case heard in a court, giving the main points in the judgment, esp. as prepared for publication.

PHRASES **on report** (esp. of a prisoner or member of the armed forces) on a disciplinary charge: *the first time you step out of line, you'll be on report.*

▶**report a bill out** (of a committee of Congress) return a bill to the legislative body for action: *if the committee chooses to report a bill out they must choose whether or not to incorporate amendments.*

ORIGIN late Middle English: from Old French *reporter* (verb), *report* (noun), from Latin *reportare* 'bring back,' from *re-* 'back' + *portare* 'carry.'

rep•re•sent /ˌrepri'zent/ ▶ v. [trans.] **1** be entitled or appointed to act or

speak for (someone), esp. in an official capacity, as a lawyer for a client: *for purposes of litigation, an infant can and must be represented by an adult.*
■ be an elected member of a legislature for (a particular constituency, party, or group): *she became the first woman to represent her district.*
2 [with clause] allege; claim: *the vendors have represented that such information is accurate.*
ORIGIN late Middle English: from Old French *representer* or Latin *repraesentare*, from *re-* (expressing intensive force) + *praesentare* 'to present.'

re•pu•di•ate /ri'pyo͞odē,āt/ ▶ v. [trans.] refuse to fulfill or discharge (an agreement, obligation, or debt): *breach of a condition by one party gives the other party the right to repudiate a contract.*
DERIVATIVES **re•pu•di•a•tion** /ri,pyo͞odē'āsHən/ n.; **re•pu•di•a•tor** /ri'pyo͞odē,ātər/ n.
ORIGIN late Middle English (originally an adjective in the sense 'divorced'): from Latin *repudiatus* 'divorced, cast off,' from *repudium* 'divorce.'

res•er•va•tion /,rezər'vāsHən/ ▶ n. a right or interest retained in an estate being conveyed: *the agreement does not contain a specific reservation of appellee's right to seek appointment as co-executrix of the estate.*
ORIGIN late Middle English (denoting the pope's right of nomination to a benefice): from Old French, or from late Latin *reservatio(n-)*, from *reservare* 'keep back.'

res ges•tae /'räz 'gestī; 'rēz 'jestē/ ▶ plural n. the events, circumstances, remarks, etc., that relate to a particular case, esp. as constituting admissible evidence in a court of law: *these declarations were admissible as part of the res gestae* | [as adj.] *the court held that the officers were not res gestae witnesses because they arrived at the scene after the crime allegedly took place.*
ORIGIN Latin, literally 'things done.'

re•sid•u•ar•y /ri'zijo͞o,erē/ ▶ adj. of or relating to the residue of an estate: *a residuary legatee.*

res•i•due /'rezə,d(y)o͞o/ ▶ n. the part of an estate that is left after the payment of charges, debts, and bequests: *this bequest directs that either all or a percentage of your estate's residue be paid to the San Jose Cathedral Foundation.*
ORIGIN late Middle English: from Old French *residu*, from Latin *residuum* 'something remaining.'

res ip•sa lo•qui•tur /,räz ,ipsə 'läkwitər; 'lōkwə,to͞or/ ▶ n. the principle that the occurrence of an accident implies negligence if circumstances were such that it would not ordinarily otherwise have happened: *the court said res ipsa loquitur did not apply when the anesthesiologist introduced evidence that broken teeth are a normal risk of a laryngoscopic procedure.*
ORIGIN Latin, literally 'the matter speaks for itself.'

res ju•di•ca•ta /ˌräz ˌjo͞odiˈkätə/ ▶ n. (pl. **res ju•di•ca•tae** /ˈräz ˌjo͞odi ˈkätē; -ˈkätī/) a matter that has been adjudicated by a competent court and may not be pursued further by the same parties: *res judicata also bars subsequent actions on claims that should have been—but were not—raised in the first proceeding.*
ORIGIN Latin, literally 'judged matter.'

re•spond•ent /riˈspändənt/ ▶ n. a defendant in a lawsuit, esp. one in an appeal or in a divorce case: *the respondent is a telecommunications corporation.*
▶ **adj.** [attrib.] in the position of defendant in a lawsuit: *the plaintiff says he has worked for the respondent party for many years.*
ORIGIN from Latin *respondent-* 'answering, offering in return.'

rest /rest/ ▶ v. [intrans.] conclude the case for the prosecution or the defense in a law case: *the prosecution rests.* See also **rest one's case** below.
PHRASES **rest one's case** conclude one's presentation of evidence and arguments in a lawsuit.
ORIGIN Old English *ræst, rest* (noun), *ræstan, restan* (verb), of Germanic origin, from a root meaning 'league' or 'mile' (referring to a distance after which one rests).

res•ti•tu•tion /ˌrestəˈt(y)o͞osHən/ ▶ n. return of a benefit received: *he was ordered to pay $6,000 in restitution.*
■ the restoring of both parties to their original position after recission of a contract.
DERIVATIVES **res•ti•tu•tive** /ˈrestəˌt(y)o͞otiv/ **adj.**
ORIGIN Middle English: from Old French, or from Latin *restitutio(n-),* from *restituere* 'restore,' from *re-* 'again' + *statuere* 'establish.'

re•straint of trade /riˈstränt əv ˈträd/ ▶ n. action that interferes with free competition in a market.

re•stric•tive cov•e•nant /riˈstriktiv ˈkəvənənt/ ▶ n. a covenant imposing a restriction on the occupancy or use of land, typically so that the value and enjoyment of adjoining land will be preserved.
■ a covenant in an employment contract that forbids the employee from working for a competitor if he or she leaves the first employer.

re•tain /riˈtān/ ▶ v. [trans.] secure the services of (a person, esp. an attorney) with a preliminary payment: *retain an attorney to handle the client's business.*
ORIGIN late Middle English: via Anglo-Norman French from Old French *retenir,* from Latin *retinere,* from *re-* 'back' + *tenere* 'hold.'

re•tain•er /riˈtānər/ ▶ n. a fee paid in advance to an attorney in order to secure or keep their services when required.

re•tri•al /rēˈtrīəl; ˈrēˌtrīəl/ ▶ n. a second or further trial.

ret•ro•ac•tive /ˌretrōˈæktiv/ ▶ adj. (esp. of legislation) taking effect from a date in the past: *a big retroactive tax increase.*
DERIVATIVES **ret•ro•ac•tion** /ˌretrōˈæksHən/ n.; **ret•ro•ac•tive•ly** adv.; **ret•ro•ac•tiv•i•ty** /ˌretrōækˈtivətē/ n.

ret•ro•spec•tive /ˌretrə'spektiv/ ▶ **adj.** (of a statute or legal decision) taking effect from a date in the past; retroactive: *retrospective pay awards.*

re•try /rē'trī/ ▶ **v.** (**re•tries, re•tried**) [trans.] try (a defendant or case) again: *the state of Alabama then retried one of the accused, and once again convicted him.*

re•turn /ri'tərn/ ▶ **v.** [trans.] (of a judge or jury) state or present (a verdict) in response to a formal request: *the jury of nine women and three men returned the verdict within hours.*

▶ **n.** an endorsement or report by a court officer or sheriff on a writ: *the officer shall promptly make a return of the facts to the court.*

ORIGIN Middle English: the verb from Old French *returner,* from Latin *re-* 'back' + *tornare* 'to turn'; the noun via Anglo-Norman French.

re•turn date /'ritərn ˌdāt/ ▶ **n.** the day on which process is due or an order is to be answered. Also called **return day**: *Stevens failed to appear in court on the return date.*

re•ver•sal /ri'vərsəl/ ▶ **n.** an annulment of a judgment, sentence, or decree made by a lower court or authority: *the Court has upheld the appellate justices in their reversal of the trial court judgment.*

ORIGIN late 15th cent. (as a legal term): from the verb REVERSE + *-al.*

re•verse /ri'vərs/ ▶ **v.** [trans.] revoke or annul (a judgment, sentence, or decree made by a lower court or authority): *the court reversed his conviction.*

ORIGIN Middle English: from Old French *revers, reverse* (nouns), *reverser* (verb), from Latin *reversus* 'turned back,' past participle of *revertere,* from *re-* 'back' + *vertere* 'to turn.'

re•ver•sion /ri'vərzHən/ ▶ **n.** the right, esp. of the original owner or their heirs, to possess or succeed to property on the death of the present possessor or at the end of a lease: *the reversion of property.*

■ a property to which someone has such a right.

DERIVATIVES **re•ver•sion•ar•y** /ti'vərzHəˌnerē/ **adj.**

ORIGIN late Middle English (denoting the action of returning to or from a place): from Old French, or from Latin *reversio(n-),* from *revertere* 'turn back' (see REVERSE).

re•ver•sion•er /ri'vərzHənər/ ▶ **n.** a person who possesses the reversion to a property or privilege.

re•vert /ri'vərt/ ▶ **v.** [intrans.] (**revert to**) (of property) return or pass to (the original owner) by reversion: *the title to the property shall revert to and be vested in the state of Mississippi.*

DERIVATIVES **re•vert•er** n.

ORIGIN Middle English: from Old French *revertir* or Latin *revertere* 'turn back.' Early senses included 'recover consciousness,' 'return to a position,' and 'return to a person (after estrangement).'

re•view /ri'vyo͞o/ ▶ **n.** a reconsideration of a judgment, sentence, etc., by a higher court or authority: *a review of her sentence | his case comes up for review in January.* Compare with JUDICIAL REVIEW.

▶ **v.** [trans.] (of a higher court or authority) reconsider (the action of a lower court or authority): *the attorney general asked the court to review the sentence.*

ORIGIN late Middle English (as a noun denoting a formal inspection of military or naval forces): from obsolete French *reveue*, from *revoir* 'see again.'

Rex /reks/ ▸ n. (in the UK) the reigning king (used following a name or in the titles of lawsuits, e.g., *Rex v. Jones*: the Crown versus Jones).

ORIGIN Latin, literally 'king.'

RICO /'rēkō/ ▸ abbr. (in the US) Racketeer Influenced and Corrupt Organizations Act.

rid•er /'rīdər/ ▸ n. an addition or amendment to a document, esp. a piece of legislation or a contract: *the rules of Congress make it difficult to attach a rider to an appropriations bill | a rider to an eligible life insurance policy.*

ORIGIN late Old English *rīdere* 'mounted warrior, knight.'

right /rīt/ ▸ n. a moral or legal entitlement to have or obtain something or to act in a certain way: [with infinitive] *you're quite **within your rights** to ask for your money back | there is no **right of** appeal against the decision.*

■ (**rights**) one's civil liberties. ■ (**rights**) the authority to perform, publish, film, or televise a particular work, event, etc.: *they sold the paperback rights.*

PHRASES **be in the right** be morally or legally justified in one's views, actions, or decisions. (**as**) **of right** (or **by right**) as a result of having a moral or legal claim or entitlement: *the state will be obliged to provide health care and education as of right.*

ORIGIN Old English *riht* (adjective and noun), *rihtan* (verb), *rihte* (adverb), of Germanic origin; related to Latin *rectus* 'ruled,' from an Indo-European root denoting movement in a straight line.

right of way /'rīt əv 'wā/ (also **right-of-way**) ▸ n. 1 the legal right, established by usage or grant, to pass along a specific route through grounds or property belonging to another.

■ a path or thoroughfare subject to such a right.

2 the legal right of a pedestrian, rider, or driver to proceed with precedence over other road users at a particular point: *he waves on other drivers, even when it's not their right of way.*

■ the right of a ship, boat, or aircraft to proceed with precedence over others in a particular situation.

3 the right to build and operate a railroad line, road, or utility on land belonging to another.

■ the land on which a railroad line, road, or utility is built: *the right of way of the South Penn Railroad was a section that ran between Harrisburg and Pittsburgh.*

Ri•ot Act /'rīət ˌækt/ a law passed by the British government in 1715 and repealed in 1967, designed to prevent civil disorder. The act made it a felony for an assembly of more than twelve people to refuse to disperse after being ordered to do so and having been read a specified portion of the act by lawful authority.

ri•par•i•an /rə'perēən; rī-/ ▸ **adj.** of, relating to, or situated on the banks of a river: *all the riparian states must sign an agreement.*

PHRASES **riparian rights** legal entitlement to use of flowing water.

ORIGIN mid 19th cent.: from Latin *riparius* (from *ripa* 'bank') + *-an.*

rise /rīz/ ▸ **v.** (past **rose** /rōz/; past part. **ris•en** /'rizən/) [intrans.] chiefly Brit. (of a meeting or a session of a court) adjourn: *the judge's remark heralded the signal for the court to rise.*

ORIGIN Old English *rīsan* 'make an attack,' 'wake, get out of bed,' of Germanic origin; related to Dutch *rijzen* and German *reisen.*

rob /räb/ ▸ **v.** (**robbed, rob•bing**) [trans.] take property unlawfully from (a person or place) by force or threat of force: *he tried, with three others, to rob a bank* | *she was **robbed** of her handbag* | [intrans.] *he was convicted of assault with intent to rob.*

ORIGIN Middle English: from Old French *rober*, of Germanic origin; related to the verb *reave.*

USAGE: In law, to **rob** is to take something from someone by causing fear of harm, whether or not actual harm occurs. The term is widely, but incorrectly, used to mean **theft**: *our house was robbed while we were away.* Technically, the more correct statement would be *our house was burglarized while we were away.*

rob•ber /'räbər/ ▸ **n.** a person who commits robbery.

ORIGIN Middle English: from Anglo-Norman French and Old French *robere*, from the verb *rober* (see ROB).

rob•ber•y /'räb(ə)rē/ ▸ **n.** (pl. **rob•ber•ies**) the action of robbing a person or place: *he was involved in drugs, violence, extortion, and robbery* | *an armed robbery.*

▪ the felonious taking of personal property from someone using force or the threat of force.

ORIGIN Middle English: from Anglo-Norman French and Old French *roberie*, from the verb *rober* (see ROB).

Ro•man law /'rōmən 'lô/ ▸ **n.** the law code of the ancient Romans, which forms the basis of civil law in many countries today.

rule /rool/ ▸ **n.** 1 a regulation or principle of law.

2 ▪ an order made by a judge or court with reference to a particular case only.

▸ **v.** [with clause] pronounce authoritatively and legally to be the case: *a federal court ruled that he was unfairly dismissed from his job.*

PHRASES **rule of law** the restriction of the arbitrary exercise of power by subordinating it to well-defined and established laws. ▪ a doctrine or precedent applied to the facts of a case under consideration: *what rule of law applies, given these facts?*

ORIGIN Middle English: from Old French *reule* (noun), *reuler* (verb), from late Latin *regulare*, from Latin *regula* 'straight stick.'

rule of the road /ˈro͞ol əv T͟Hə ˈrōd/ ▸ n. (usu. **rules of the road**) a custom or law regulating the direction in which two vehicles (or riders or ships) should move to pass one another on meeting, or which should yield to the other, so as to avoid collision.

WHAT TO DO IF YOU'RE BEING SUED . . . OR THINKING OF SUING

Before you are sued . . .

. . . you might receive advance warning, typically in the form of a lawyer's letter stating that you will be sued unless you satisfy certain demands. This is seldom an idle threat. It is a final chance to resolve a dispute without the expense and turmoil of litigation. Sometimes you can do this yourself—for example, when the claim is for a sum of money that you know you owe and are prepared to pay. In more complex situations, a lawyer might be able to help you stave off the suit—for example, by negotiating a lower sum, arranging for you to pay in installments, or arranging for mediation or arbitration. In each case, a properly drafted agreement can assure that the suit will not be filed, as long as you hold up your end of the agreement. If you negotiate directly with your opponent's lawyer, you will be at a disadvantage; remember: that lawyer's job is not to reach a fair result, but to make you pay.

If you are sued . . .

. . . you'll know it. You will receive a summons or other court order requiring you to appear and respond to the plaintiff's allegations. If you receive notice of an actual lawsuit, you have to shift into high gear. There are two overriding principles:

1. Do not ignore it. The summons says that if you do not answer by a certain date, judgment will be entered against

you—and it most certainly will. Even if the suit is baseless, your lack of response results in a default judgment, which may be difficult to overturn; your wages may be garnished or your property seized to satisfy it. And if the judgment is justified, it would have been better to settle the case than to have a judgment clouding your credit record for years to come.

2. Unless the case is in small claims court—and maybe even if it is—get a lawyer. (See *Choosing a Lawyer*, p. 18.) A lawyer can advise on your rights, prepare necessary court papers, assert defenses you might not know about, file claims against other parties to help reduce your liability, and negotiate from a position of strength. If necessary, you can phone the plaintiff's lawyer and ask for time to hire a lawyer. Most lawyers will grant an extension, but be sure to get it in writing.

The next steps depend upon the nature of the case. If the IRS is suing or auditing you over a tax return prepared by a paid preparer, send notice of the action to the tax preparer. If the suit is for personal injury or property damage and you have any kind of liability insurance that could conceivably apply, send copies of the summons and complaint to your insurance company immediately, together with a demand that they "defend and indemnify" you—that is, provide a lawyer and pay any judgment. Most liability policies require the insurance company to provide a lawyer for you, so you will not have to get one on your own. But the time limits for making such demands can be short. Do not hold back just because you are unsure whether the incident is actually covered; that can be sorted out later.

Get together any documents and other evidence that you have relating to the case. Your lawyer will need them, and you will have to produce them during the "discovery" phase of the suit. Do not even think of forging, altering, or destroying evidence. When such potentially criminal shenanigans come to light (and don't think they won't!), they are devastating to your case.

Tell your lawyer everything. Your lawyer needs all the facts—especially the bad ones!—right up front in order to plan the best strategy, give the best advice, and get the best result. The last thing you want is for your lawyer to be blindsided at a deposition, in settlement talks, or at trial. Bear in mind also that your lawyer is not allowed to present evidence that he or she knows to be false; and if you lie on the witness stand and your lawyer finds out later in the proceeding, the lawyer is required to set the record straight. Don't sandbag your own lawyer and your own case.

If you are thinking of suing . . .

. . . think twice. Being a plaintiff in a lawsuit is almost as bad as being the defendant. The time and expense, the physical and emotional strain, and the disruption of your life and relationships can be just as painful.

If you have a consumer complaint or business dispute, explore other options: direct negotiation, the Better Business Bureau, or a consumer protection agency. Discuss mediation or arbitration with your lawyer. Use small claims court if possible.

But if someone has injured you or damaged your property, you must get a lawyer involved promptly. Every state limits the time you have to bring a suit, and the limit can be as short as a few months. If there is an invasion of your rights that you want stopped—for example, your tenant refuses to vacate an apartment at the end of the lease's term—any delay at all in running to court can jeopardize your position.

Whether you sue or are sued, try to be objective in evaluating your case. Nearly all cases settle; except for rare cases brought for the purpose of establishing a precedent or for the vindication of one's feelings, winning is less important than getting the best deal you can at the lowest cost.

S

s ▶ **abbr.** ■ section (of an act).

safe con•duct /'sāf 'kän‚dəkt/ ▶ **n.** immunity from arrest or harm when passing through an area: *the article provides safe conduct at sea for medical equipment intended for wounded and sick members of the armed forces.*

■ a document securing such a privilege.

sal•vage /'sælvij/ (also **salvage payment**) ▶ **n.** payment made or due to a person who has saved a ship or its cargo.

ORIGIN mid 17th cent.: from French, from medieval Latin *salvagium*, from Latin *salvare* 'to save.'

sanc•tion /'sæNG(k)SHən/ ▶ **n. 1** a penalty for disobeying a law or rule: *a range of sanctions aimed at deterring insider abuse.*

2 official confirmation or ratification of a law.

■ historical a law or decree, esp. an ecclesiastical decree.

▶ **v.** [trans.] **1** impose a sanction or penalty on: *the client is hereby sanctioned.*

2 officially confirm; uphold as legal: *in* Plessy v. Ferguson, *the court sanctioned segregation in public facilities.*

DERIVATIVES **sanc•tion•a•ble adj.**

ORIGIN late Middle English (as a noun denoting an ecclesiastical decree): from French, from Latin *sanctio(n-)*, from *sancire* 'ratify.' The verb dates from the late 18th cent.

sanc•tu•ar•y /'sæNG(k)CHŌŌ‚erē/ ▶ **n.** (pl. **sanc•tu•ar•ies**) immunity from arrest: *he has been **given sanctuary** in the US Embassy in Beijing.*

ORIGIN from Old French *sanctuaire*, from Latin *sanctuarium*, from *sanctus* 'holy.' The early sense 'a church or other sacred place where a fugitive was immune, by the law of the medieval church, from arrest' gave rise to the sense 'immunity from arrest.'

sat•is•fac•tion /‚sæṯis'fækSHən/ ▶ **n.** the payment of a debt or fulfillment of an obligation or claim: *in **full and final satisfaction** of the claim.*

ORIGIN Middle English: from Old French, or from Latin *satisfactio(n-)*, from *satisfacere* 'satisfy, content.'

sav•ing /'sāviNG/ ▶ **n.** a reservation; an exception.

sav•ing clause /'sāviNG ‚klôz/ ▶ **n.** an exception in a statute preserving prior law from repeal: *section 8 includes a saving clause intended to* *make clear that the copyright protection of a private work is not affected if the work is published by the government.*

■ a clause in a contract or agreement containing an exemption from one or more of its conditions.

seal /sēl/ ▸ n. a piece of wax, lead, or other material with an individual design stamped into it, attached to a document to show that it has come from the person who claims to have issued it.

■ a design embossed in paper for this purpose. ■ an engraved device used for stamping a design that authenticates a document.

▸v. [trans.] fix a piece of wax or lead stamped with a design to (a document) to authenticate it.

PHRASES **under seal** under legal protection of secrecy: *the judge ordered that the videotape be kept under seal.*

ORIGIN Middle English: from Old French *seel* (noun), *seeler* (verb), from Latin *sigillum* 'small picture,' diminutive of *signum* 'a sign.'

search war•rant /'sərCH ,wôrənt; ,wärənt/ ▸ n. a legal document authorizing a police officer or other official to enter and search premises.

sec•ond-de•gree /'sekən(d) də,grē/ ▸ adj. [attrib.] denoting a category of a crime, esp. murder, that is less serious than a first-degree crime: *the jury returned a verdict of second-degree murder.*

se•di•tion /si'diSHən/ ▸ n. conduct or speech inciting people to rebel against the authority of a state or monarch.

ORIGIN late Middle English (in the sense 'violent strife'): from Old French, or from Latin *seditio(n-)*, from *sed-* 'apart' + *itio(n-)* 'going' (from the verb *ire*).

se•di•tious /si'diSHəs/ ▸ adj. inciting or causing people to rebel against the authority of a state or monarch: *the letter was declared seditious.*

DERIVATIVES **se•di•tious•ly** adv.

ORIGIN late Middle English: from Old French *seditieux* or Latin *seditiosus*, from *seditio* 'mutinous separation' (see **SEDITION**).

se•di•tious li•bel /si'diSHəs 'lībəl/ ▸ n. a published statement that is seditious: *Zenger was charged with publishing seditious libel.*

■ the action or crime of publishing such a statement: *the doctrine of seditious libel was upheld in the American colonies.*

sei•sin /'sēzin/ (also **sei•zin**) ▸ n. possession of land by freehold.

■ Brit., historical possession, esp. of land: *Richard Fitzhugh did not take seisin of his lands until 1480.*

ORIGIN Middle English: from Old French *seisine*, from *saisir* 'seize.'

seize /sēz/ ▸ v. [trans.] **1** (of the police or another authority) take possession of (something) by warrant or legal right; confiscate; impound: *police have seized 726 lb of cocaine.*

2 (also **seise**) (**be seized of**) English Law be in legal possession of: *the court is currently seized of custody applications.*

■ historical have or receive freehold possession of (property): *any person who is seized of land has a protected interest in that land.*

ORIGIN Middle English: from Old French *seizir* 'give seisin,' from medieval Latin *sacire*, in the phrase *ad proprium sacire* 'claim as one's own,' from a Germanic base meaning 'procedure.'

self-de•fense /'self di'fens/ ▶ n. the defense of one's person or interests, esp. through the use of physical force, which is permitted in certain cases as an answer to a charge of violent crime or a tort: *he claimed self-defense in the attempted murder charge* | [as adj.] *self-defense classes.*

DERIVATIVES **self-de•fen•sive** adj.

self-prov•ing /'self 'prōōviNG/ ▶ adj. (of a will) accompanied by a witnesses' affidavit for which no oral testimony is needed to be admitted to probate: *we recommend that all wills be self-proving.*

■ of or relating to an affidavit that makes a will self-proving: *attached to the will offered for probate was a self-proving affidavit and certificate executed by the testatrix, the two witnesses to the will, and a notary public.*

sen•a•tor /'senətər/ ▶ n. a member of a senate.

DERIVATIVES **sen•a•to•ri•al** /ˌsenə'tôrēəl/ adj.; **sen•a•tor•ship** /'senətər,SHip/ n.

ORIGIN Middle English (denoting a member of the ancient Roman senate): from Old French *senateur*, from Latin *senator*.

sen•tence /'sent(ə)ns/ ▶ n. the punishment assigned to a defendant found guilty by a court: *her husband is **serving** a three-year **sentence** for fraud.*

■ the punishment fixed by law for a particular offense: *slander of an official carried an eight-year prison sentence.*

▶ v. [trans.] declare the punishment decided for (an offender): *ten army officers were **sentenced to** death.*

PHRASES **under sentence of** having been condemned to: *he was under sentence of death.*

ORIGIN Middle English (in the senses 'way of thinking, opinion,' 'court's declaration of punishment,' and 'gist (of a piece of writing)'): via Old French from Latin *sententia* 'opinion,' from *sentire* 'feel, be of the opinion.'

sep•a•ra•tion /ˌsepə'rāSHən/ ▶ n. the state in which a husband and wife remain married but live apart: *legal grounds for divorce or separation* | *she and her husband have agreed to a **trial separation**.* See also LEGAL SEPARATION (sense 1).

ORIGIN late Middle English: via Old French from Latin *separatio(n-)*, from *separare* 'disjoin, divide.'

sep•a•ra•tion of pow•ers /ˌsepə'rāSHən əv 'powərz/ ▶ n. phrase the vesting of the legislative, executive, and judicial powers of government in separate bodies: *the separation of powers insures that the authority of the president may not encroach upon that of the Congress or the Supreme Court.*

se•ques•ter /si'kwestər/ ▶ v. [trans.] **1** isolate (a jury) from outside influences during a trial: *the jurors had been sequestered since Monday.*

2 take legal possession of (assets) until a debt has been paid or other claims have been met: *the power of courts to sequester the assets of unions.*
■ legally place (the property of a bankrupt) in the hands of a trustee for division among the creditors: [as adj.] (**sequestered**) *a trustee in a sequestered estate.* ■ declare (someone) bankrupt: *two more poll tax rebels were sequestered.*
ORIGIN late Middle English: from Old French *sequestrer* or late Latin *sequestrare* 'commit for safekeeping,' from Latin *sequester* 'trustee.'

se•ques•trate /'sēkwi,strāt; 'sek-; si'kwestrāt/ ▶ v. [trans.] another term for SEQUESTER (sense 2).
DERIVATIVES **se•ques•tra•ble** /si'kwestrəbəl/ **adj.**
ORIGIN late Middle English (in the sense 'separate from general access'): from late Latin *sequestrat-* 'given up for safekeeping,' from the verb *sequestrare* (see SEQUESTER).

se•ques•tra•tion /,sēkwi'strāsHən; ,sek-/ ▶ n. **1** the action of taking legal possession of assets until a debt has been paid or other claims have been met: *if such court injunctions are ignored, sequestration of trade union assets will follow.*
■ an act of declaring someone bankrupt.
2 the action of isolating a jury during a trial: *either party may move for sequestration of the jury.*

ser•geant-at-arms /'särjənt æt 'ärmz; ət/ (Brit. **ser•jeant-at-arms**) ▶ n. (pl. **sergeants-at-arms**) an official of a legislative or other assembly whose duty includes maintaining order and security.

serve /sərv/ ▶ v. [trans.] **1** spend (a period) in jail or prison: *he is serving a ten-year jail sentence.*
2 deliver (a document such as a summons or writ) in a formal manner to the person to whom it is addressed: *a warrant was **served on** Jack Sherman.*
■ deliver a document to (someone) in such a way: *they were just about to **serve** him **with** a writ.*
PHRASES **serve one's time** (also **serve time**) spend time in jail or prison.
ORIGIN Middle English: from Old French *servir*, from Latin *servire*, from *servus* 'slave.'

serv•ice /'sərvis/ ▶ n. the formal delivery of a document such as a writ or summons.

ser•vi•tude /'sərvi,t(y)o͞od/ ▶ n. the subjection of property to an easement or other restriction: *the deed of easement granted a public forest servitude to the state.*
ORIGIN late Middle English: via Old French from Latin *servitudo*, from *servus* 'slave.'

set a•side /'set ə'sīd/ ▶ phrasal verb overrule or annul (a legal decision or process): *the Supreme Court has set aside the order in its entirety.*

set-off /'set ˌôf/ ▸ n. a counterbalancing debt pleaded by the defendant in an action to recover money due *the set-off may diminish or entirely cancel the claim of the plaintiff.*

set•tle /'setl/ ▸ v. end (a legal dispute) by mutual agreement: *the matter was settled out of court* | [intrans.] *he sued for libel and then settled out of court.*

PHRASES **settle one's affairs** (or **estate**) make any necessary arrangements, such as writing a will, before one's death.

ORIGIN Old English *setlan* 'to seat, place.'

set•tle•ment /'setlmənt/ ▸ n. 1 a formal arrangement made between the parties to a lawsuit in order to resolve it, esp. out of court: *the owner reached an out-of-court settlement with the plaintiffs.*

2 an arrangement whereby property passes to a person or succession of people as dictated by the settlor.

■ the amount or property given: *a generous settlement.*

set•tlor /'setl-ər; 'setlər/ ▸ n. a person who makes a settlement, esp. of property.

sev•er•al /'sev(ə)rəl/ ▸ adj. applied or regarded separately.Often contrasted with JOINT.

DERIVATIVES **sev•er•al•ly** adv.

ORIGIN late Middle English: from Anglo-Norman French, from medieval Latin *separalis*, from Latin *separ* 'separate, different.'

sev•er•al•ty /'sev(ə)rəltē/ ▸ n. the tenure of land held by an individual, not jointly or in common with another.

■ the condition of land so held: *the Dawes Severalty Act provides for the allotment of lands **in severalty** to Indians on the various reservations* ■ a piece of land so held.

ORIGIN late Middle English: from Anglo-Norman French *severalte,* from *several* (see SEVERAL).

sev•er•ance /'sev(ə)rəns/ ▸ n. the action of ending a connection or relationship, especially a property interest among co-owners: *a portion of the property may be sold through a severance.*

ORIGIN late Middle English: from Anglo-Norman French, based on Latin *separare* 'disjoin, divide.'

sex crime /'seks ˌkrīm/ ▸ n. informal a crime involving sexual assault or having a sexual motive.

sex dis•crim•i•na•tion /'seks disˌkriməˌnāSHən/ (also **sexual discrimination**) ▸ n. discrimination in employment and opportunity against a person (typically a woman) on grounds of sex.

sex•u•al ha•rass•ment /'sekSHŌŌəl həˈræsmənt/ ▸ n. harassment (typically of a woman) in a workplace, or other professional situation, usually involving the making of unwanted sexual advances or obscene remarks.

SG ▸ abbr. solicitor general.

sher•iff /'sHerif/ ▸ n. (in the US) an elected officer in a county who is responsible for law enforcement and judicial administration.

■ (also **high sheriff**) (in England and Wales) the chief executive officer of the Crown in a county, having various administrative and judicial functions. ■ an honorary officer elected annually in some English towns. ■ (in Scotland) a judge.
DERIVATIVES **sher•iff•dom** /'sHerifdəm/ n.
ORIGIN Old English *scīrgerēfa* (see **SHIRE, REEVE**[1]).

shop•lift•ing /'sHäp,liftiNG/ ▸ n. the criminal action of stealing goods from a store while pretending to be a customer.
DERIVATIVES **shop•lift** v.; **shop•lift•er** /-,liftər/ n.

side•bar /'sīd,bär/ (also **sidebar conference**) ▸ n. (in a court of law) a discussion between the lawyers and the judge held out of earshot of the jury.

silk /silk/ ▸ n. Brit., informal a Queen's (or King's) Counsel. [ORIGIN: so named because of the right accorded to wear a gown made of this cloth.]

si•ne di•e /'sīnə 'dī,ē; 'sēnā 'dē,ā/ ▸ adv. (with reference to business or proceedings that have been adjourned) with no appointed date for resumption: *the case was adjourned sine die.*
ORIGIN Latin, literally 'without a day.'

si•tus /'sīṯəs; 'sē-/ ▸ n. the place to which, for purposes of legal jurisdiction or taxation, an act occurred or a property belongs: *finally, the court held that the situs of these ferries was Norfolk, where the company had its principal place of business.* | *a vehicle has situs for taxation in the City if it is garaged, parked, or stored in the City.*

slan•der /'slændər/ ▸ n. the tortious act of making a false spoken statement damaging to a person's reputation: *he is suing the TV network for slander.* Compare with **LIBEL**.
▸ v. [trans.] make false and damaging statements about (someone): *they were accused of slandering the head of state.*
DERIVATIVES **slan•der•er** n.; **slan•der•ous** /'slændərəs/ adj.; **slan•der•ous•ly** /'slændərəslē/ adv.
ORIGIN Middle English: from Old French *esclandre*, alteration of *escandle*, from late Latin *scandalum* 'cause of offense,' from Greek *skandalon* 'snare, stumbling block.'

small-claims court /'smôl 'klāmz ,kôrt/ ▸ n. a local court in which claims for small sums of money can be heard and decided quickly and cheaply, without legal representation.

so•lic•it /sə'lisit/ ▸ v. (**so•lic•it•ed, so•lic•it•ing**) [intrans.] incite or persuade (a person) to commit an illegal or insubordinate act.
■ accost someone and offer one's or someone else's services as a prostitute: [as n.] (**soliciting**) *although prostitution was not itself an offense, soliciting was.*
DERIVATIVES **so•lic•i•ta•tion** /sə,lisi'tāsHən/ n.
ORIGIN late Middle English: from Old French *solliciter*, from Latin *sollicitare* 'agitate,' from *sollicitus* 'anxious,' from *sollus* 'entire' + *citus* (past participle of *ciere* 'set in motion').

so•lic•i•tor /sə'lisit̩ər/ ▸ n. the chief law officer of a city, town, or government department.
■ Brit. a member of the legal profession qualified to deal with conveyancing, the drawing up of wills, and other legal matters. Compare with **BARRISTER**.
ORIGIN late Middle English (denoting an agent or deputy): from Old French *solliciteur*, from *solliciter* (see **SOLICIT**).

so•lic•i•tor gen•er•al /sə'lisit̩ər 'jen(ə)rəl/ ▸ n. (pl. **so•lic•i•tors gen•er•al**) in the US Department of Justice, the law officer responsible for arguing cases before the US Supreme Court.

spe•cial ver•dict /'speSHəl 'vərdikt/ ▸ n. a verdict that states facts as proved but leaves the court to draw conclusions from them in order to render judgment.

spe•cie /'spēSHē; -sē/ ▸ n. (as **in specie**) in the real, precise, or actual form specified: *the plaintiff could not be sure of recovering his goods in specie.*
ORIGIN mid 16th cent.: from Latin, ablative of *species* 'form, kind,' in the phrase *in specie* 'in the actual form.'

spe•cif•ic per•for•mance /spə'sifik pər'fôrməns/ ▸ n. the performance of a contractual duty, as ordered in cases where damages would not be adequate remedy: *a decree for specific performance may include any terms and conditions as to payment of the rent, damages, or other relief that the court deems just.*

speed lim•it /'spēd ˌlimit/ ▸ n. the maximum speed at which a vehicle may legally travel on a particular stretch of road.

speed•y tri•al /'spēdē 'trīəl/ ▸ n. a criminal trial held after minimal delay, as a citizen's constitutional right.

split de•ci•sion /'split di'siZHən/ ▸ n. a decision based on a majority verdict rather than on a unanimous one: *a split decision has been reached in the malpractice trial filed by a Rockville woman.*

spo•li•a•tion /ˌspōlē'āSHən/ ▸ n. **1** the action of destroying, mutilating, or altering a document (e.g., a will) or evidence unfavorable to oneself: *the plaintiff's alleged spoliation of evidence.*
2 the action of taking goods or property from somewhere by illegal or unethical means: *the spoliation of the Church.*
ORIGIN late Middle English (denoting pillaging): from Latin *spoliatio(n-)*, from the verb *spoliare* 'strip, deprive.'

spous•al /'spowzəl/ ▸ adj. [attrib.] of or relating to marriage or to a husband or wife: *the spousal benefits of married couples.*

stale /stāl/ ▸ adj. (**stal•er, stal•est**) (of a check or legal claim) invalid because not acted on within a reasonable time: *nonpayment of a stale claim is not actionable.*
ORIGIN Middle English (describing beer in the sense 'clear from long standing, strong'): probably from Anglo-Norman French and Old French, from *estaler* 'to halt.'

stand /stænd/ ▸ n. (**the stand**) a witness stand: *Sergeant Harris took the stand.*

▸**v.** [trans.] undergo or submit to, as in **stand trial** (see below).

PHRASES **stand trial** be tried in a court of law: *one of the suspects died before standing trial.*

▸**stand down** (of a witness) leave the witness stand after giving evidence: *the witness may stand down.*

ORIGIN Old English *standan* (verb), *stand* (noun), of Germanic origin, from an Indo-European root shared by Latin *stare* and Greek *histanai*, also by the noun *stead.*

Star Cham•ber /'stär 'CHămbər/ an English court of civil and criminal jurisdiction that developed in the late 15th century, trying esp. those cases affecting the interests of the Crown. It was noted for its arbitrary and oppressive judgments and was abolished in 1641.

sta•re de•ci•sis /'sterē də'sīsis/ ▸**n.** the legal principle that courts should abide by precedent.

ORIGIN Latin, literally 'stand by things decided.'

state /stāt/ ▸**n. 1** the particular condition that someone or something is in at a specific time: *the state of the company's finances* | *we're worried about her state of mind.*

2 the civil government of a country: *services provided by the state* | [in combination] *state-owned companies.*

▸**adj.** [attrib.] of, provided by, or concerned with the civil government of a country: *the future of state education* | *a state secret.*

▸**v.** [trans.] specify the facts of (a case) for consideration: *judges must give both sides an equal opportunity to state their case.*

ORIGIN Middle English (as a noun): partly a shortening of ESTATE, partly from Latin *status* 'manner of standing, condition.'

state•ment /'stātmənt/ ▸**n.** a formal account of events given by a witness, defendant, or other party to the police or in a court of law: *she made a statement to the police.*

state's at•tor•ney /'stāts ə'tərnē/ ▸**n.** a lawyer representing a state in court.

state's ev•i•dence /'stāts 'evidns/ ▸**n.** evidence for the prosecution given by a participant in or accomplice to the crime being tried.

PHRASES **turn state's evidence** give such evidence: *persuading one-time gang members to turn state's evidence.*

stat•ute /'stæCHoōt/ ▸**n.** a written law passed by a legislative body: *violation of the hate crimes statute* | *the tax is not specifically disallowed by statute.*

ORIGIN Middle English: from Old French *statut*, from late Latin *statutum*, neuter past participle of Latin *statuere* 'set up,' from *status* 'standing.'

stat•ute book /'stæCHoōt ,boŏk/ ▸**n.** a book in which laws are written.

stat•ute law /'stæCHoōt ,lô/ ▸**n.** the body of principles and rules of law laid down in statutes. Compare with COMMON LAW, CASE LAW.

stat•ute of lim•i•ta•tions /'stæCHoōt əv ,limi'tāsHənz/ ▸**n.** a statute prescribing a period of time limitation for the bringing of certain kinds of legal action: *California's statute of limitations in personal injury cases is one year.*

stat•utes at large /'stæcʜo͞ots æt 'lärj; ət/ ▸ **plural n.** a country's statutes in their original version, regardless of later modifications or codification.

stat•u•to•ry /'stæcʜə͵tôrē/ ▸ **adj.** required, permitted, or enacted by statute: *the courts did award statutory damages to each of the plaintiffs.*
■ (of a criminal offense) defined by, or carrying a penalty prescribed by, statute: *statutory theft.* ■ of or relating to statutes: *constitutional and statutory interpretation.*
DERIVATIVES **stat•u•to•ri•ly** /'stacʜə͵tôrəlē/ adv.

stat•u•to•ry rape /'stæcʜə͵tôrē 'rāp/ ▸ **n.** sexual intercourse with a person under the age of consent.

stay /stā/ ▸ **v.** [trans.] stop, delay, or prevent (something), in particular suspend or postpone (judicial proceedings or a particular procedure) or refrain from pressing (charges): *their appeal will not stay proceedings.*
▸ **n.** a suspension or postponement of judicial proceedings or a particular procedure: *a stay of prosecution.*
PHRASES **a stay of execution** a delay in carrying out a court order.

strict con•struc•tion /'strikt kən'strəksʜən/ ▸ **n.** a literal interpretation of a statute or document (e.g., a constitution) by a court.
DERIVATIVES **strict con•struc•tion•ist** n.

strict li•a•bil•i•ty /'strikt ͵līə'bilitē/ ▸ **n.** liability that arises from certain actions without a showing of actual negligence or intent to harm: *this is a classic dog-bite case that turns on whether there is strict liability for violating a leash law.*

strike /strīk/ ▸ **v.** (past and past part. **struck** /strək/; past part. **stricken** 'strikən) [trans.] cancel, remove, or cross out with or as if with a pen, particularly testimony or remarks in court: *strike his name **from** the list* | *these remarks will be stricken from the record.*
■ (**strike down**) abolish or invalidate (a law or regulation) by judicial decision: *the law was struck down by the Supreme Court.*
ORIGIN Old English *strīcan* 'go, flow' and 'rub lightly,' of West Germanic origin; related to German *streichen* 'to stroke.'

sub ju•di•ce /͵so͞ob 'yo͞odi͵kā; ͵səb 'jo͞odi͵sē/ ▸ **adj.** under judicial consideration and therefore prohibited from public discussion elsewhere: *the cases were still sub judice.*
ORIGIN Latin, literally 'under a judge.'

sub•lease ▸ **n.** /'səb͵lēs/ a lease of a property by a tenant to a subtenant.
▸ **v.** /͵səb'lēs/ another term for SUBLET.

sub•les•see /͵səble'sē/ ▸ **n.** a person who holds a sublease.

sub•les•sor /͵səble'sôr/ ▸ **n.** a person who grants a sublease.

sub•let ▸ **v.** /͵səb'let/ (**sub•let•ting**; past and past part. **sub•let**) [trans.] lease (a property) to a subtenant: *I quit my job and sublet my apartment.*
▸ **n.** /'səb͵let/ another term for SUBLEASE.
■ informal a property that has been subleased.

sub•mis•sion /səbˈmiSHən/ ▶ n. a proposition or argument presented by a lawyer to a judge or jury: *the defense lawyer for murder suspect P. D. Jones will make her last submission before the jury.*
ORIGIN late Middle English: from Old French, or from Latin *submissio(n-)*, from the verb *submittere* (see **SUBMIT**).

sub•mit /səbˈmit/ ▶ v. (**sub•mit•ted, sub•mit•ting**) [trans.] present (a proposal, application, or other document) to a person or body for consideration or judgment: *the panel's report was **submitted to** a parliamentary committee.*
■ [with clause] (esp. in judicial contexts) suggest; argue: *he submitted that such measures were justified.*
DERIVATIVES **sub•mit•ter** n.
ORIGIN late Middle English: from Latin *submittere*, from *sub-* 'under' + *mittere* 'send, put.' The sense 'present for judgment' dates from the mid 16th cent.

sub•orn /səˈbôrn/ ▶ v. [trans.] bribe or otherwise induce (someone) to commit an unlawful act such as perjury: *he was accused of conspiring to suborn witnesses.*
■ obtain (perjury or another unlawful act) by such inducement: *I thought it was a ludicrous suggestion that I had urged someone to lie or tried to suborn perjury in other ways.*
DERIVATIVES **sub•or•na•tion** /ˌsəbôrˈnāSHən/ n.; **sub•orn•er** n.
ORIGIN mid 16th cent.: from Latin *subornare* 'incite secretly,' from *sub-* 'secretly' + *ornare* 'equip.'

sub•poe•na /səˈpēnə/ ▶ n. (in full **subpoena ad testificandum**) a writ ordering a person to attend a court: *a subpoena may be issued to compel their attendance* | *they were all **under subpoena** to appear.*
▶ v. (**sub•poe•nas, sub•poe•naed** /səˈpēnəd/, **sub•poe•na•ing** /səˈpēnə ˌiNG/) [trans.] summon (someone) with a subpoena: *the Queen is above the law and cannot be subpoenaed.*
■ require (a document or other evidence) to be submitted to a court of law: *the decision to subpoena government records.*
ORIGIN late Middle English (as a noun): from Latin *sub poena* 'under penalty' (the first words of the writ). Use as a verb dates from the mid 17th cent.

sub•poe•na du•ces te•cum /səˈpēnə ˈdo͞osēz ˈtēkəm/ ▶ n. a writ ordering a person to attend a court and bring relevant documents.
ORIGIN Latin, literally 'under penalty you shall bring with you.'

sub•ro•ga•tion /ˌsəbrəˈgāSHən/ ▶ n. the substitution of one person or group by another in respect of a debt or insurance claim, accompanied by the transfer of any associated rights and duties: *the right of subrogation entitles a surety to step into the shoes of any party whose obligations it assumed.*
DERIVATIVES **sub•ro•gate** /ˈsəbrəˌgāt/ v.
ORIGIN late Middle English (in the general sense 'substitution'): from

late Latin *subrogatio(n-)*, from *subrogare* 'choose as substitute,' from *sub-* 'in place of another' + *rogare* 'ask.'

sub•stan•tive /'səbstəntiv/ ▸ **adj.** defining rights and duties as opposed to giving the rules by which such things are established.

DERIVATIVES **sub•stan•ti•val** /ˌsəbstən'tīvəl/ **adj.**; **sub•stan•tive•ly adv.**

ORIGIN late Middle English (in the sense 'having an independent existence'): from Old French *substantif*, *-ive* or late Latin *substantivus*, from *substantia* 'essence.'

sub•sti•tute /'səbstiˌt(y)o͞ot/ ▸ **n.** (in litagation) a party who acts or serves in place of another.
▸**v.** [trans.] (in litagation) replace one party with another.

DERIVATIVES **sub•sti•tut•a•bil•i•ty** /ˌsəbstəˌt(y)o͞otə'bilite͞/ **n.**; **sub•sti•tut•a•ble adj.**; **sub•sti•tu•tive** /'səbstiˌt(y)o͞otiv/ **adj.**

ORIGIN late Middle English (denoting a deputy or delegate): from Latin *substitutus* 'put in place of,' past participle of *substituere*, based on *statuere* 'set up.'

suc•ces•sion /sək'seSHən/ ▸ **n.** the action or process of inheriting a title, office, property, etc.
■ the right or sequence of inheriting a position, title, etc.: *the succession to the vice presidency was disputed.* ■ the body of law dealing with inheritance.

PHRASES **in succession to** inheriting or elected to the place of: *he is not first in succession to the presidency.* **settle the succession** determine who shall succeed someone.

DERIVATIVES **suc•ces•sion•al** /sək'seSHənl/ **adj.**

ORIGIN Middle English (denoting legal transmission of an estate or the throne to another, also in the sense 'successors, heirs'): from Old French, or from Latin *successio(n-)*, from the verb *succedere* 'come close after,' from *sub-* 'close to' + *cedere* 'go.'

sue /so͞o/ ▸ **v.** (**sues**, **sued**, **su•ing**) [trans.] institute legal proceedings against (a person or institution), typically for redress: *she is to sue the baby's father* | [intrans.] *I sued for breach of contract.*

DERIVATIVES **su•er** /'so͞oər/ **n.**

ORIGIN Middle English: from Anglo-Norman French *suer*, based on Latin *sequi* 'follow.' Early senses were very similar to those of the verb *follow.*

suf•fer•ance /'səf(ə)rəns/ ▸ **n.** the condition of the holder of an estate who continues to hold it after the title has ceased, without the express permission of the owner: *an estate at sufferance.*

su•i ju•ris /ˌso͞oˌī 'jo͞oris; ˌso͞oˌe͞/ ▸ **adj.** of full age and capacity; independent: *the beneficiaries are all sui juris.*

ORIGIN Latin, literally 'of one's own right.'

suit /so͞ot/ ▸ **n.** short for LAWSUIT.

sum•ma•ry /'səməre͞/ ▸ **adj.** (of a judicial process) conducted without the customary legal formalities: *summary arrest.*

■ (of a conviction or judgment) made by a judge or magistrate without a trial.

PHRASES **summary judgment** judgment of the court prior to trial, because the law is clear and the case presents no genuine issues of material fact.

DERIVATIVES **sum•mar•i•ly** /sə'merəlē; 'səmərəlē/ **adv.**

ORIGIN late Middle English (as an adjective): from Latin *summarius,* from *summa* 'sum total' (see SUM).

sum•ma•tion /sə'mᴀSHən/ ▶ n. an attorney's closing speech at the conclusion of the giving of evidence: *the state was allowed a rebuttal to the defense summation.*

sum•mon /'səmən/ ▶ v. [trans.] authoritatively or urgently call on (someone) to be present, esp. as a defendant or witness in a court of law: *the victim's ex-wife has been summoned to appear in court on Thursday.*

DERIVATIVES **sum•mon•a•ble adj.; sum•mon•er n.**

ORIGIN Middle English: from Old French *somondre,* from Latin *summonere* 'give a hint,' later 'call, summon,' from *sub-* 'secretly' + *monere* 'warn.'

sum•mons /'səmənz/ ▶ n. (pl. **sum•mons•es**) an order to appear before a judge or magistrate, or the writ containing it: *a summons for nonpayment of a parking ticket.*

▶v. [trans.] serve (someone) with a summons: [with obj. and infinitive] *he has been summonsed to appear in court next month.*

ORIGIN Middle English: from Old French *sumunse,* from an alteration of Latin *summonita,* feminine past participle of *summonere* (see SUMMON).

sum up /ˌsəm 'əp/ ▶ v. (**summed up, sum•ming up**) (of a judge) review the evidence at the end of a case, and direct the jury regarding points of law.

■ give a brief summary of something: *Gerard will open the debate and I will sum up.*

DERIVATIVES **sum•ming-up** /'səmiNG 'əp/ **n.**

ORIGIN Middle English: via Old French from Latin *summa* 'main part, sum total,' feminine of *summus* 'highest.'

sun•set law /'sənset ˌlô/ ▶ n. a law that automatically terminates a regulatory agency, board, or function of government on a certain date, unless renewed: *in accordance with the state sunset law, the act sets the expiration date for the committee three years after the date of its creation.*

sun•shine law /'sən,SHīn ˌlô/ ▶ n. a law requiring certain proceedings of government agencies to be open or available to the public.

su•pe•ri•or court /sə'pirēər/ ▶ n. **1** (in many states of the US) a court of appeals or a court of general (original) jurisdiction.

2 a court with general jurisdiction over other courts; a higher court.

Su•preme Court /sə'prēm 'kôrt; soo-/ ▶ n. the highest judicial court in most US states.

■ a court of original jurisdiction in some states, including New York.

■ (in full **US Supreme Court**) the highest federal court in the US, consisting of nine justices and having appellate jurisdiction over all cases involving questions of federal law.

sur•e•ty /'sʜǒǒritē/ ▶ n. (pl. **sur•e•ties**) a person who takes responsibility for another's performance of an undertaking, for example their appearing in court or the payment of a debt.

■ money given to support an undertaking that someone will perform a duty, pay their debts, etc.; a guarantee: *the judge granted bail with a surety of $500.*

DERIVATIVES **sur•e•ty•ship** /sʜǒǒritē,sʜip/ n.

ORIGIN Middle English (in the sense 'something given to support an undertaking that someone will fulfill an obligation'): from Old French *surte*, from Latin *securitas*, from *securus* 'free from care.'

sur•ren•der /sə'rendər/ ▶ v. [intrans.] cease resistance to an enemy or opponent and submit to their authority: *three of the suspects surrendered to the authorities.*

■ [trans.] give up or hand over (a person, right, or possession), typically on compulsion or demand: *we have never ceded or surrendered title to our lands, rights to our resources, or the power to make decisions within our territory.*

▶ n. the action of surrendering.

■ the action of surrendering a life insurance policy.

ORIGIN late Middle English (chiefly in legal use): from Anglo-Norman French.

sur•ro•gate /'sərəgit; -,gāt/ ▶ n. a substitute, esp. a person deputizing for another in a specific role or office: *she was regarded as the **surrogate** for the governor during his final illness.*

■ in many states, a public official with responsibility for administration of estates. ■ a judge in charge of probate, inheritance, and guardianship.

ORIGIN early 17th cent.: from Latin *surrogatus*, past participle of *surrogare* 'elect as a substitute,' from *super-* 'over' + *rogare* 'ask.'

sur•vi•vor /sər'vīvər/ ▶ n. a joint tenant who has the right to the whole estate on the other's death: *making substantial gifts to children reduces estate taxes on the survivor's estate.*

sur•vi•vor•ship /sər'vīvər,sʜip/ ▶ n. a right depending on survival, esp. the right of a survivor of holders of a joint interest to take the whole on the death of the others: *in some states the survivorship position is created automatically when the property is acquired by two or more people.*

sus•pend /sə'spend/ ▶ v. [trans.] (usu. **be suspended**) prevent from continuing or being in force or effect, in particular:

■ officially prohibit (someone) from holding their usual post or carrying out their usual role for a particular length of time: *two officers were **suspended from** duty pending the outcome of the investigation.*

■ defer or delay (an action, event, or judgment): *the judge suspended judgment until January 15.* ■ (of a judge or court) cause (an imposed

sentence) to be unenforced as long as no further offense is committed within a specified period: *the sentence was suspended for six months* | [as adj.] (**suspended**) *a suspended jail sentence.*
ORIGIN Middle English: from Old French *suspendre* or Latin *suspendere*, from *sub-* 'from below' + *pendere* 'hang.'

sus•tain /sə'stān/ ▸ v. [trans.] uphold, affirm, or confirm the justice or validity of (especially an objection to the introduction of evidence in court): *the allegations of discrimination were sustained.*
ORIGIN Middle English: from Old French *soustenir*, from Latin *sustinere*, from *sub-* 'from below' + *tenere* 'hold.'

swear /swer/ ▸ v. (past **swore** /swôr/; past part. **sworn** /swôrn/) [trans.] take a solemn oath as to the truth of (a statement): *I asked him if he would swear a statement to this effect.* Compare with AFFIRM.
■ [trans.] (**swear someone in**) admit someone to a particular office or position by directing them to take a formal oath: *he was sworn in as a witness.*
▸**swear something out** obtain the issue of (a warrant for arrest) by making a charge on oath: *if the police don't make an arrest, you may swear out a warrant.*
DERIVATIVES **swear•er** n.
ORIGIN Old English *swerian*, of Germanic origin; related to Dutch *zweren*, German *schwören*, also to *answer.*

syl•la•bus /'siləbəs/ ▸ n. (pl. **syllabuses** or **syllabi** /'silə,bī/) a summary of the opinion of a court.
ORIGIN mid 17th cent. (in the sense 'concise table of headings of a discourse'): modern Latin, originally a misreading of Latin *sittybas*, accusative plural of *sittyba*, from Greek *sittuba* 'title slip, label.'

T

tar•iff /'tærif; 'ter-/ ▸ n. a tax or duty to be paid on a particular class of imports or exports.
■ a list of these taxes. ■ a table of the fixed charges made by a business, esp. in a hotel or restaurant.
▸v. [trans.] fix the price of (something) according to a tariff: *these services are tariffed by volume.*
ORIGIN late 16th cent. (also denoting an arithmetical table): via French from Italian *tariffa*, based on Arabic *'arrafa* 'notify.'

tax /tæks/ ▸ n. a compulsory contribution to federal, state, or municipal revenue, levied by the government on income and business profits or added to the cost of some goods, services, and transactions.
▸v. [trans.] **1** impose a tax on (someone or something): *hardware and software is **taxed at** 7.5 percent.*
2 examine and assess (the costs of a case).
DERIVATIVES **tax•a•ble adj.**
ORIGIN Middle English (also in the sense 'estimate or determine the amount of a penalty or damages,' surviving in sense 2): from Old French *taxer*, from Latin *taxare* 'to censure, charge, compute,' perhaps from Greek *tassein* 'fix.'

tax a•void•ance /'tæks ə,voidns/ ▸ n. the arrangement of one's financial affairs to minimize tax liability within the law. Compare with TAX EVASION.

tax e•va•sion /'tæks i,vāzHən/ ▸ n. the illegal nonpayment or underpayment of tax. Compare with TAX AVOIDANCE.

tech•ni•cal /'teknikəl/ ▸ adj. according to a strict application or interpretation of the law or rules: *the arrest was a technical violation of the treaty.*

tech•ni•cal•i•ty /,tekni'kælitē/ ▸ n. (pl. **tech•ni•cal•i•ties**) a precise, usually procedural point of law or a small detail of a set of rules: *their convictions were overturned **on a technicality**.*

ten•an•cy /'tenənsē/ ▸ n. (pl. **ten•an•cies**) possession of land or property as a tenant: *Holding took over the tenancy of the farm.*
■ the state, condition, or period of being a tenant: *tenancy was for less than one year.*

ten•an•cy in com•mon /'tenənsē in 'kämən/ ▸ n. a shared tenancy in which each holder has a distinct, separately transferable interest.

ten•ant /'tenənt/ ▸ **n.** a person who occupies land or property rented from a landlord.

■ a person holding real property by private ownership.

▸**v.** [trans.] (usu. **be tenanted**) occupy (property) as a tenant: [as adj.] *some insurance companies will cover the loss or damage of contents in your tenanted properties.*

DERIVATIVES **ten•ant•a•ble adj.** (formal); **ten•ant•less adj.**

ORIGIN Middle English: from Old French, literally 'holding,' present participle of *tenir*, from Latin *tenere*.

ten•ant at will /'tenənt æt 'wil/ ▸ **n.** (pl. **ten•ants at will**) a tenant who has no stated lease term and can be evicted, or can vacate, at any time, provided statutory notice requirements are met.

ten•ure /'tenyər/ ▸ **n. 1** the conditions under which land or buildings are held or occupied: *our focus is on agricultural land use and land tenure within the city.*

2 the holding of an office: *his tenure of the premiership would be threatened.*

■ a period for which an office is held.

3 guaranteed permanent employment, esp. as a teacher or professor, after a probationary period.

▸**v.** [trans.] give (someone) a permanent post, esp. as a teacher or professor: *I had recently been tenured and then promoted to full professor.*

■ [as adj.] (**tenured**) having or denoting such a post: *a tenured faculty member.*

ORIGIN late Middle English: from Old French, from *tenir* 'to hold,' from Latin *tenere*.

term /tərm/ ▸ **n. 1** (also **term for years** or Brit. **term of years**) a tenancy of a fixed period.

2 (**terms**) conditions under which an action may be undertaken or agreement reached; stipulated or agreed-upon requirements: *the union and the company agreed upon the contract's terms.*

ORIGIN Middle English (denoting a limit in space or time, or (in the plural) limiting conditions): from Old French *terme*, from Latin *terminus* 'end, boundary, limit.'

ter•ri•to•ri•al /ˌteriˈtôrēəl/ ▸ **adj. 1** of or relating to the ownership of an area of land or sea: *territorial disputes.*

2 of or relating to a particular territory, district, or locality: *territorial public health departments*

DERIVATIVES **ter•ri•to•ri•al•i•ty** /ˌteriˌtôreˈælitē/ n.; **ter•ri•to•ri•al•ly adv.**

ORIGIN early 17th cent.: from late Latin *territorialis*, from Latin *territorium* (see TERRITORY).

ter•ri•to•ri•al wa•ters /ˌteriˈtôrēəl 'wôtərz; 'wätərz/ ▸ **plural n.** the waters under the jurisdiction of a state, esp. the part of the sea within a stated distance of the shore (traditionally three miles from low-water mark, but extended in the 20th century by most countries).

ter•ri•to•ry /ˈterəˌtôrē/ ▸ n. (pl. **ter•ri•to•ries**) an area of land under the jurisdiction of a ruler or state: *the government was prepared to give up the nuclear weapons on its territory.*
ORIGIN late Middle English: from Latin *territorium*, from *terra* 'land.' The word originally denoted the district surrounding and under the jurisdiction of a town or city, specifically a Roman or provincial city.

tes•ta•ment /ˈtestəmənt/ ▸ n. a person's will, esp. the part relating to personal property: *the testament said that the ex-wives get nothing and his children get enough money to just pay off all of their debts.*
ORIGIN Middle English: from Latin *testamentum* 'a will' (from *testari* 'testify'), in Christian Latin also translating Greek *diathēkē* 'covenant.'

tes•ta•men•ta•ry /ˌtestəˈmen(t)ərē/ ▸ adj. of, relating to, or bequeathed or appointed through a will: *a testamentary gift to your alma mater.*
ORIGIN late Middle English: from Latin *testamentarius*, from *testamentum* 'a will,' from *testari* 'testify.'

tes•tate /ˈtestāt/ ▸ adj. [predic.] having made a valid will before one dies: *Marjorie died testate and in her will she named her son as the personal representative.*
■ denoting property settled by will: *if a will has been left, you will be dealing with a testate estate.*
▸ n. a person who has died leaving such a will: *it is incumbent upon the executor and the court to honor the testate's wishes.*
ORIGIN late Middle English (as a noun): from Latin *testatus* 'testified, witnessed,' past participle of *testari*, from *testis* 'a witness.'

tes•ta•tion /teˈstāsHən/ ▸ n. the disposal of property by will: *restrictions on testation.*

tes•ta•tor /ˈtesˌtātər/ ▸ n. a person who has made a will.
ORIGIN Middle English: from Anglo-Norman French *testatour*, from Latin *testator*, from the verb *testari* 'testify.'

test case /ˈtest ˌkās/ ▸ n. a case initiated to set a precedent for other cases involving similar questions of law: *civil servant wins test case to stop wearing necktie.*

tes•ti•fy /ˈtestəˌfī/ ▸ v. (**tes•ti•fies, tes•ti•fied**) [intrans.] give evidence as a witness in a law court: *he testified against his own commander* | [with clause] *he testified that he had supplied Barry with crack.*
DERIVATIVES **tes•ti•fi•er** n.
ORIGIN late Middle English: from Latin *testificari*, from *testis* 'a witness.'

tes•ti•mo•ny /ˈtestəˌmōnē/ ▸ n. (pl. **tes•ti•mo•nies**) a formal written or spoken statement, esp. one given in a court of law.
ORIGIN Middle English: from Latin *testimonium*, from *testis* 'a witness.'

theft /THeft/ ▸ n. the action or crime of stealing: *he was convicted of theft* | *the latest theft happened at a garage.*
ORIGIN Old English *thīefth*, *thēofth*, of Germanic origin; related to THIEF.

USAGE: See usage at ROB.

thief /THēf/ ▸ n. (pl. **thieves** /THēvz/) a person who steals another person's property, esp. by stealth and without using force or violence.
ORIGIN Old English *thīof*, *thēof*, of Germanic origin; related to Dutch *dief* and German *Dieb*, also to THEFT.

thieve /THēv/ ▸ v. [intrans.] be a thief; steal something: *they began thieving again.*
ORIGIN Old English *thēofian*, from *thēof* 'thief.' Transitive uses began in the late 17th cent.

thiev•er•y /'THēv(ə)rē/ ▸ n. the action of stealing another person's property: *livestock thievery is still afoot in the state.*

third-de•gree /'THərd di'grē/ ▸ n. (**the third degree**) long and harsh questioning, esp. by police, to obtain information or a confession: *Officer Lee observed Lieutenant Billings **giving** the suspect **the third degree.***

third par•ty /'THərd 'pärtē/ ▸ n. a person or group besides the two primarily involved in a situation, esp. a dispute or contract.
▸ adj. [attrib.] of or relating to a person or group besides the two primarily involved in a situation: *third-party suppliers.*

third per•son /'THərd 'pərsən/ ▸ n. a third party.

threat /THret/ ▸ n. **1** a statement of an intention to inflict pain, injury, damage, or other hostile action on someone in retribution for something done or not done: *members of her family have received **death threats**.* **2** a person or thing likely to cause damage or danger.
ORIGIN Old English *thrēat* 'oppression,' of Germanic origin; related to Dutch *verdrieten* 'grieve,' German *verdriessen* 'irritate.'

three strikes /'THrē 'strīks/ ▸ n. [usu. as adj.] (**three-strikes**) legislation providing that an offender's third felony is punishable by life imprisonment or another severe sentence: [as adj.] *they are in favor of limiting the three-strikes law to only violent and serious offenders.*
ORIGIN 1990s: from the phrase *three strikes and you're out* (with allusion to baseball).

tip•staff /'tip‚staef/ ▸ n. a bailiff.
ORIGIN mid 16th cent. (first denoting a metal-tipped staff): contraction of *tipped staff* (carried by a bailiff).

ti•tle /'tītl/ ▸ n. a right or claim to the ownership of property or to a rank or throne: *a local family had **title** to the property | the buyer acquires a good title to the merchandise.*
■ short for TITLE DEED.
ORIGIN Old English *titul*, reinforced by Old French *title*, both from Latin *titulus* 'inscription, title.' The word originally denoted a placard or inscription placed on an object, giving information about it, hence a descriptive heading in a book or other composition.

ti•tle deed /'tītl ‚dēd/ ▸ n. a legal deed or document constituting evidence of a right, esp. to ownership of property.

Tor•rens sys•tem /'tôrənz ‚sistəm; 'tär-/ ▸ n. a system of land title registration, adopted originally in Australia and later in some states of the

US, under which a judicial decree and registration obviate the need for title insurance.

ORIGIN mid 19th cent.: named after Sir Robert *Torrens*(1814-84), first premier of South Australia.

tort /tôrt/ ▶ n. a noncriminal breach of a duty imposed by law (rather than by contract) that gives the right of action for damages: *the common-law torts of assault and trespass.*

ORIGIN Middle English (in the general sense 'wrong, injury'): from Old French, from medieval Latin *tortum* 'wrong, injustice,' neuter past participle of Latin *torquere* 'to twist.'

tort•fea•sor /'tôrt,fēzər; -zôr/ ▶ n. a person who commits a tort.

ORIGIN mid 17th cent.: from Old French *tort-fesor*, from *tort* 'wrong' and *fesor* 'doer.'

tor•tious /'tôrsHəs/ ▶ adj. constituting or pertaining to a tort: *tortious breach of contract.*

DERIVATIVES **tor•tious•ly** adv.

ORIGIN late Middle English: from Anglo-Norman French *torcious*, from the stem of *torcion* 'extortion, violence,' from late Latin *tortio(n-)* 'twisting, torture,' from Latin *torquere* 'to twist.' The original sense was 'injurious.'

trade•mark /'trād,märk/ ▶ n. a symbol, device, or words legally registered or established by use as representing a company or product.

▶v. [trans.] [usu. as adj.] (**trademarked**) provide with a trademark: *they are counterfeiting trademarked goods.*

trans•fer ▶ v. /træns'fər; 'træns,fər/ (**trans•ferred, trans•fer•ring**) [trans.] make over the possession of (property, a right, or a responsibility) to someone else: *more than 400 acres of unspoiled forest was transferred to the Conservancy.*

▶n. /'træns,fər/ a conveyance of property, esp. stocks, from one person to another: *the transfer of ownership is legal and binding.*

DERIVATIVES **trans•fer•ee** /,trænsfə'rē/ n.; **trans•fer•or** /træns'fərər; 'træns,fərər/ n.

ORIGIN late Middle English (as a verb): from French *transférer* or Latin *transferre*, from *trans-* 'across' + *ferre* 'to bear.' The earliest use of the noun (late 17th cent.) was as a legal term in the sense 'conveyance of property.'

trav•erse /trə'vərs/ ▶ v. [trans.] deny (an allegation) in pleading: *the defendant might have traversed the plaintiff's allegation that he was a citizen of the State of Missouri.*

DERIVATIVES **tra•vers•a•ble** adj.

ORIGIN Middle English: from Old French *traverser*, from late Latin *traversare*; the noun is from Old French *travers* (masculine), *traverse* (feminine), partly based on *traverser*.

trea•son /'trēzən/ ▶ n. (also **high treason**) the crime of betraying one's country, esp. by attempting to kill the sovereign or overthrow the government: *they were convicted of treason.*

■ (**petty treason**) historical the crime of murdering someone to whom the murderer owed allegiance, such as a master or husband.

DERIVATIVES **trea•son•ous** /ˈtrēzənəs/ **adj.**

ORIGIN Middle English: from Anglo-Norman French *treisoun*, from Latin *traditio(n-)* 'handing over,' from the verb *tradere*.

USAGE: In British law, there were formerly two types of crime to which the term **treason** was applied: **petty treason** (the crime of murdering one's master or husband) and **high treason** (the crime of betraying one's country). As a classification of offense, the crime of **petty treason** was abolished in 1828. In modern use, the term **high treason** is now often simply called **treason**. In American law, **treason** is defined in Article 3, Section 3, of the US Constitution.

treas•ure trove /ˈtreZHər ˌtrōv/ ▶ **n.** valuables of unknown ownership that are found hidden, in some cases declared the property of the finder.

ORIGIN late Middle English: from Anglo-Norman French *tresor trové*, literally 'found treasure.'

trea•ty /ˈtrētē/ ▶ **n.** (pl. **trea•ties**) a formally concluded and ratified agreement between countries.

ORIGIN late Middle English: from Old French *traite*, from Latin *tractatus* 'treatise.'

tres•pass /ˈtrespəs; -ˌpæs/ ▶ **v.** [intrans.] enter the owner's land or property without permission: *there is no excuse for* **trespassing on** *railroad property*.

▶ **n.** entry to a person's land or property without their permission: *the defendants were guilty of trespass | a mass trespass on the hills*.

■ an unlawful act deliberately committed against the person or property of another.

DERIVATIVES **tres•pass•er n.**

ORIGIN from Old French *trespasser* 'pass over, trespass,' *trespas* 'passing across.'

tri•a•ble /ˈtrīəbəl/ ▶ **adj.** able to be tried in court; liable to trial.

■ (of a case or issue) able to be investigated and decided judicially: *a triable issue of fact.*

ORIGIN late Middle English: from Anglo-Norman French, from Old French *trier* 'sift' (see TRY).

tri•al /ˈtrī(ə)l/ ▶ **n.** a formal examination of evidence by a judge or tribunal, especially a jury, in order to determine the facts in criminal or civil proceedings: *the newspaper accounts of the trial.*

PHRASES **on trial** being tried in a court of law: *this is the first time the Church of Scientology itself and its recruitment methods have gone on trial.* **stand trial** see STAND.

ORIGIN late Middle English: from Anglo-Norman French, or from medieval Latin *triallum*.

tri•al court /ˈtrīəl ˌkôrt/ ▶ **n.** a court of law where cases are tried in the first place, as distinguished from an appeals court.

tri•al law•yer /'trīəl ˌloiər; ˌlôyər/ ▶ n. a lawyer who practices in a trial court.

tri•bu•nal /trī'byo͞onl; trə-/ ▶ n. a court of justice: *an international war crimes tribunal.*
■ a seat or bench for a judge or judges.
ORIGIN late Middle English (denoting a seat for judges): from Old French, or from Latin *tribunal* 'raised platform provided for magistrates' seats,' from *tribunus,* literally 'head of a tribe.'

tri•er /'trīər/ ▶ n. a person or body responsible for investigating and deciding a case judicially: *the jury is the trier of fact.*

-trix /triks/ ▶ suffix (pl. **-tri•ces** /'trīsēz/ or **-trix•es**) forming feminine agent nouns corresponding to masculine nouns ending in *-tor* (such as *executrix* corresponding to *executor*).
ORIGIN from Latin.

true bill /'tro͞o 'bil/ ▶ n. a bill of indictment found by a grand jury to be supported by sufficient evidence to justify the hearing of a case.

trust /trəst/ ▶ n. **1** an arrangement whereby one person is the nominal owner of property that is to be held or used for the benefit of one or more others: *a trust was set up | the property is to be **held in trust** for his son.* **2** a body of trustees.
■ an organization or company managed by trustees: *a charitable trust* | [in names] *the National Trust for Historic Preservation.* ■ dated a large company that has or attempts to gain monopolistic control of a market.
ORIGIN Middle English: from Old Norse *traust,* from *traustr* 'strong'; the verb from Old Norse *treysta,* assimilated to the noun.

trust com•pa•ny /'trəst ˌkəmpənē/ ▶ n. a company formed to act as a trustee or to deal with trusts.

trust deed /'trəst ˌdēd/ ▶ n. a deed of conveyance creating and setting out the conditions of a trust.
■ (in certain states) the equivalent of a mortgage. Also called DEED OF TRUST.

trust•ee /ˌtrəs'tē/ ▶ n. an individual person or member of a board given control or powers of administration of property in trust with a legal obligation to administer it solely for the purposes specified.
DERIVATIVES **trust•ee•ship** /ˌtrəs'tē,SHip/ n.

trust•ee in bank•rupt•cy /ˌtrəs'tē 'bæNGkrəp(t)sē/ ▶ n. a person taking administrative responsibility for the financial affairs of a bankrupt and the distribution of assets to creditors.

try /trī/ ▶ v. (**tries, tried**) [trans.] (usu. **be tried**) subject (someone) to trial: *he was arrested and tried for the murder.*
■ investigate and decide (a case or issue) in a formal trial: *the most serious criminal cases must be tried by a jury.*
ORIGIN Middle English: from Old French *trier* 'sift,' of unknown origin.

UNDERSTANDING WILLS, TRUSTS, AND INTESTATE SUCCESSION

Ancient Egyptian kings were laid to rest in tombs filled with priceless objects for their enjoyment in the afterlife. Most of us today prefer to leave our wealth behind for the people, institutions, and causes we care about. The primary legal mechanisms for satisfying this desire are wills, trusts, and the laws of intestate succession.

Wills

A *will* is a formal expression of intent regarding the distribution of one's property at death. The person who makes the will is called the *testator* (or in older usage, in the case of a woman, the *testatrix*). The will can also be called a *testament*, and wills are traditionally captioned "Last Will and Testament," although today many people choose the simpler "Will."

As with so much else in American law, what constitutes a valid will depends on where you live. The law of your home state governs most aspects of your will, but any provisions that concern real estate are governed by the law of the state where that property is located. Your will should satisfy the laws not only where you live but in any state where you own land or a house. Some states recognize oral (*nuncupative*) or unwitnessed handwritten (*holographic*) wills in some circumstances, but the only sure course is to execute a *formal* will—one that is signed and witnessed in strict conformity with state statutes.

In general, you can leave your money and property to anyone you want, with one important qualification: your spouse is ordinarily entitled to a portion (usually one-third to one-half) of your estate no matter what your will says. But anyone named in your will can *disclaim* the gift; for example, the child who married an heiress can decline his share of the estate so that more money will go to your other children.

In addition to disposing of assets, a will normally designates an *executor*—an individual or institution to be responsible for carrying out the instructions in the will. Parents of young children also use their wills to nominate a *guardian* for minor children in case both parents die before the children are grown. The courts follow these desires whenever they can.

Some amount of judicial action will be required even if there are no minor children. Before the will can be acted upon, it must be validated in a probate proceeding. Broadly, *probate* refers to the entire court-supervised process in which the executor marshals the assets in the estate, pays the testator's debts, and distributes what is left according to the will. Probate used to be a long and expensive proposition, but simplified probate procedures are now available for most small estates.

Trusts

A *trust* is an arrangement where one person or institution, the *trustee,* holds, manages, and distributes assets for the benefit of another, the *beneficiary.* There can be multiple trustees and multiple beneficiaries. The person who establishes the trust by providing the original money or property is called the *grantor, settlor, donor,* or *trustor.* The assets held in trust are called the trust *corpus* or *principal* or *res.*

A *testamentary trust* is one created by will—specifically, by a clause that gives all or part of the estate to a designated trustee to be held for the benefit of specified beneficiaries. Typical examples include a trust for the support of one's children until they are old enough to be given the entire principal; a trust for the support of one's spouse for the rest of the spouse's life, after which any money left goes to the children; or a *charitable trust* created to benefit a public purpose. Unlike other trusts, a charitable trust may last indefinitely.

A trust established during the grantor's lifetime is called an *inter vivos trust* or *living trust*. This can serve the same purposes as a testamentary trust. In addition, you can create a living trust in which you are not only the grantor but also the trustee and the beneficiary: in effect, you give yourself your own money with instructions to use it for your own benefit and enjoyment. As absurd as this sounds, it might save probate expenses later on; the trust instrument can direct that, upon your death, the trust will be taken over by a successor trustee for the purpose of distributing the assets according to your wishes, so that the assets will pass through the trust rather than through your will.

There are many other devices besides wills and trusts for transferring wealth at death, including joint accounts, life insurance, and IRAs with named beneficiaries. With such a range of options, it is best to have a knowledgeable lawyer help in creating an overall estate plan and drafting the necessary documents.

Intestate succession

Someone who dies without a will is said to die *intestate*. Each state has laws of *intestate succession* that dictate who will inherit your property if you die without a will. These rules of inheritance represent the legislature's guess as to how you would want your property distributed. Generally, it goes to your spouse, children, or closest blood relatives. For example, in some states the estate of a person survived only by a spouse and parents is split between the spouse and the parents; in other states it all goes to the spouse.

The court will appoint an administrator to oversee distribution of an intestate estate in accordance with the law. If no surviving relative who qualifies under the statute can be found, the property goes to the state—a process called *escheat*.

U

ul•tra vi•res /ˌəltrə ˈvīrēz/ ▶ **adj. & adv.** beyond one's (typically, a corporation's) legal power or authority: [as adj.] *jurisdictional errors render the decision ultra vires.*
ORIGIN Latin, literally 'beyond the powers.'

un•al•ien•a•ble /ˌənˈālyənəbəl; -ˈālēə-/ ▶ **adj.** another term for INALIENABLE.

un•ap•peal•a•ble /ˌənəˈpēləbəl/ ▶ **adj.** (of a case or ruling) not able to be referred to a higher court for review: *the jury verdict in a recent tobacco case may be unappealable.*

un•charged /ˌənˈCHärjd/ ▶ **adj.** not accused of an offense under the law: *she was released uncharged.*

un•cor•rob•o•rat•ed /ˌənkəˈräbəˌrātid/ ▶ **adj.** not confirmed or supported by other evidence or information: *the unreliability of uncorroborated confessions.*

un•de•fend•ed /ˌəndiˈfendid/ ▶ **adj.** not defended: *legal aid for undefended divorces.*

un•der•sher•iff /ˈəndərˌsherif/ ▶ **n.** a deputy sheriff.

un•der the in•flu•ence /ˈəndər THē ˈinflo͞oəns/ ▶ **adverbial phrase** informal affected by alcoholic drink or other intoxicants: *he was charged with driving under the influence.*

un•due in•flu•ence /ˈənˌd(y)o͞o ˈinflo͞oəns/ ▶ **n.** influence by which a person is induced to act subject to coercion or without adequate attention to the consequences: *it shall be presumed that the transfer of property by the dependent elderly owner was the result of undue influence.*

un•en•cum•bered /ˌənenˈkəmbərd/ ▶ **adj.** not having any burden or impediment: *the land was unencumbered by mortgages.*
■ free of debt or other financial liability: *the objective is to start their working lives unencumbered by debt.*

un•en•force•a•ble /ˌənenˈfôrsəbəl/ ▶ **adj.** (esp. of an obligation or law) impossible to enforce: *such contracts may be declared unenforceable by the courts.*

u•ni•cam•er•al /ˌyo͞oniˈkæm(ə)rəl/ ▶ **adj.** (of a legislative body) having a single legislative chamber: *the unicameral system favors rule by the majority.*
ORIGIN mid 19th cent.: from *uni-* 'one' + Latin *camera* 'chamber' + *-al.*

un•law•ful /ˌənˈlawfəl/ ▸ **adj.** not conforming to, permitted by, or recognized by law or rules: *the use of unlawful violence* | *they claimed the ban was unlawful.*
  DERIVATIVES **un•law•ful•ly** /ənˈlôfəlē/ **adv.**; **un•law•ful•ness** n.
un•liq•ui•dat•ed /ˌənˈlikwiˌdātid/ ▸ **adj.** (of a debt) not cleared or paid off.
  ■ not calculated precisely: *unliquidated damages.*
un•served /ˌənˈsərvd/ ▸ **adj.** (of a writ or summons) not officially delivered to a person: *there is no point in leaving a writ unserved.*
un•sworn /ˌənˈswôrn/ ▸ **adj.** (of testimony or evidence) not given under oath: *unsworn statements in criminal trials.*
un•tried /ˌənˈtrīd/ ▸ **adj.** (of an accused person) not yet subjected to a trial in court: *untried suspects.*
un•writ•ten /ˌənˈritn/ ▸ **adj.** (esp. of a law) resting originally on custom or judicial decision rather than on statute: *an unwritten constitution.*
us•er /ˈyoozər/ ▸ **n.** the continued use or enjoyment of a right.
u•su•rer /ˈyoozHərər/ ▸ **n.** a person who lends money at unreasonably high rates of interest.
  ORIGIN Middle English: from Anglo-Norman French, from Old French *usure*, from Latin *usura* (see USURY).
u•su•ri•ous /yooˈzHoorēəs/ ▸ **adj.** of or relating to the practice of usury: *they lend money at usurious rates.*
  DERIVATIVES **u•su•ri•ous•ly adv.**
u•su•ry /ˈyoozH(ə)rē/ ▸ **n.** the illegal action or practice of lending money at unreasonably high rates of interest.
  ■ archaic interest at such rates.
  ORIGIN Middle English: from Anglo-Norman French *usurie*, or from medieval Latin *usuria*, from Latin *usura*, from *usus* 'a use' (see USE).
ut•ter /ˈətər/ ▸ **v.** [trans.] put (forged money) into circulation: *he knowingly uttered and possessed counterfeit securities beyond a reasonable doubt.*
  ORIGIN late Middle English: from Middle Dutch *ūteren* 'speak, make known, give currency to (coins).'

V

v. ▶**abbr.** versus.

va•cant /'vākənt/ ▶**adj.** (of premises) having no fixtures, furniture or inhabitants; empty: *a vacant warehouse.*

ORIGIN Middle English: from Old French, or from Latin *vacant-* 'remaining empty,' from the verb *vacare.*

va•cate /'vākāt/ ▶**v.** [trans.] **1** leave (a place that one previously occupied): *the Ludds will vacate the premises before March 15.*

2 cancel or annul (a judgment, contract, or charge): *the administrator argues that the judge's decision should be vacated.*

ORIGIN mid 17th cent.: from Latin *vacat-* 'left empty,' from the verb *vacare.*

val•id /'vælid/ ▶**adj.** legally binding due to having been executed in compliance with the law: *a valid contract.*

■ legally acceptable: *the visas are valid for thirty days.*

DERIVATIVES **va•lid•i•ty** /və'liditē/ n.; **val•id•ly** adv.

ORIGIN late 16th cent.: from French *valide* or Latin *validus* 'strong,' from *valere* 'be strong.'

val•u•a•ble con•sid•er•a•tion /'væy(oo)əbəl kən‚sidə'rāsHən/ ▶**n.** legal consideration having some economic value, in order to make a contract enforceable: *the airline prohibits the sale or auction of travel-related documents for cash or other valuable consideration.*

var•i•ance /'verēəns/ ▶**n.** a discrepancy between two statements or documents.

■ an official dispensation from a rule or regulation, typically a building regulation.

ORIGIN Middle English: via Old French from Latin *variantia* 'difference.'

vend /vend/ ▶**v.** [trans.] sell (something): *bottled water will be vended throughout the event.*

DERIVATIVES **vend•i•ble** (also **vend•a•ble**) adj.

ORIGIN early 17th cent. (in the sense 'be sold'): from French *vendre* or Latin *vendere* 'sell,' from *venum* 'something for sale' + a variant of *dare* 'give.'

ven•dor /'vendər; -dôr/ (also **vend•er**) ▶**n.** the seller in a sale, esp. of property.

ORIGIN late 16th cent.: from Anglo-Norman French *vendour* (see **VEND**).

ven•ue /'venyōō/ ▸ n. the county or district within which a criminal or civil case must be heard: *the public defender is not seeking a jury trial and has not asked for a change of venue.*

ORIGIN late 16th cent. (denoting a thrust or bout in fencing; also in the Law sense): from Old French, literally 'a coming,' feminine past participle of *venir* 'come,' from Latin *venire.*

ver•dict /'vərdikt/ ▸ n. the jury's decision on a disputed issue in a civil or criminal case or an inquest: *the jury returned a verdict of 'not guilty.'*

ORIGIN Middle English: from Anglo-Norman French *verdit*, from Old French *veir* 'true' (from Latin *verus*) + *dit* (from Latin *dictum* 'saying').

ver•sus /'vərsəs; -səz/ (abbr.: **v.** or **vs.**) ▸ prep. against: *the State of Pennsylvania versus Jefferson-King Industries.*

ORIGIN late Middle English: from a medieval Latin use of Latin *versus* 'toward.'

vest•ed in•ter•est /'vestid 'int(ə)rist/ ▸ n. [usu. in sing.] an interest (usually in land or money held in trust) recognized as belonging to a particular person: *the unmarried minor child held a vested interest in the income and capital.*

ve•to /'vētō/ ▸ n. (pl. **ve•toes**) a constitutional right to reject a decision or proposal made by a lawmaking body: *Congress can override the president's veto.*

■ such a rejection.

▸ v. (**ve•toes, ve•toed**) [trans.] exercise a veto against (a decision or proposal made by a lawmaking body): *the president vetoed the bill.*

DERIVATIVES **ve•to•er** n.

ORIGIN early 17th cent.: from Latin, literally 'I forbid,' used by Roman tribunes of the people when opposing measures of the Senate.

vex•a•tious /vek'sāSHəs/ ▸ adj. denoting an action or the bringer of an action that is brought without sufficient grounds for winning, purely to cause annoyance to the defendant: *there was no vexatious action by either party* | *a vexatious litigant.*

DERIVATIVES **vex•a•tious•ly** adv.; **vex•a•tious•ness** n.

vice chan•cel•lor /,vīs 'CHæns(ə)lər/ ▸ n. **1** a deputy chancellor, esp. one of a British university who discharges most of its administrative duties.

2 a judge appointed to assist a chancellor, esp. in chancery court or court of equity.

vic•i•nage /'visənij/ ▸ n. the area from which cases may be brought to a court: *he has been the assignment judge for the Morris/Sussex vicinage for 17 years.*

ORIGIN Middle English: from Old French *vis(e)nage*, from an alteration of Latin *vicinus* 'neighbor.'

view /vyōō/ ▸ n. (in court proceedings) a formal inspection by the judge and jury of the scene of a crime or property mentioned in evidence: *if you are going to have a view, it is desirable you do it together with the control and cooperation of the court.*

PHRASES **in plain view** capable of being seen on open inspection: *officers may seize property that they find in plain view, if they have probable cause to believe it is evidence of a crime.*

ORIGIN Middle English: from Anglo-Norman French *vieue*, feminine past participle of *veoir* 'see,' from Latin *videre*.

vi•o•lence /'vī(ə)ləns/ ▸ n. the unlawful exercise of physical force.

PHRASES **do violence to** damage or adversely affect: *he used visitation and custody issues to harass and do violence to her.*

ORIGIN Middle English: via Old French from Latin *violentia*, from *violent-* 'vehement, violent' (see **VIOLENT**).

vi•o•lent /'vī(ə)lənt/ ▸ adj. involving an unlawful exercise of force: *violent behavior | violent crimes.*

DERIVATIVES **vi•o•lent•ly adv.**

ORIGIN Middle English (in the sense 'having a marked or powerful effect'): via Old French from Latin *violent-* 'vehement, violent.'

vis•it•a•tion /ˌvizi'tāsHən/ ▸ n. a person's right to spend time with their children who are in the custody of the other parent, a foster parent, or other legal guardian.

ORIGIN Middle English: from Old French, or from late Latin *visitatio(n-)*, from the verb *visitare* 'go to see.'

void /void/ ▸ adj. not valid or legally binding: *the contract was void.*

▸v. [trans.] declare that (something) is not valid or legally binding: *the Supreme court voided the statute.*

DERIVATIVES **void•a•ble adj.**

ORIGIN Middle English (in the sense 'unoccupied'): from a dialect variant of Old French *vuide*; related to Latin *vacare* 'vacate'; the verb partly a shortening of *avoid*, reinforced by Old French *voider*.

voir dire /'vwär 'dir/ ▸ n. a preliminary examination of a witness or a juror by a judge or counsel: *was there bias on the part of the juror who concealed information on voir dire? | [as adj.] the voir dire session is not meant to intrude on your privacy.*

■ an oath taken by such a witness.

ORIGIN Law French, from Old French *voir* 'true' + *dire* 'say.'

vouch•er /'vowcHər/ ▸ n. a small printed piece of paper that entitles the holder to a discount or that may be exchanged for goods or services.

WATCHING
LAWYER SHOWS

L awyer shows on television are about entertainment first
and law second. Enjoy the entertainment; take the law
with a grain of salt.

The model for a long line of lawyer shows was *Perry Mason,*
which ran from 1957 to 1966. The title character was a defense
attorney who conveniently had one client at a time—always an
accused murderer, always innocent, always able to afford a
good lawyer. Through insight and clever sleuthing, Mason
always discovered the real murderer, and through brilliant
cross-examination and dramatic courtroom maneuvers, he
always trapped the culprit into confessing. In a decade of
shows, nothing remotely resembling reality ever occurred.

In 1986, *L.A. Law* burst onto the screen and changed everything. For eight years, this show presented the adventures of an
entire fictional law firm. It expanded popular television's view
of law to include civil as well as criminal law; one of the charac-
ters was even a tax lawyer. It dealt with topical issues such as
gun control, sexual harassment, and the right to die. It
employed lawyers as writers and consultants to try to keep the
show in touch with legal reality. It raised issues of legal ethics
and practice that even some law professors found useful as
springboards for class discussion. But the writers never lost
sight of television's first principle: to entertain. After decades of
the law show as a whodunit, *L.A. Law* started a new trend—the
law show as relationship drama, with plenty of sex, glamour,

and intrigue. It made practicing law look like a Hollywood fantasy. Applications to law schools surged.

After *L.A. Law*, television could never go back to the simplistic days of *Perry Mason*. Modern law shows often do a commendable job of highlighting serious legal and ethical issues. And they are generally careful about specific points of law: if a lawyer character quotes a statute, the quote is probably accurate. But in case of a conflict, dramatic development wins out over legal plausibility. If the plot calls for a lawyer to discuss a case with the judge outside the presence of opposing counsel—something no judge who values his or her career would allow—the writers simply have the judge say, "We shouldn't be talking like this," and then proceed to discuss the case anyway.

Television presents a distorted view of legal practice for one simple reason: most of what lawyers do—however intellectually satisfying for the lawyers themselves—has less visual and dramatic appeal than watching grass grow. To get around this,

- Television emphasizes trial work, as distinguished from the business and personal legal work that most lawyers do.

- Television focuses on criminal law, even though most legal work involves civil matters. Drafting wills, negotiating contracts, and poring over tax regulations are not the stuff of great television.

The nature of a trial lawyer's work is itself distorted:

- Time is compressed. An hour of television equals a year of legal work on a case.

- Most of the work—including legal research, motions, pleadings, document exchanges, depositions, trial preparation, post-trial motions, and appeals—is eliminated.

- Television lawyers act as detectives. Real lawyers seldom go out and find clues. They rely upon police reports or, in civil cases, documentary evidence and interviews. Lawyers with rich clients sometimes hire a private detective to help gather evidence, but very few criminal defendants can afford anything like that.

- Legal cases on television actually go to trial. In real life, the vast majority of civil cases are settled, and the vast majority of criminal cases end with a plea bargain.

Courtroom scenes—the core of most television law shows—are also unrealistic. Elementary courtroom decorum is regarded as too dull for a television audience. In a real court,

- Lawyers do not argue with each other. First, one addresses the judge. Then, the other addresses the judge. Interruptions are not allowed.

- Lawyers do not suddenly confront witnesses with exhibits pulled out of thin air. A new exhibit must be marked with a letter or number for identification, shown to the opposing attorney, identified by the witness, and admitted into evidence by the judge; only then is the lawyer allowed to interrogate the witness about it.

- Lawyers do not approach the witness unless they need to do so (say, to point to a line in an exhibit)—and even then only after asking and receiving permission from the judge.

- Judges do not bark commands like "My chambers. Now!" Even less do lawyers bark out demands, like "Sidebar!" A lawyer desiring a sidebar conference would typically say, "May we approach?" (referring to approaching the bench). But in fact, judges discourage such conferences because they disrupt the trial and make the jurors feel left out.

- Jurors do not retire to deliberate without first listening to detailed, tedious, and often confusing instructions on the law.

"Reality-based" law shows should be viewed with equal skepticism. News programs can give only oversimplified summaries; "news magazine" shows and "docudramas" are interested only in sensational cases; police video shows select only the car chases that make the police look good and not those that end in tragedy. Even Court TV does not show typical trials.

A particularly odd kind of "reality" show is the pseudo-court show, of which there are many examples. Typically, people squabble about some petty dispute in front of the star of the show, who plays the role of a "judge" but who often berates and belittles them. In return, the disputing parties get some money and 15 minutes of fame—almost to the minute. The courtroom is fake, the bailiff is fake, the robed judge is at best a former judge, the "proceedings" are an unruly caricature of judicial proceedings, and any "judgment" is paid by the producers of the show.

To get a feeling for the real thing, go to a courthouse. It will not be as exciting as television, but it will be dramatic in a different way. It will be the American legal system at work.

W

waiv•er /'wāvər/ ▸ n. an act or instance of knowingly relinquishing a right or claim: *waiver of landlord's claim to annexed fixtures.*
■ a document recording such waiving of a right or claim: *participants are asked to sign a waiver on all Sierra Club outings.*

ward /wôrd/ ▸ n. **1** a person, usually a minor, under the care and control of a guardian appointed by their parents or a court.
2 one of the divisions of a prison.
PHRASES **ward of the court** a person, usually a minor or of unsound mind, for whom a guardian has been appointed by a court or who has become directly subject to the authority of that court.
DERIVATIVES **ward•ship** /'wôrd,SHip/ n.
ORIGIN Old English *weard*, *weardian* 'keep safe, guard,' of Germanic origin; reinforced in Middle English by Old Northern French *warde* (noun), *warder* (verb) 'guard.'

war•rant /'wôrənt; 'wä-/ ▸ n. a document issued by a legal or government official authorizing the police or some other body to make an arrest, search premises, or carry out some other action relating to the administration of justice: *magistrates issued a warrant for his arrest | an extradition warrant.*
■ a document that entitles the holder to receive goods, money, or services: *we'll issue you with a travel warrant.*
DERIVATIVES **war•rant•er** n.
ORIGIN from variants of Old French *guarant* (noun), *guarantir* (verb), of Germanic origin.

war•ran•tee /ˌwôrən'tē; ˌwä-/ ▸ n. a person to whom a warranty is given.

USAGE: **Warrantee** means 'person to whom a warranty is made'; it is not a spelling variant of **warranty**.

war•ran•tor /'wôrəntôr; 'wä-/ ▸ n. a person or company that provides a warranty.

war•ran•ty /'wôrəntē; 'wä-/ ▸ n. (pl. **war•ran•ties**) a written guarantee, issued to the purchaser of an article by its manufacturer, promising to repair or replace it if necessary within a specified period of time: *the car comes with a three-year warranty | as your machine is under warranty, I suggest getting it checked.*

■ (in contract law) a promise that something in furtherance of the contract is guaranteed by one of the contractors, esp. the seller's promise that the thing being sold is as promised or represented. ■ (in an insurance contract) an engagement by the insured party that certain statements are true or that certain conditions shall be fulfilled, the breach of it invalidating the policy. ■ (in property law) a covenant by which the seller binds themselves and their heirs to secure to the buyer the estate conveyed in the deed.

ORIGIN Middle English: from Anglo-Norman French *warantie*, variant of *garantie* . Early use was as a legal term denoting a covenant annexed to a conveyance of property, in which the vendor affirmed the security of the title.

USAGE: See usage at GUARANTEE and WARRANTEE.

waste /wāst/ ▶ n. damage to an estate caused by an act or by neglect, esp. by a life-tenant.
■ damage to the value of assets being held or managed, as by a trustee.
ORIGIN Middle English: from Old Northern French *wast(e)* (noun), *waster* (verb), based on Latin *vastus* 'unoccupied, uncultivated.'

where•as /(h)wer'æz/ ▶ conj. (esp. in legal preambles) taking into consideration the fact that: *whereas, under the right conditions, community service offers great benefits to both the service providers and recipients.*

will /wil/ ▶ n. a legal document containing instructions as to what should be done with one's property and to provide for one's minor children after one's death.
▶ v. [trans.] (**will something to**) bequeath something to (someone) by the terms of one's will.
■ [with clause] leave specified instructions in one's will: *he willed that his body be given to the hospital.*
PHRASES **at will** subject to termination at any time: *employment at will | tenancy at will | contract at will.*
ORIGIN Old English *willa* (noun), *willian* (verb), of Germanic origin; related to Dutch *wil*, German *Wille* (nouns), also to the modal verb *will* and the adverb *well.*

wit•ness /'witnis/ ▶ n. **1** a person who sees an event, typically a crime or accident, take place: *police are appealing for **witnesses to** the accident.*
■ a person giving sworn testimony to a court of law or the police. See also EXPERT WITNESS. ■ a person who is present at the signing of a document and who also signs it to confirm this.
2 used to refer to confirmation or evidence given by signature, under oath, or otherwise: *in witness thereof, the parties sign this document.*
▶ v. [trans.] see (an event, typically a crime or accident) take place: *a bartender who witnessed the murder.*

■ be present as someone signs (a document) or gives (their signature) to a document and sign it oneself to confirm this: *the clerk witnessed her signature.*

wit•ness stand /'witnis ,stænd/ (Brit. **wit•ness box**) ▶ n. the place in a court from which a witness gives evidence.

writ /rit/ ▶ n. a form of written command in the name of a court or other legal authority to act, or abstain from acting, in some way.

■ **(one's writ)** one's power to enforce compliance or submission; one's authority: *you have business here which is out of my writ and competence.*

ORIGIN Old English, as a general term denoting written matter, from the Germanic base of *write*.

writ of cer•ti•o•ra•ri /'rit əv ,sərsH(ē)ə'rärē/ ▶ n. see CERTIORARI.

writ of ex•e•cu•tion /'rit əv ,eksi'kyōōsHən/ ▶ n. a judicial order that a judgment be enforced: *applicant requests the court issue a writ of execution against the property of the following person.*

wrong /rôNG/ ▶ n. a breach, by commission or omission, of one's legal duty: *environmental wrongs.*

■ an invasion of a right to the damage or prejudice of another: *the women and children in this pseudo-religious community suffered numerous wrongs.*

ORIGIN late Old English *wrang*, from Old Norse *rangr* 'awry, unjust.'

wrong•ful /'rôNGfəl/ ▶ adj. constituting a wrong; not fair, just, or legal: *an action for wrongful death.*

■ not entitled to a position or claimed standing: *the wrongful heir.*

DERIVATIVES **wrong•ful•ly adv.**; **wrong•ful•ness n.**

APPENDICES

LEGAL AID ORGANIZATIONS

Alabama

Alabama Legal Services Programs
http://www.alabamalegalservices.org
info@alsp.org

Offices:
Legal Services Corporation of
  Alabama, Inc.
500 Bell Building
207 Montgomery Street
Montgomery, AL 36104

Legal Services of Metro
  Birmingham, Inc.
1820 Seventh Avenue North
P.O. Box 11765
Birmingham, AL 35202

Legal Services of North-Central
  Alabama, Inc.
2000-C Vernon Street
P. O. Box 2465
Huntsville, AL 35804

Alaska

Alaska Legal Services Corporation
http://www.alsc-law.org

Offices:
1016 West Sixth Avenue, Suite 200
Anchorage, AK 99501
(907) 272-9431; (800) 478-9431
anchorage3@alsc-law.org

P.O. Box 248
Bethel, AK 99559-0248
(907) 543-2237; (800) 478-2230
alscbthl@unicom-alaska.com

P.O. Box 176
Dillingham, AK 99576-0176
(907) 842-1452; (888) 391-1475
dillingham@alsc-law.org

P.O. Box 1429
Nome, AK 99762-1429
(907) 443-2230 *or* (888) 495-6663
nome@alsc-law.org

1648 Cushman, Suite 300
Fairbanks, AK 99701-6202
(907) 452-5181; (800) 478-5401
fairbanks@alsc-law.org

416 6th Street, Suite 322
Juneau, AK 99801-1096
(907) 586-6425; (800) 789-6426
alscjno@alaska.net

306 Main Street #218
Ketchikan, AK 99901-6483
(907) 225-6420
alscket@ptialaska.net

P.O. Box 526
Kotzebue, AK 99752-0526
(907) 442-3500; (887) 622-9797
alsckotz@yahoo.com

Arizona

DNA–Legal People's Services, Inc.
*[Provides free legal services in civil
matters to qualified low-income
residents on and near the Navajo
Nation.]*
http://www.dnalegalservices.org/
information@dnalegalservices.org

William E. Morris Institute for
Justice
http://www.azji.org/

Offices:
305 South Second Avenue
Phoenix, AZ 85001
(602) 252-3432

100 North Stone, Suite 305
Tucson, AZ 85701
(520) 740-1207

Arkansas

Arkansas Legal Services Programs
http://www.arlegalservices.org/

Offices:
Center for Arkansas Legal Services
303 West Capital, Suite 200
Little Rock, AR 72201
(501) 376-3423

Legal Aid of Arkansas
4083 North Shiloh Drive, Suite 3
Fayetteville, AR 72703
(479) 442-0600

California

Bay Area Legal Aid
http://www.baylegal.org/
405 14th Street, 9th Floor
Oakland, CA 94612
(510) 663-4755; (510) 663-4744;
 (800) 551-5554

Bet Tzedek Legal Services
http://www.bettzedek.org

Offices:
145 South Fairfax Avenue
Suite 200
Los Angeles, CA 90036
(323) 939-0506

12821 Victory Boulevard
North Hollywood, CA 91606
(818) 769-0136

California Indian Legal Services,
 Inc.
*[Services for Native Americans and
 Indian Tribes in California]*
http://www.calindian.org
510 16th Street, Fourth Floor
Oakland, CA 94612
(510) 835-0284; (800) 829-0284

787 North Main Street, Suite D
Bishop, CA 93514
(760) 873-3581; (800) 736-3582

609 S. Escondido Boulevard
Escondido, CA 92025
(760) 746-8941; (800) 743-8941

324 F Street
Eureka, CA 95501
(707) 443-8397; (800) 347-2402

510 16th Street, Fourth Floor
Oakland, CA 94612
(510) 835-0284; (800)829-0284

37 Old Courthouse Square
Suite 207
Santa Rosa, CA 95404
(707) 573-8016

California Rural Legal Assistance,
Inc.
631 Howard Street, Suite 300
San Francisco, CA 94105-3907
(415) 777-2752

Central California Legal Services
http://www.las.org/

Offices:
1999 Tuolumne St.
Suite 700
Fresno, CA 93721
(559) 570-1200

357 W. Main St.
Suite 201
Merced, CA 95340
(209) 723-5466

208 W. Main St.
Suite U-1
Visalia, CA 93291
(559) 733-8770; (800) 350-3654

Greater Bakersfield Legal
Assistance, Inc.
615 California Avenue
Bakersfield, CA 93304
(661) 325-5943

Inland Counties Legal Services,
Inc.
http://www.iellaaid.org/pages/
icls_link.html
1737 Atlanta Avenue, Suite H-3
Riverside, CA 92507
(909) 368-2531; (909) 368-2555

Legal Aid Foundation of Los
Angeles
http://www.lafla.org
1102 South Crenshaw Boulevard
Los Angeles, CA 90019-3111
(323) 801-7990; (800) 399-4529

Legal Aid Society of Orange
County, Inc.
902 North Main Street
Santa Ana, CA 92701
(714) 571-5233; (800) 834-5001

Legal Aid Society of San Diego, Inc.
110 South Euclid Avenue
San Diego, CA 92114
(619) 471-2620, (619) 262-0896

Legal Services of Northern
California
http://www.lsnc.net/
517 12th Street
Sacramento, CA 95814
(916) 551-2150

Napa County Legal Assistance
Agency
1227 Coombs St.
Napa, CA 94559
(707) 255-4933

Neighborhood Legal Services of
Los Angeles County
http://www.nls-la.org
13327 Van Nuys Boulevard

Pacoima, CA 91331-3099
(818) 834-7590; (818) 896-5211

Colorado

Colorado Legal Services
1905 Sherman Street
Suite 400
Denver, CO 80203
(303) 837-1313; (303) 837-1321

Connecticut

Statewide Legal Services of
  Connecticut, Inc.
http://www.slsct.org
425 Main Street, 4th Floor
Middletown, CT 06457
(860) 344-8096; (800) 453-3320

Delaware

Legal Services Corporation of
  Delaware, Inc.
http://www.lscd.com
100 West 10th Street
Suite 203
Wilmington, DE 19801
(302) 575-0408

District of Columbia

Neighborhood Legal Services
  Program of the District of
  Columbia
http://www.nlsp.org
701 Fourth Street, N.W.
Washington, DC 20001
(202) 682-2720

Florida

Bay Area Legal Services, Inc.
http://www.bals.org
Riverbrook Center, 2nd Floor
829 W. Dr. Martin Luther King
Tampa, FL 33603
(813) 232-1343

Central Florida Legal Services, Inc.
http://www.cfls.org
128-A Orange Avenue
Daytona Beach, FL 32114-4310
(386) 255-6573

Florida Rural Legal Services, Inc.
http://www.frls.org
963 East Memorial Boulevard
P.O. Box 24688
Lakeland, FL 33802-4688
(863) 688-7376; (800) 277-7680

Greater Orlando Area Legal
  Services, Inc.
1036 West Amelia Street
Orlando, FL 32805
(407) 841-7777

Gulfcoast Legal Services, Inc.
http://www.gulfcoastlegal.org
641 First Street South
St. Petersburg, FL 33701-5003
(727) 821-0726; (800) 230-5920

Jacksonville Area Legal Aid, Inc.
http://www.jaxlegalaid.org
126 West Adams Street
Jacksonville, FL 32202-3849
(904) 356-8371

Legal Aid Service of Broward
  County
609 Southwest First Avenue
Fort Lauderdale, FL 33301
(954) 765-8957; (954) 765-8950

Legal Services of Greater
  Miami, Inc.
http://www.lsgmi.org
3000 Biscayne Boulevard, Suite
  500
Miami, FL 33137-4129
(305) 576-0080

Legal Services of North
  Florida, Inc.
2119 Delta Boulevard
Tallahassee, FL 32303-4209
(850) 385-9007

Northwest Florida Legal
  Services, Inc.
701 South J Street
P.O. Box 1551
Pensacola, FL 32597-1551
(850) 432-1750; (850) 432-2336

Three Rivers Legal Services, Inc.
http://www.trls.org
214 W. University Avenue
Primrose Square, Suite A
Gainesville, FL 32601
(352) 372-0519

Withlacoochee Area Legal
  Services, Inc.
222 S.W. Broadway Street
Ocala, FL 34474-4151
(352) 629-0105

Georgia

Atlanta Legal Aid Society, Inc.
151 Spring Street, N.W.
Atlanta, GA 30303-2097
(404) 614-3990; (404) 524-5811

Georgia Legal Services Program
http://www.glsp.org
1100 Spring Street, Suite 200A
Atlanta, GA 30309-2848
(404) 206-5175; (800) 498-9469

Guam

Guam Legal Services Corporation
113 Bradley Place
Hagatna, GU 96910-4911
(671) 477-9811

Hawaii

Legal Aid Society of Hawaii
924 Bethel Street
P.O. Box 37375
Honolulu, HI 96837-0375
(808) 536-4302

Native Hawaiian Legal
  Corporation
*[Serving Native Americans in
  Hawaii]*
1164 Bishop Street, Suite 1205
Honolulu, HI 96813-2826
(808) 521-2302

Idaho

Idaho Legal Aid Services, Inc.
http://www.idaholegalaid.org
310 North Fifth Street
P.O. Box 913
Boise, ID 83701-0913
(208) 336-8980; (208) 345-0106

Illinois

Land of Lincoln Legal Assistance
Foundation, Inc.
http://www.lollaf.org
2420 Bloomer Drive
Alton, IL 62002-4809
(618) 462-0036

Legal Assistance Foundation of
Metropolitan Chicago
http://www.lafchicago.org
111 W. Jackson Boulevard
Suite 300
Chicago, IL 60604-3502
(312) 341-1070

Prairie State Legal Services, Inc.
975 North Main Street
Rockford, IL 61103-7064
(815) 965-2134

Indiana

Indiana Legal Services, Inc.
http://www.indianajustice.org
Market Square Ctr., Suite 1640
151 North Delaware Street
Indianapolis, IN 46204-2517
(317) 631-9410; (800) 869-0212

Iowa

Legal Services Corporation of Iowa
1111 Ninth Street, Suite 230
Des Moines, IA 50314-2527
(515) 243-2151; (800) 532-1275

Legal Aid Society of Polk County
Human Services Campus
1111 Ninth Street, Suite 380
Des Moines, IA 50314-2527
(515) 243-1193

Kansas

Kansas Legal Services, Inc.
712 S. Kansas Ave., Ste. 200
Topeka, KS 66603
(785) 233-2068; (800) 723-6953

Kentucky

Appalachian Research and Defense
Fund of Kentucky
120 North Front Avenue
Prestonsburg, KY 41653
(606) 886-3876; (800) 556-3876

Cumberland Trace Legal Services,
Inc.
http://www.klaid.org
KLAid@KLAid.org
520 East Main Street
P.O. Box 1776
Bowling Green, KY 42102-1776
(270) 782-1924; (866) 452-9243;
(800) 782-1924

Central Kentucky Legal Services
Inc.
498 Georgetown Street
P.O. Box 12947
Lexington, KY 40583-2947
(800) 928-4556

Legal Aid of the Blue Grass
302 Greenup Street
Covington, KY 41011-1740
(859) 431-8200

Legal Aid Society
http://www.laslou.org
425 West Muhammad Ali Blvd
Louisville, KY 40202-2353
(502) 584-1254; (800) 292-1862

Louisiana

Acadiana Legal Service
  Corporation
http://www.la-law.org
1020 Surrey Street
P.O. Box 4823
Lafayette, LA 70502-4823
(337) 237-4320; (800) 256-1175

Capital Area Legal Services
  Corporation
http://www.calscla.org
calsc@calscla.org
200 Third Street
P.O. Box 3273
Baton Rouge, LA 70821
(225) 338-9797; (800) 256-1900

Kisatchie Legal Services
  Corporation
134 St. Denis Street
P.O. Drawer 1189
Natchitoches, LA 71458-1189
(800) 960-9109

Legal Services of North Louisiana,
  Inc.
http://www.lsnl.org
720 Travis Street
Shreveport, LA 71101
(318) 222-7186; (800) 826-9265

New Orleans Legal Assistance
  Corporation
http://www.nolac.org/
144 Elk Place Suite 1000
New Orleans, LA 70112-2635
(504) 529-1000

North Louisiana Legal Assistance
  Corporation
200 Washington Street

P.O. Box 3325
Monroe, LA 71210-3325
(800) 256-1262

Northwest Louisiana Legal
  Services Inc.
720 Travis Street
Shreveport, LA 71101
(800) 826-9265

Southeast Louisiana Legal Services
  Corporation
1200 Derek Drive Suite 100
P. O. Drawer 2867
Hammond, LA 70404-2867
(985) 345-2130; (800) 349-0886

Southwest Louisiana Legal
  Services Society Inc.
1011 Lakeshore Drive Suite 402
P.O. Box 3002
Lake Charles, LA 70602-3002
(800) 256-1955

Maine

Pine Tree Legal Assistance, Inc.
http://www.ptla.org
88 Federal Street
P.O. Box 547
Portland, ME 04112-0547
(207) 774-4753; (207) 774-8211

Maryland

Legal Aid Bureau, Inc.
http://www.mdlab.org
500 East Lexington Street
Baltimore, MD 21202
(410) 539-5340

Massachusetts

Legal Services for Cape Cod and
Islands, Inc.
http://www.lscci.org
460 West Main Street
Hyannis, MA 02601-3695
(508) 775-7020; (800) 742-4107

Massachusetts Justice Project, Inc.
57 Suffolk Street
Suite 401
Holyoke, MA 01040
(413) 533-2660; (800) 639-1209

Merrimack Valley Legal
Services, Inc.
http://www.mvlegal.org
35 John Street, Suite 302
Lowell, MA 01852-1101
(978) 458-1465

New Center for Legal Advocacy,
Inc.
257 Union Street
New Bedford, MA 02740
(508) 979-7160; (800) 244-9023

South Middlesex Legal Services,
Inc.
http://www.smlegal.org
354 Waverly Street
Framingham, MA 01702
(508) 620-1830; (800) 696-1501

Volunteer Lawyers Project of the
Boston Bar Association
http://www.vlpnet.org
29 Temple Place
Boston, MA 02111
(617) 423-0648

Michigan

Center for Civil Justice
320 S. Washington (2nd floor)
Saginaw, MI 48607
(517) 755-3120; (800) 724-7441

Lakeshore Legal Aid
Robert A. Verkuilen Building
21885 Dunham Road, Suite 4
Clinton Twp., MI 48036
(586) 469-5185

Legal Aid and Defender
Association, Inc.
http://www.ladadetroit.org
645 Griswold
Suite 3466
Detroit, MI 48226-4216
(313) 965-4553; (313) 965-9419

Legal Services of South Central
Michigan, Inc.
420 North Fourth Avenue
Ann Arbor, MI 48104-1197
(734) 665-6181

Legal Services of Eastern Michigan
http://www.lsem-mi.org
436 South Saginaw Street
Flint, MI 48502
(810) 234-2621; (800) 339-9513

Legal Services of Northern
Michigan, Inc.
1349 S. Otsego Avenue Unit 7B
Parkside Mini-Mall
Gaylord, MI 49735
(989) 705-1067; (888) 645-9993

Michigan Indian Legal Services, Inc.
[Provides legal aid to low-income Indian individuals and tribes]
814 South Garfield Avenue
Suite A
Traverse City, MI 49686-3430
(231) 947-0122; (800) 968-6877

Michigan Legal Services
220 Bagley Avenue, Suite 900
Detroit, Michigan 48226
(313) 964-4130; (800) 875-4130

Oakland Livingston Legal Aid
35 West Huron Street, 5th Floor
Pontiac, MI 48342-2125
(248) 456-8861; (248) 456-8888

Western Michigan Legal Services
Cornerstone Bldg., Suite 400
89 Ionia Avenue,N.W.
Grand Rapids, MI 49503
(616) 774-0672; (800) 442-2777

Minnesota

Central Minnesota Legal Services, Inc.
430 First Avenue North
Suite 359
Minneapolis, MN 55401-1780
(612) 332-8151; (612) 783-4970

Judicare of Anoka County, Inc.
1201 89th Avenue, N.E., Suite 310
Blaine, MN 55434
(763) 783-4970; (612) 783-4970

Legal Aid Service of Northeastern Minnesota
http://www.lasnem.org
302 Ordean Building

424 West Superior Street
Duluth, MN 55802
(218) 726-4800; (800) 622-7266

Legal Services of Northwest Minnesota Corporation
1015 7th Avenue North
P.O. Box 838
Moorhead, MN 56561-0838
(218) 233-8585; (800) 450-8585

Southern Minnesota Regional Legal Services, Inc.
http://www.smrls.org
700 Minnesota Building
46 East Fourth Street
St. Paul, MN 55101-1112
(651) 228-9823

Mississippi

Central Mississippi Legal Services Corporation
414 South State St., 3rd Floor
P.O. Box 951
Jackson, MS 39205-0951
(601) 948-6752; (800) 959-6752

North Mississippi Rural Legal Services, Inc.
http://www.nmrls.com
2134 West Jackson Avenue
P.O. Box 767
Oxford, MS 38655-0767
(662) 234-8731; (800) 959-6752

Southeast Mississippi Legal Services Corporation
111 East Front Street
P.O. Drawer 1728
Hattiesburg, MS 39403-1728
(601) 545-2950

South Mississippi Legal Services
Corporation
203 Fountain Square Building
P.O. Box 1386
Biloxi, MS 39533-1386
(228) 374-4160

Southwest Mississippi Legal
Services Corporation
P. O. Box 1242
221 Main Street
McComb, MS 39649-1242
(601) 684-0578

Micronesia

Micronesian Legal Services, Inc.
Chalon Kanoa Village, Dist. #2
P.O. Box 500269
Saipan, MP 96950-0269
(670) 234-6471; (670) 234-6243

Missouri

Legal Aid of Western Missouri
http://www.lawmo.org
1125 Grand Avenue, Suite 1900
Kansas City, MO 64106
(816) 474-6750; (816) 474-6750

Legal Services of Eastern Missouri,
Inc.
http://www.lsem.org
info@lsem.org
4232 Forest Park Avenue
St. Louis, MO 63108
(314) 534-4200; (800) 444-0514

Legal Services of Southern
Missouri
http://www.lsosm.org
la@lsosm.org
2872 South Meadowbrook Avenue

Springfield, MO 65807
(417) 881-1397; (800) 444-4863

Mid-Missouri Legal Services
Corporation
legalaid@mmls.org
205 East Forest Avenue
Columbia, MO 65203
(573) 442-0116; (800) 568-4931

Montana

Montana Legal Services
Association
http://www.montanalegalservices.com
616 Helena Ave., Suite 100
Helena, MT 59601
(406) 442-9830; (800) 666-6124

Nebraska

Nebraska Legal Services
http://www.nebls.com
500 South 18th St.
Suite 300, The Law Bldg.
Omaha, NE 68102-2533
(402) 348-1069; (402) 348-1060

Nevada

Nevada Legal Services, Inc.
530 South 6th Street
Las Vegas, NV 89101
(702) 386-0404

New Hampshire

Legal Advice & Referral Center,
Inc.
http://www.larcnh.org
33 North Main St., 2nd Floor
P.O. Box 4147
Concord, NH 03302-4147
(603) 224-5723; (800) 639-5290

New Jersey

Bergen County Legal Services
61 Kansas Street
Hackensack, NJ 07601
(201) 487-2166

Camden Regional Legal Services
Inc.
745 Market Street
Camden, NJ 08102-1117
(609) 964-2010

Cape-Atlantic Legal Services, Inc.
26 So. Pennsylvania Ave.
Atlantic City, NJ 08401
(800) 870-7547

Central New Jersey Legal Services
http://www.lsnj.org
78 New Street, 3rd Floor
New Brunswick, NJ 08901-2584
(732) 249-7600

Essex-Newark Legal Services
Project, Inc.
http://www.lsnj.org
5 Commerce Street, 2nd Floor
Newark, NJ 07102
(973) 624-4500

Hudson County Legal Services
Corporation
574 Summit Avenue
Jersey City, NJ 07306-2797
(201) 792-6363

Hunterdon County Legal Service
Corporation
82 Park Avenue
Flemington, NJ 08822-1170
(908) 782-7979

Legal Aid Society of Mercer
County
198 West State Street
Trenton, NJ 08608-1103
(609) 695-6249

Legal Aid Society of Morris
County
30 Schuyler Place 2nd Floor
P.O. Box 900
Morristown, NJ 07963-0900
(973) 285-6911

Legal Services of New Jersey
http://www.lsnj.org
P.O. Box 1357
Edison, NJ 08818-1357
732-572-9100

Legal Services of Northwest Jersey
http://www.lsnj.org
91 Front Street
P.O. Box 65
Belvidere, NJ 07823-0065
(908) 475-2010

Middlesex County Legal Services
Corporation
78 New Street 3rd Floor
New Brunswick, NJ 08901-2584
(732) 249-7600

Northeast New Jersey Legal
Services Corporation
http://www.lsnj.org
574 Summit Avenue
Jersey City, NJ 07306-2797
(201) 792-6363

Ocean-Monmouth Legal Services,
Inc.
http://www.lsnj.org
9 Robbins Street, Suite 2A

Toms River, NJ 08753
(732) 866-0020; (732) 341-2727

Passaic County Legal Aid Society
175 Market Street 4th Floor
Paterson, NJ 07505
(973) 345-7171

Somerset-Sussex Legal Services
  Corporation
78 Grove Street
Somerville, NJ 08876
(908) 231-0840

South Jersey Legal Services
http://www.lsnj.org
745 Market Street
Camden, NJ 08102-1117
(856) 964-2010

Union County Legal Services
  Corporation
60 Prince Street
Elizabeth, NJ 07208
(908) 354-4340

Warren County Legal Services Inc.
91 Front Street
P.O. Box 65
Belvidere, NJ 07823-0065
(908) 475-2010

New Mexico

Community and Indian Legal
  Services Inc.
805 Early Street Building F
P.O. Box 5175
Santa Fe, NM 87502-5175
(800) 373-9881

Legal Aid Society of Albuquerque
  Inc.
121 Tijeras Ave. NE Suite 3100
P.O. Box 25486
Albuquerque, NM 87125-5486
(505) 243-7871

New Mexico Legal Aid
500 Cooper NW Suite 300
P.O. Box 25486
Albuquerque, NM 87125-5486
(505) 243-7871

Southern New Mexico Legal
  Services Inc.
300 North Downtown Mall
Las Cruces, NM 88001-1216
(800) 376-5727

New York

Chemung County Neighborhood
  Legal Services, Inc.
215 E. Church Street, Suite 301
Elmira, NY 14901-2889
(607) 734-1647

Legal Aid for Broome and
  Chenango
http://www.wnylc.net
30 Fayette Street
Binghamton, NY 13901
(607) 723-7966

Legal Aid Society of Mid-New
  York, Inc.
255 Genesee Street, 2nd Floor
Utica, NY 13501
(315) 732-2131

Legal Aid Society of Northeastern
New York, Inc.
55 Colvin Avenue
Albany, NY 12206
(518) 462-6765; (800) 462-2922

Legal Aid Society of Rockland
County, Inc.
http://www.wnylc.net
2 Congers Road
New City, NY 10956-0314
(845) 634-3627

Legal Services for New York City
http://www.legalsupport.org
350 Broadway, 6th Floor
New York, NY 10013-9998
(212) 431-7200

Legal Services of Central New
York, Inc.
http://www.wnylc.net
472 South Salina Street, #300
Syracuse, NY 13202
(315) 475-3127

Monroe County Legal Assistance
Corporation
http://www.wnylc.net
80 St. Paul Street, Suite 700
Rochester, NY 14604-1350
(716) 325-2520

Nassau/Suffolk Law Services
Committee, Inc.
http://www.wnylc.net
One Helen Keller Way
5th Floor
Hempstead, NY 11550
(516) 292-8100

Neighborhood Legal Services, Inc.
http://www.nls.org
Ellicott Square Building
295 Main Street, Room 495
Buffalo, NY 14203-2473
(716) 847-0650

Niagara County Legal Aid Society,
Inc.
http://www.wnylc.net
775 Third Street
P.O. Box 844
Niagara Falls, NY 14302-0844
(716) 284-8831

North Country Legal Services, Inc.
http://www.wnylc.net
100 Court Street
P.O. Box 989
Plattsburgh, NY 12901-0989
(518) 563-4022; (800) 722-7380

Southern Tier Legal Services
http://www.wnylc.net
104 East Steuben Street
Bath, NY 14810
(607) 776-4126

Westchester/Putnam Legal
Services, Inc.
http:///www.wpls.org
4 Cromwell Place
White Plains, NY 10601
(914) 949-1305

North Carolina

Legal Aid of North Carolina, Inc.
http://www.legalaidnc.org
224 South Dawson St.
Raleigh, NC 27611-6087
(919) 856-2130

Legal Aid Society of Northwest
  North Carolina Inc.
Patten Building
216 West Fourth Street
Winston-Salem, NC 27101-2824
(800) 660-6663

Legal Services of Southern
  Piedmont Inc.
1431 Elizabeth Avenue
Charlotte, NC 28204
(704) 376-1600

North Central Legal Assistance
  Program Inc.
212 North Mangum Street
P.O. Box 2101
Durham, NC 27702-2101
(800) 331-7594

North Dakota

Legal Assistance of North Dakota,
  Inc.
http://www.legalassist.org
1025 Third Street North
P.O. Box 1893
Bismarck, ND 58502-1893
(701) 222-2110; (800) 634-5263

North Dakota Legal Services Inc.
Main Street
P.O. Box 217
New Town, ND 58763-0217
(701) 627-4719

Ohio

Community Legal Aid Services,
  Inc.
http://www.communitylegalaid.org
The Rose Building, 3rd Floor
265 South Main Street

Akron, OH 44308
(330) 535-4191; (866) 584-2350

Legal Aid Society of Greater
  Cincinnati
http://www.lascinti.org
215 East Ninth Street
Suite 200
Cincinnati, OH 45202
(513) 241-9400; (800) 582-2682

The Legal Aid Society of Cleveland
http://www.lasclev.org
1223 West Sixth St., 4th Floor
Cleveland, OH 44113-1301
(216) 687-1900

The Legal Aid Society of
  Columbus
http://www.columbuslegalaid.org
40 West Gay Street
Columbus, OH 43215-2896
(614) 737-0135; (614) 224-8374

Legal Services of Northwest Ohio,
  Inc.
640 Spitzer Building
520 Madison Avenue
Toledo, OH 43604-1371
(419) 724-0030; (877) 894-4599

Ohio State Legal Services
http://www.oslsa.org
555 Buttles Avenue
Columbus, OH 43215-1137
(614) 221-7201; (800) 589-5888

Western Ohio Legal Services
  Association
http://www.wolsaoh.org
311 East Market St., Suite 307
Lima, OH 45801-4565
(419) 224-9070

Oklahoma

Oklahoma Indian Legal Services, Inc.
[Providing legal services to Native Americans in Oklahoma]
http://www.oilsonline.org
4200 Perimeter Center Drive
Suite 222
Oklahoma City, OK 73112
(405) 943-6457; (800) 658-1497

Legal Aid Services of Oklahoma, Inc.
http://www.legalaidok.org
2915 North Classen Boulevard
Suite 110
Oklahoma City, OK 73106
(405) 557-0020; (800) 421-1641

Legal Services of Eastern Oklahoma Inc.
http://www.lseo.org/
115 West Third St., Suite 701
Tulsa, OK 74103-3403
(800) 299-3338

Oregon

Lane County Legal Aid Service Inc.
http://www.lanecountylegalservices.org
376 East 11th Avenue
Eugene, OR 97401-3246
(541) 342-6056

Legal Aid Services of Oregon
700 S.W. Taylor St., Suite 310
Portland, OR 97205
(503) 224-4094

Marion-Polk Legal Aid Service Inc.
http://www.mplas.org
1655 State Street
Salem, OR 97301-4258
(800) 359-1845

Pennsylvania

Laurel Legal Services, Inc.
306 South Pennsylvania Avenue
Greensburg, PA 15601-3066
(724) 836-2211; (800) 253-9558

Legal Aid of Southeastern Pennsylvania
http://www.lasp.org
317 Swede Street
Norristown, PA 19401-4801
(610) 275-5400

MidPenn Legal Services, Inc.
http://www.midpenn.org
3540 North Progress Avenue
Suite 102
Harrisburg, PA 17110
(717) 541-8141; (717) 232-0581

Montgomery County Legal Aid Service
317 Swede Street
Norristown, PA 19401-4801
(610) 275-5400

Neighborhood Legal Services Association
928 Penn Avenue
Pittsburgh, PA 15222-3799
(412) 644-7450; (412) 255-6700

North Penn Legal Services, Inc.
http://www.northpennlegal.org
65 E. Elizabeth Ave, STE 903
Bethlehem, PA 18018
(610) 317-5312; (800) 982-4387

Northwestern Legal Services
http://www.nwls.org
Renaissance Center, Suite 1200
1001 State Street
Erie, PA 16501-1833
(814) 452-6949; (800) 665-6957

Philadelphia Legal Assistance
  Center
http://www.philalegal.org
1424 Chestnut Street
2nd Floor
Philadelphia, PA 19102
(215) 981-3808; (215) 981-3800

Southwestern Pennsylvania Legal
  Services, Inc.
10 West Cherry Avenue
Washington, PA 15301
(724) 225-6170; (800) 846-0871

Puerto Rico

Community Law Office, Inc.
170 Calle Federico Costa
Box 194735
San Juan, PR 00919-4735
(787) 751-1600

Puerto Rico Legal Services, Inc.
http://www.servicioslegales.org
1859 Ave. Ponce de León-Pda 26
Apartado 9134
San Juan, PR 00908-9134
(787) 728-9561; (800) 981-5342

Rhode Island

Rhode Island Legal Services, Inc.
http://www.rils.org
56 Pine Street, 4th Floor
Providence, RI 02903
(401) 274-2652; (800) 662-5034

South Carolina

Carolina Regional Legal Services
  Corporation
http://www.sclegalservicesprograms
  .org/crls/index.html
279 West Evans Street
P.O. Box 479
Florence, SC 29503-0479
(803) 667-1896

Legal Services Agency of Western
  Carolina Inc.
http://www.sclegalservicesprograms
  .org/lsawc/index.html
1 Pendleton Street
Greenville, SC 29601
(864) 467-3232

Neighborhood Legal Assistance
  Program Inc.
http://www.sclegalservicesprograms
  .org/programs.html
438 King Street
Charleston, SC 29403-6283
(803) 722-0107

Palmetto Legal Services
http://www.netside.com/~plslex/
  index2.html
2109 Bull Street
P.O. Box 2267
Columbia, SC 29202-2267
(800) 273-1200

Piedmont Legal Services Inc.
http://www.sclegalservicesprograms
  .org/plsinc/index.html
148 East Main Street
Spartanburg, SC 29306
(800) 922-8176

The South Carolina Centers for
  Equal Justice
1 Pendleton Street
Greenville, SC 29601
(864) 679-3232

South Dakota

Black Hills Legal Services Inc.
528 Kansas City Street
P.O. Box 1500
Rapid City, SD 57709
(800) 742-8602

Dakota Plains Legal Services, Inc.
160 Second Street
P.O. Box 727
Mission, SD 57555-0727
(605) 856-4444; (800) 658-2297

East River Legal Services
335 North Main Ave., Suite 300
Sioux Falls, SD 57104
(605) 336-9230; (800) 952-3015

Tennessee

Knoxville Legal Aid Society Inc.
http://korrnet.org/klas/
502 South Gay Street Suite 404
Knoxville, TN 37902-1502
(423) 637-0484

Legal Aid of East Tennessee
http://www.laet.org
502 South Gay St.
Suite 404
Knoxville, TN 37902-1502
(865) 637-0484

Legal Aid Society of Middle
  Tennessee and the Cumberlands
211 Union Street, Suite 800

Nashville, TN 37201-1504
(615) 780-7123; (615) 244-6610

Legal Services of South Central
  Tennessee Inc.
104 West Seventh Street
P.O. Box 1256
Columbia, TN 38402-1256
(931) 381-5533

Legal Services of Upper East
  Tennessee Inc.
311 West Walnut Street
P.O. Box 360
Johnson City, TN 37605-0360
(423) 928-8311

Memphis Area Legal Services, Inc.
Claridge House, Suite 200
109 North Main Street
Memphis, TN 38103-5013
(901) 523-8822

Rural Legal Services of Tennessee
  Inc.
226 Broadway Jackson Square
P.O. Box 5209
Oak Ridge, TN 37831-5209
(423) 483-8454

West Tennessee Legal Services, Inc.
http://www.wtls.org
210 West Main Street
P.O. Box 2066
Jackson, TN 38302-2066
(731) 426-1311; (800) 372-8346

Texas

Bexar County Legal Aid
  Association Inc.
http://www.barrera.atfreeweb.com/
434 South Main Ave. Suite 300

San Antonio, TX 78204
(210) 227-0111

Coastal Bend Legal Services
102 Pueblo Street
Corpus Christi, TX 78405
(800) 840-3379

East Texas Legal Services Inc.
http://www.etls.org/
414 East Pillar Street
P.O. Box 631070
Nacogdoches, TX 75963-1070
(800) 354-1889

El Paso Legal Assistance Society
1301 N. Oregon
El Paso, TX 79902
(800) 373-9028

Gulf Coast Legal Foundation
http://www.gclf.org/
1415 Fannin Avenue 3rd Floor
Houston, TX 77002
(800) 733-8394

Legal Aid of Central Texas
http://www.lact.org/
2201 Post Road, Suite 104
Austin, TX 78704
(800) 369-9270

Legal Aid of NorthWest Texas
600 East Weatherford Street
Fort Worth, TX 76102
(817) 877-0609; (800) 955-3959

Legal Services of North Texas
http://www.lsnt.org/
1515 Main Street
Dallas, TX 75201-4803
(214) 748-1234

Lone Star Legal Aid
414 East Pilar Street
P.O. Box 631070
Nacogdoches, TX 75963-1070
(936) 560-1455; (800) 354-1889

Texas Rural Legal Aid, Inc.
http://www.trla.org
300 South Texas Boulevard
Weslaco, TX 78596
(956) 968-6574; (800) 968-8823

West Texas Legal Services, Inc.
600 East Weatherford Street
Fort Worth, TX 76102
(800) 955-3959

Utah

Utah Legal Services, Inc.
http://www.andjusticeforall.org
205 North 400 West
Salt Lake City, UT 84103-1125
(801) 328-8891; (800) 662-4245

Vermont

Legal Services Law Line of
  Vermont, Inc.
http://www.lawlinevt.org
30 Elmwood Avenue
Burlington, VT 05401
(802) 863-7153; (800) 639-8857

Vermont Legal Aid
(800) 889-2047

Offices:
264 North Winooski Avenue
Burlington, VT 05402

7 Court Street
Montpelier, VT 05601

1111 Main Street, Suite B
St. Johnsbury, VT 05819

57 North Main Street
Rutland, VT 05701

56 Main Street, Suite 301
Springfield, VT 05156

Virginia

Blue Ridge Legal Services, Inc.
http://www.brls.org
204 North High Street
P.O. Box 551
Harrisonburg, VA 22803
(540) 433-1830; (800) 237-0141

Central Virginia Legal Aid Society,
  Inc.
http://www.cvlas.org
101 West Broad St., Suite 101
P.O. Box 12206
Richmond, VA 23241-2206
(804) 648-1012; (800) 868-1012

Legal Services of Eastern Virginia,
  Inc.
http://www.legalaidva.org
2017 Cunningham Dr., Suite 300
P.O. Box 7502
Hampton, VA 23666
(757) 827-0350; (800) 944-6624

Legal Services of Northern Virginia
  Inc.
http://members.aol.com/lsnvmain/
6400 Arlington Blvd. Suite 630
Falls Church, VA 22042
(703) 534-4343

Potomac Legal Aid Society, Inc.
allstaff@potomaclegalaid.org
6400 Arlington Blvd
Suite 600
Falls Church, VA 22042
(703) 538-3975

Potomac Legal Aid Society, Inc.
allstaff@potomaclegalaid.org
6400 Arlington Blvd
Suite 600
Falls Church, VA 22042
(703) 538-3975

Southwest Virginia Legal Aid
  Society, Inc.
http://www.svlas.org
227 West Cherry Street
Marion, VA 24354
(276) 783-6576; (800) 277-6754

Tidewater Legal Aid Society
125 St. Paul's Blvd.
Suite 400
Norfolk, VA 23510
(757) 627-5423

Virginia Legal Aid Society, Inc.
http://www.vlas.org
513 Church Street
P.O. Box 6058
Lynchburg, VA 24505-6058
(434) 528-4722; (888) 528-8527

Virgin Islands

Legal Services of the Virgin Islands,
  Inc.
3017 Orange Grove
Christiansted
St. Croix, VI 00820-4375
(340) 773-2626

Washington

Northwest Justice Project
http://www.nwjustice.org
401 Second Avenue South
Suite 407
Seattle, WA 98104
(888) 201-1014; (206) 464-1519

West Virginia

Appalachian Legal Services, Inc.
922 Quarrier Street, 4th Floor
Charleston, WV 25301
(304) 343-4481

Legal Aid of West Virginia, Inc.
http://www.wvlegalservices.org
922 Quarrier Street, 4th Floor
Charleston, WV 25301
(800) 642-8279; (304) 342-6814

Wisconsin

Legal Action of Wisconsin, Inc.
http://www.legalaction.org
230 West Wells St., Room 800
Milwaukee, WI 53203-1866
(414) 278-7722; (414) 278-7777

Legal Services of Northeastern
  Wisconsin Inc.
201 W. Walnut Street
Suite 203
Green Bay, WI 54303
(800) 236-1127

Western Wisconsin Legal Services
  Inc.
http://www.mhtc.net/~wwlsdvo/
205 5th Avenue, Suite 300
P.O. Box 2617
La Crosse, WI 54602-2617
(608) 785-2809; (800) 873-0927

Wisconsin Judicare, Inc.
http://www.judicare.org
300 Third Street, Suite 210
P.O. Box 6100
Wausau, WI 54402-6100
(800) 472-1638; (715) 842-1681

Wyoming

Wyoming Legal Services, Inc.
P.O. Box 1160
1017 East Main Street
Lander, WY 82520
(800) 442-6170; (307) 332-6626

FURTHER READING

A short list, by no means comprehensive, of interesting and informative books about American law and lawyers.

General Books About the Law

Abraham, H.J. *The Judicial Process*, 6th ed. Oxford University Press, 1993.

Bogus, Carl T. *Why Lawsuits are Good for America: Disciplined Democracy, Big Business, and the Common Law*. New York University Press, 2001.

Farnsworth, E. Allan. *An Introduction to the Legal System of the United States*, 2nd ed. Oceana, 1996.

Feinman, Jay M. *Law 101: Everything You Need To Know About the American Legal System*. Oxford University Press, 2000.

Hall, Kermit L. *Oxford Companion to American Law*. Oxford University Press, 2002.

Hall, Kermit L., James W. Ely, and Joel B. Grossman (eds.). *The Oxford Companion to the Supreme Court of the United States*. Oxford University Press, 1992.

Jasanoff, Sheila. *Science at the Bar: Law, Science, and Technology in America*. Harvard University Press, 1996.

Kairys, D., (ed). *The Politics of Law*. 3rd ed. Pantheon Books, 1998.

Lazarus, Edward. *Closed Chambers: The Rise, Fall, and Future of the Modern Supreme Court*. Penguin, 1999.

Levi, Edward H. *An Introduction to Legal Reasoning*. University of Chicago Press, 1962.

Rehnquist, William H. *The Supreme Court*. Vintage Books, 2002.

Schwartz, Bernard. *Decision: How the Supreme Court Decides Cases*. Oxford University Press, 1996.

Tarr, G. Alan. *Judicial Process and Judicial Policymaking*. Wadsworth, 2002.

Wice, P. *Judges and Lawyers*. HarperCollins, 1991.

History of the Law

Auerbach, Jerold S. *Unequal Justice—Lawyers and Social Change in Modern America*. Oxford University Press, 1976.

Brophy, Alfred L. and Randall Kennedy. *Reconstructing the Dreamland: The Tulsa Race Riot of 1921, Race Reparations, and Reconciliation*. Oxford University Press, 2003.

Friedman, Lawrence M. *American Law in the Twentieth Century*. Yale University Press, 2002.

Friedman, Lawrence M. *A History of American Law*, 2nd ed. Touchstone, 1985.

Horwitz, Morton J. *The Transformation of American Law, 1870-1960*. Oxford University Press, 1992.

Levy, Leonard Williams. *Origins of the Bill of Rights*. Yale University Press, 2001.

Patterson, James T. *Brown vs Board of Education: A Civil Rights Milestone and Its Troubled Legacy*. Oxford University Press, 2001.

Schwartz, Bernard. *A Book of Legal Lists*. Oxford University Press, 1997.

Schwartz, Bernard. *A History of the Supreme Court*. Oxford University Press, 1995.

Semonche, John E. *Keeping the Faith: A Cultural History of the U.S. Supreme Court*. Rowman and Littlefield, 1998.

Simon, James F. *What Kind of Nation: Thomas Jefferson, John Marshall, and the Epic Struggle to Create a United States*. Simon and Schuster, 2002.

White, G. Edward. *Tort Law in America*, 2nd ed. Oxford University Press, 2003.

Lawyers and the Legal Profession

Abel, R. *American Lawyers*. Oxford University Press, 1989.

Arron, Deborah. *Running From the Law: Why Good Lawyers Are Getting Out of the Legal Profession*. Niche Press, 1997.

Dershowitz, Alan M. *Letters to a Young Lawyer*. Basic Books, 2001.

Glendon, Mary Ann. *A Nation Under Lawyers: How the Crisis in the Legal Profession Is Transforming American Society*. Harvard University Press, 1996.

Hagan, J., and F. Kay. *Gender in Practice*. Oxford University Press, 1995.

Kronman, Anthony T. *The Lost Lawyer: Failing Ideas of the Legal Profession*. Harvard University Press, 1995.

Margolick, David. *At the Bar: The Passions and Peccadilloes of American Lawyers*. Touchstone Books, 1995.

Linowitz, Sol M., and Martin Mayér. *The Betrayed Profession: Lawyering at the End of the Twentieth Century*. Johns Hopkins University Press, 1996.

Nader, Ralph and Wesley J. Smith. *No Contest: Corporate Lawyers and the Perversion of Justice in America*. Random House, 1999.

Rhode, Deborah. *In the Interests of Justice: Refining the Legal Profession*. Oxford University Press, 2001.

Rosenthal, D.E. *Lawyer and Client*. Russell Sage Foundation, 1974.

Selles, Benjamin. *The Soul of the Law: Understanding Lawyers and the Law*. Vega Books, 2002.

Simenoff, Mark (ed.). *My First Year As a Lawyer*. Signet, 1996.

Zitrin, Richard A. and Carol M. Langford. *The Moral Compass of the American Lawyer: Truth, Justice, Power, and Greed*. Ballantine Books, 2000.

Biographies

Gunther, Gerald. *Learned Hand: The Man and the Judge*. Belknap Press, 1995.

Harbaugh, William H. *Lawyer's Lawyer: The Life of John W. Davis*. Oxford University Press, 1985.

Holmes, Jr. Oliver Wendell, and Richard A. Posner. *The Essential Holmes: Selections from the Letters, Speeches, Judicial Opinions, and Other Writings of Oliver Wendell Holmes, Jr.* University of Chicago Press, 1996.

Kalman, Laura. *Abe Fortas: A Biography*. Yale University Press, 1990.

Newman, Roger K. *Hugo Black: A Biography*. Fordham University Press, 1997.

Polenberg, Richard. *The World of Benjamin Cardozo: Personal Values and the Judicial Process*. Harvard University Press, 1999.

Weinberg, Arthur, William O. Douglas, and Clarence Darrow. *Attorney for the Damned: Clarence Darrow in the Courtroom*. University of Chicago Press, 1989.

White, G. Edward. *The American Judicial Tradition: Profiles of Leading American Judges*. Oxford University Press, 1998.

White, G. Edward. *Oliver Wendell Holmes: Sage of the Supreme Court*. Oxford University Press, 1999.

Williams, Juan. *Thurgood Marshall: American Revolutionary*. Random House, 2000.

Interesting Cases

Black, Roy. *Black's Law: A Criminal Lawyer Reveals His Defense Strategies in Four Cliffhanger Cases*. Simon and Schuster, 1999.

Harr, Jonathan. *A Civil Action*. Vintage Books, 1996.

Jones, Rodney R. *Disorderly Conduct: Verbatim Excerpts from Actual Cases*. W.W. Norton, 1999.

Lewis, Anthony. *Gideon's Trumpet*. Vintage Books, 1989.

McLynn, Frank. *Famous Trials: Cases That Made History*. Reader's Digest, 1995.

Sayer, John William. *Ghost Dancing the Law: The Wounded Knee Trials*. Harvard University Press, 1997.

Stern, Gerald M. *The Buffalo Creek Disaster*. Knopf, 1977.

Werth, Barry. *Damages: One Family's Legal Struggles in the World of Medicine*. Simon and Schuster, 1998.

International Law

Arend, Anthony Clark. *Legal Rules and International Society*. Oxford University Press 1999

Brownlie, Ian. *Principles of Public International Law*. Oxford University Press, 1998.

Steiner, Henry J, and Philip Alston. *International Human Rights in Context*. Oxford University Press, 2000.

Theory of the Law

Bobbit, Philip. *Constitutional Fate : Theory of the Constitution*. Oxford University Press, 1984.

Duxbury, Neil. *Patterns of American Jurisprudence*. Oxford University Press, 1995.

Epstein, Richard A. *Simple Rules for a Complex World*. Harvard University Press, 1997.

Kennedy, Duncan. *A Critique of Adjudication (fin de siecle)*. Harvard University Press, 1997.

Llewellyn, Karl N. *Bramble Bush: On Our Law and Its Study*. Oceana Publications, 1981.

Minda, Gary. *Postmodern Legal Movements*. New York University Press, 1995.

Patterson, Dennis. *Companion to Philosophy of Law and Legal Theory*. Blackwell, 1999.

Posner, Richard A. *Overcoming Law*. Harvard University Press, 1996.

Schlag, Pierre. *Laying Down the Law: Mysticism, Fetishism, and the American Legal Mind*. New York University Press, 1998.

Sunstein, Cass R. *Legal Reasoning and Political Conflict*. Oxford University Press, 1998.

Tushnet, Mark V. *Taking the Constitution Away From the Courts*. Princeton University Press, 2000.

Tushnet, Mark V. *The New Constitutional Order*. Princeton University Press, 2002.

White, Jefferson and Dennis Patterson. *Introduction to the Philosophy of Law*. Oxford University Press, 1998.

Criminal Law

Humes, Edward. *No Matter How Loud I Shout: A Year in the Life of Juvenile Court.* Touchstone Books, 1997.

Morris, Norval and David Rothman (eds.). *Oxford History of the Prison: The Practice of Punishment in Western Society.* Oxford University Press, 1997.

Morris, Norval. *The Brothel Boy and Other Parables of the Law.* American Philological Association, 1992.

Prejean, Helen. *Dead Man Walking: An Eyewitness Account of the Death Penalty in the United States.* Vintage Books, 1996.

Tonry, Michael. Handbook of Crime and Punishment. Oxford University Press, 2001.

Zimring, Franklin. *The Contradictions of American Capital Punishment.* Oxford University Press, 2003.

Law School

Osborn, John J. *The Paper Chase.* Whitson Publishing Company, 2003.

Turow, Scott. *One L: The Turbulent True Story of a First Year at Harvard Law School.* Warner Books, 1977.

Stevens, Robert B. *Law School: Legal Education in America from the 1850s to the 1980s.* University of North Carolina Press, 1990

Practical Law Advice

Brill, Steven. *The Court TV Cradle-to-Grave Legal Survival Guide.* Little, Brown, 1995.

Irving, Shae, and Kathleen Michon. *Nolo's Encyclopedia of Everyday Law.* Nolo Press, 2002.